About Me! Sobre Mí!

Write your name.
_____
_____

Date
_____

Hey! Paste your picture here!

Age?

Greatness! In this oval, write something that is great about you!
_____
_____
_____

Where do you live?
Your city _____
Your state _____

Who is your best friend?
My best friend is:
_____

Top 5 Vacation Spots
List the top 5 places that you would like to visit.
_____
_____
_____
_____
_____

Welcome to *Bridges*, where building partnerships between home and school is an important part of ensuring that all children perform at their true academic potential.

Bridges is a unique workbook series developed by classroom teachers and based on national standards in language arts and mathematics. *Bridges* workbooks (available for students in grade/skill levels Pre-K–Grade 5-6) review basic skills in reading, writing, math, and language arts from the grade students are leaving and preview upcoming skills to help prepare students for the grade ahead.

Bridges begins with a pre-assessment test module to help determine student skill level and a parents' guide to help parents become more involved with their children's education. The parents' guide provides tips and on how to encourage interest in reading and a "Blueprint" for success that discusses how to use the workbook most effectively.

Bridges is divided into three sections that progress in difficulty. Each section begins with an incentive contract calendar to help generate excitement and interest in completing assignments and to give parents and teachers a tool to gauge progress. Exercises are typically in half-page increments to give students with shorter attention spans or those who do not yet have a full mastery of the English language a variety of skills and manageable assignments. Exercise instructions are presented in English and Spanish to allow Spanish-speaking parents to become more involved with their children's assignments and overall education.

A post-assessment module is also included to help evaluate student progress. Each *Bridges* workbook includes a certificate of completion that can be awarded by a teacher or parent to recognize and reinforce the student achievement.

We wish you, and your child or students, success this year.

Level Red = Transition from Grade 5 to Grade 6

All rights reserved.
Copyright 1998, 2004 Federal Education Publishing

Reproduction in any manner, in whole or in part, in English or in other languages,
or otherwise without written permission of the publisher is prohibited.

For information, write: Bridges • PO Box 57936 • Salt Lake City, Utah 84157-0936 • 801-313-0332

Please visit our website at www.BridgesProgram.com for supplements, additions, and corrections to this book.

Second Edition 2004
Printed in the United States of America

ISBN: 1-932210-66-0

Table of Contents

Parents' Guide—Getting the Most from *Bridges* iv
Using the Spanish Instructions in *Bridges* x
How to Encourage Children to Pick Up a Book and Read xi
Bridges Assessment Tests xii
Reading Book List xxviii
Ready for Reading xxx

1st Section
Incentive Contract Calendar 1
Try Something New 2
Daily Activities in Math, Reading, Writing, and Language 3

2nd Section
Incentive Contract Calendar 33
Try Something New 34
Daily Activities in Math, Reading, Writing, and Language 35

3rd Section
Incentive Contract Calendar 65
Try Something New 66
Daily Activities in Math, Reading, Writing, and Language 67

High-Frequency Word List 97
Words to Sound Out, Read, and Spell 98
Glossary 101
Answer Pages 105

Flashcards 130

Parents' Guide

"Getting the Most from Bridges"

You are the most important teacher your child will ever have. *Bridges* is a guided daily workbook to help you succeed in this role.

Studies indicate that basic learning skills are more easily acquired early in life, and small successes can have a lifelong effect on a child's accomplishments. In fact, the more often you tell your children they are intelligent, the more likely they are to become just that. Chances to make such comments present themselves every day, especially during summer or off-track breaks.

You can encourage your children's intellectual development by involving them in things you do. When you cook, point out what ingredients you use and what effect they have on the meal—you've taught vocabulary and science. Take time to explain the newscast—you've taught social studies. Take your child shopping and point out price, brand, and weight differences—you've taught math, economics, and consumer skills.

Of course, you can also encourage your children to learn by getting directly involved in their schoolwork with a book like *Bridges*. This workbook contains:

- Over 200 specially designed, self-motivating activities to keep your child busy, happy, and learning. Each day includes an activity in reading, writing, arithmetic, and language. There are forty-five days in all.
- A Parents' Guide containing ideas for getting the most out of *Bridges*.
- A carefully selected book list full of works children love to read.
- An Incentive Contract to motivate and reward your child's efforts.
- "Try Something New" lists of creative ideas for when your child says, "What can I do? I'm bored."
- High-Frequency Word Lists with vocabulary to sound out, read, and spell.
- A frameable Official Certificate for successfully completing the workbook activities.
- A Spanish Glossary of terms used in the book. (Glossary words are marked with a ‡.)
- Instructions translated into Spanish to help you help your child.

Bridges is packed with ideas for extracurricular activities, as well as fun and challenging math, reading, writing, spelling, and identification exercises that will take your children a step ahead and help them reach for the stars.

Bridges Blueprint for Success

Summer Reading

- There is a suggested reading list on pages xxviii–xxix.
- Experts recommend that you read to your pre-kindergarten through first grade children 5–10 minutes each day and ask questions about the story. For older children, the recommended daily reading times are—

    Grades 1–2, 10–20 minutes; Grades 2–3, 20–30 minutes; Grades 3–4, 30–45 minutes; Grades 4–5, 45–60 minutes; and Grades 5–6, 45–60 minutes.
- You and your child should decide the length of reading time and fill it in on the Incentive Contract Calendar.

Summer Activity Calendar

- An Incentive Contract Calendar is located at the beginning of each section.
- You and your child should sign an agreement for an incentive or reward before your child begins each section.
- When your child completes the agreed reading time each day, he/she colors or initials the box below the 📘. When your child completes a day of *Bridges,* he/she colors or initials the box below the 📔.
- Let your child explore and experiment with the "Try Something New" activities lists.

Sections of Bridges

- There are three sections in *Bridges*.
- Each section becomes progressively more challenging.
- There are four activities each day.
- Your child will need a pencil, eraser, ruler, and crayons to complete the activities.

Words to Sound Out, Read, and Spell

At the end of each book (except Pre-K and K-1) are lists of words to sound out, read, and spell. You can use these for a number of activities and word games you can play with your child:

- Choose your child's favorite words, make two sets of flash cards, and play the matching game (in order to keep the two matching cards, you have to know the word's meaning or spelling).
- Draw pictures of exciting words.
- Use as many words as you can from the list to make up five questions, statements, or explanations.
- Write a story using as many words as you can from the word list.
- Write a list of words you have a hard time spelling.
- Write a list of action verbs.
- Close your eyes, try to remember as many words as you can from the word list, and write them down.
- Practice writing each word five times.
- Write a list of words you find while traveling to the mountains, on vacation, or on the way to a friend's house.

© Federal Education Publishing   Level Red

10 Hints on How to Maximize *Bridges*

 Let your child explore the book by flipping through the pages and looking at the activities.

 Help select a good time for reading or working on the activities. Suggest a time before your child has played outside and becomes too tired to do his/her work.

 Provide any necessary materials. A pencil, ruler, eraser, and crayons are all that are required.

 Offer positive guidance. Children need a great deal of guidance. Remember, the activities are not meant to be tests. You want to create a relaxed and positive attitude toward learning. Work through at least one example on each page with your child. "Think aloud" and show your child how to solve problems.

 Give your child plenty of time to think. You may be surprised by how much children can do on their own.

 Stretch your child's thinking beyond the page. If you are reading a storybook, you might ask, "What do you think will happen next?" or "What would you do if this happened to you?" Encourage your child to name objects that begin with certain letters, or count the number of items in your shopping cart. Also, children often enjoy making up their own stories with illustrations.

 Reread stories and occasionally flip through completed pages. Completed pages and books will be a source of pride to your child and will help show how much he/she accomplished over the summer.

 Read and work on activities while outside. Take the workbook out in the backyard, to the park, or to a family campout. It can be fun wherever you are!

 Encourage siblings, baby-sitters, and neighborhood children to help with reading and activities. Other children are often perfect for providing the one-on-one attention necessary to reinforce reading skills.

 Give plenty of approval! Stickers and stamps, or even a hand-drawn funny face are effective for recognizing a job well done. At the end of the summer, your child can feel proud of his/her accomplishments and will be eager for school to start.

Level Red — Bridges™

Guía para los padres

"Obteniendo el mayor beneficio de Bridges"

Los padres son los maestros más importantes que los niños tendrán en su vida. *Bridges* ofrece un cuaderno guía de ejercicios diarios para que usted tenga éxito en este papel.

Hay estudios que indican que las habilidades básicas de aprendizaje se obtienen con mayor efectividad durante los años formativos de la persona. Los pequeños triunfos pueden producir efectos permanentes en los logros de los niños. Mientras más a menudo les diga usted a sus hijos que son inteligentes, mayores son las posibilidades de que se conviertan justamente en ello.

Las oportunidades para hacerles tales comentarios a sus hijos se presentan a diario, especialmente durante las vacaciones de verano o los descansos entre periodos de estudio.

Puede motivar el desarrollo intelectual de sus niños al permitirles participar en actividades que usted hace. Por ejemplo, muéstreles los ingredientes que use y enséñeles el efecto que tienen en las comidas y les habrá enseñado vocabulario y ciencias. Tome tiempo para explicarles las noticias y les habrá enseñado ciencias sociales. Lleve a sus hijos de compras y enséñeles sobre las diferencias de precios, marcas y medidas, y les habrá enseñado matemáticas, economía y habilidades del consumidor.

Este cuaderno de ejercicios contiene:

- Más de 200 actividades especialmente diseñadas para incentivar a los niños a que se motiven a sí mismos y se mantengan ocupados y felices a medida de que aprenden. Esta guía está dividida en cuatro actividades diarias: lectura, escritura, aritmética y uso del idioma. La guía presenta un programa de 45 días; cada página con el número del día pertinente.
- Una Guía para los padres que contiene pautas útiles sobre cómo usar mejor el libro.
- Una lista de libros cuidadosamente seleccionados de obras que a los niños les encanta leer.
- Un Contrato de Incentivo para motivar y premiar los esfuerzos de los niños.
- Una lista de ideas creativas "Trata Algo Nuevo" para cuando los niños pregunten: "¿Qué puedo hacer?, estoy aburrido".
- Listas de palabras, con vocabulario para pronunciar, leer y escribir.
- Un Certificado Oficial para cuando el niño haya completado exitosamente todas las actividades del libro.
- Un Glosario en español de términos utilizados en el libro. (Las plalbras que se encuentran en el glosario están marcadas con una ‡).
- Instrucciones traducidas al español para ayudarlo a usted y a su niño.

Bridges contiene muchísimas ideas para actividades extracurriculares, así como también divertidos y desafiantes ejercicios de matemáticas, lectura, escritura, ortografía e identificación, que harán progresar a su niño y lo ayudarán a obtener las estrellas.

© Federal Education Publishing   Level Red

Bridges Blueprint para el éxito

Lectura para el verano

- En la página XXVIII encontrará una lista de sugerencias para lectura.
- Los expertos recomiendan que se le lea al niño entre edad preescolar y 1er grado, por 5 a 10 minutos diarios y que se le haga preguntas acerca de la historia. Para niños de mayor edad se recomienda una lectura diaria de:
    Grados 1–2: 10–20 minutos; Grados 2–3: 20–30 minutos; Grados 3–4: 30–45 minutos
    Grados 4–5: 45–60 minutos; Grados 5–6: 45–60 minutos.
- Usted y su niño deberán pactar el tiempo que dedicarán a la lectura y completar el Calendario de Incentivo de Actividades.

Contrato de Incentivo

- Al principio de cada sección se encuentra un Contrato de Incentivo.
- Usted y su niño deberán firmar un acuerdo de incentivo o recompensa antes de que el niño comience cada sección.
- Cuando el niño complete un día de *Bridges*, coloreará o escribirá sus iniciales en la ▭. Cuando su niño complete el tiempo diario de lectura pactado, coloreará o escribirá sus iniciales en el 📘.
- Deje que el niño explore y experimente la lista de actividades Trata Algo Nuevo.

Secciones de Bridges

- *Bridges* contiene 3 secciones.
- Cada sección se torna progresivamente más desafiante.
- Cada día consta de cuatro actividades.
- El niño necesitará un lápiz, una goma, y lápices de colores para completar las actividades.

Palabras para pronunciar, leer y deletrear

Después de la última sección figuran palabras para pronunciar, leer y deletrear. Usted puede utilizar estas palabras para muchas actividades y juegos de palabras que realice con su niño:

- Elija las palabras favoritas de su niño, prepare dos juegos de tarjetas y juegue al *Juego de la Memoria*. Ponga las tarjetas boca abajo y dé vuelta de a dos a la vez, tratando de recordar las coincidencias a medida que avance (para quedarse con las dos tarjetas que coinciden, se debe saber o el significado o cómo se escriben).
- Haga dibujos de las palabras interesantes.
- Utilice la mayor cantidad posible de palabras de la lista para inventar cinco preguntas, oraciones declarativas o explicaciones.
- Escriba una historia utilizando la mayor cantidad posible de palabras de la lista.
- Escriba una lista de las palabras que más le cuesta deletrear.
- Haga una lista de verbos activos.
- Cierre los ojos, trate de recordar la mayor cantidad posible de palabras de la lista y escríbalas.
- Escriba cada palabra cinco veces.
- Haga una lista de palabras que encuentre mientras viaja a las montañas, vacaciona o se dirige a la casa de un amigo.

Level Red

10 sugerencias para obtener el mayor beneficio de *Bridges*

 Deje que su niño explore el libro, hojeando las páginas y mirando las actividades.

 Seleccione un buen momento para la lectura y la realización de actividades. Sugiera un momento luego de que su niño haya jugado al aire libre y antes de que se encuentre demasiado cansado.

 Facilite el material necesario, generalmente todo lo que necesitará será: un lápiz, una regla, una goma y lápices de colores.

 Ofrezca una guía positiva. Los niños necesitan guía permanente. Recuerde que las actividades no son exámenes. Cree una actitud relajada y positiva hacia el trabajo escolar. Realice con el niño por lo menos un ejemplo de cada página. "Piense en voz alta" y muéstrele al niño cómo resolver los problemas.

 Dele al niño mucho tiempo para pensar. Se sorprenderá de cuánto pueden realizar los niños por sí solos.

 Extienda el pensamiento del niño más allá de las actividades de la página. Si está leyendo una historia puede preguntarle: "¿Qué crees que sucederá ahora?" o "¿Qué harías si te sucediera a ti?" Incentive a su niño a nombrar objetos que comiencen con ciertas letras o a que cuente los objetos de su carrito de compras. Muchas veces los niños también disfrutan inventando sus propias historias con ilustraciones.

 De vez en cuando, revise páginas ya finalizadas. Las páginas ya terminadas y los libros ya leídos serán una fuente de orgullo para su niño y lo ayudarán a demostrar lo mucho que ha logrado a través de las semanas.

 Lea y realice las actividades al aire libre. Lleve el libro de actividades al aire libre al jardín, al parque o a un campamento. ¡Puede ser divertido!

 Incentive a los hermanos, niñeras y niños del vecindario a que ayuden a su niño en las actividades y la lectura. Muchas veces otros niños son perfectos para proporcionar la atención recíproca que necesitan los lectores principiantes.

 ¡Muestre aprobación! Las calcomanías, las etiquetas y hasta una cara divertida dibujada por usted son un reconocimiento efectivo de un trabajo realizado satisfactoriamente. Cuando su niño haya completado el libro, cuelgue el certificado de logro en un lugar donde todos puedan verlo.

Using the Spanish Instructions in *Bridges*

Basic instructions in Spanish for each activity are provided in red underneath the English instructions. These are to help you as a parent understand the overall nature of the assignment and what tasks your child is supposed to complete. On pages 99–100, *Bridges* also includes a Spanish glossary of grammatical and mathematical terms that may be unfamiliar. All words included in the glossary are marked with a ‡. For example, one instruction reads:

> **Write adjectives in the blanks.**
> Escribe adjetivos‡ en los espacios en blanco.

The ‡ tells you that you will find an explanation for the word *adjective* in the glossary:

> **Adjetivo** (adjective) — una palabra que califica a un sustantivo o pronombre. Los adjetivos pueden describir cuántos, de qué tipo o cuál. En la oración "El hombre delgado cepillaba tres perros con un peine azul", *tres*, *delgado* y *azul* son adjetivos.

Note: Once he or she is old enough, your child should read the complete instructions in English. The English paragraphs sometimes contain additional information your child will need to complete the assignment. While this may be challenging at first, it will help your child develop important educational skills. As children work to understand the English instructions, they will not only strengthen their English skills; they will also develop strategies for learning, such as using context clues, a dictionary to look up unfamiliar terms, and a glossary. These are skills all students need, regardless of their native language.

Uso de las instrucciones en español en *Bridges*

Debajo de las instrucciones en inglés para cada actividad, encontrará instrucciones básicas en español escritas en rojo. El objetivo de estas instrucciones es ayudarlo a usted, como padre, a comprender la naturaleza general del trabajo y las tareas que se supone su niño debe realizar. En las páginas 99–100, *Bridges* también incluye un glosario en español de términos gramaticales y matemáticos que podrían resultarle poco comunes. Todas las palabras incluidas en el glosario se encuentran marcadas con una ‡. Por ejemplo, una de las instrucciones dice:

> **Write adjectives in the blanks.**
> Escribe adjetivos‡ en los espacios en blanco.

El ‡ le indica que encontrará una explicación de la palabra adjetivo en el glosario:

> **Adjetivo** (adjective) — una palabra que califica a un sustantivo o pronombre. Los adjetivos pueden describir cuántos, de qué tipo o cuál. En la oración "El hombre delgado cepillaba tres perros con un peine azul", tres, delgado y azul son adjetivos.

Nota: Una vez que el niño tenga la edad apropiada, deberá leer las instrucciones solamente en inglés. Muchas veces los párrafos en inglés contienen información adicional que su niño necesitará para completar la tarea. Aunque al principio esto puede resultar un desafío, ayudará a que su niño desarrolle habilidades educativas importantes. Al mismo tiempo que los niños trabajan para comprender las instrucciones en inglés, no solamente refuerzan sus habilidades con respecto al idioma, sino que también desarrollan estrategias de aprendizaje, como por ejemplo, el uso de pistas de contexto, de un glosario y de un diccionario para buscar términos desconocidos. Estas son habilidades que todos los estudiantes necesitan, sin importar cuál sea su lengua nativa.

How to Encourage Children to Pick Up a Book and Read

You can help your child develop good reading habits. Most experts agree that reading with your child is the most important thing you can do. To choose a good book, use *Bridges*' book list.

Set aside time each day to read aloud to your child at bedtime or after lunch or dinner. Read some of the books you enjoyed when you were young.

Visit the library to find books that meet your child's specific interests. Ask a librarian which books are popular among children of your child's grade. Take advantage of storytelling activities at the library. Ask the librarian about other resources, such as stories on cassettes, videotapes, records, and even computers.

Encourage and provide a variety of reading materials. Help your child read house numbers, street signs, signs in store windows, and package labels. Encourage your child to tell stories using pictures.

Best of all, show your child you like to read. Sit down with a good book. After supper, share stories and ideas that might interest your child from the newspapers and magazines you're reading.

Cómo motivar a los niños para que escojan un libro y lo lean

Usted puede ayudar a su niño a desarrollar buenos hábitos de lectura. La mayoría de los expertos coincide en que leer con su niño es lo más importante que usted puede hacer. Para elegir un buen libro, utilice la lista de libros *Bridges*.

Reserve un momento del día para leerle en voz alta a su niño: a la hora de irse a dormir o luego del almuerzo o de la cena. Lea algunos de los libros que a usted le gustaban cuando era niño. Visite la biblioteca para encontrar libros que coincidan con los intereses específicos de su niño.

Pregúntele a un bibliotecario cuáles son los libros populares entre los niños del mismo grado. Aproveche las actividades de narración de cuentos en las bibliotecas. Pregúntele al bibliotecario acerca de otros recursos, como historias en casetes, cintas de video, discos y computadoras.

Fomente y proporcione gran variedad de material de lectura. Ayúdele a su niño a leer los números de las casas, los carteles de las calles, los carteles en los escaparates y las etiquetas de envoltorios. Incentive a su niño a relatar historias basándose en dibujos.

Pero, por sobre todo, demuéstrele al niño que a usted le gusta leer. Siéntese con un buen libro. Luego de la comida comparta las historias e ideas del periódico o revistas que usted lee que puedan interesarle al niño.

© Federal Education Publishing

Assessment Tests

A Word about Assessment

The goal of the assessment test is to help you discover what skills your students have acquired and what skills they need to learn. You can use the pretest at the beginning of a new school year or during the course of the school year to give you an idea of where your students are in their development. The post-test can then be used as a follow-up. As you give the assessment, talk with your students about their thinking. Ask questions about the answers they give. If a student cannot complete the assessment, you can use the assessment as a teaching tool. Walk the student through the assessment, teaching as you go.

Keys to Positive Assessment

Your students will need the assessment page and a pencil.
Provide a quiet place free of clutter and distractions.
If parents are administering the test at home, suggest that they try answering questions with a question. For example:

    Student: *"What is this word?"*
    Parent: *"What letters do you see in the word?"* or *"What sound does each letter make?"*

Instruct parents to refrain from immediately correcting their child and to note skills that need to be taught or reinforced. They should have the child move on if he or she is having difficulty.

Assessment Tests

The assessment tests are divided into four parts:

    <u>Assessment 1</u> Assesses reading ability, including comprehension, main idea, paragraphing, cause and effect, and vocabulary.
    <u>Assessment 2</u> Assesses language skills and the ability to recognize such things as subjects and predicates, pronouns, adverbs, adjectives, and verb tenses.
    <u>Assessment 3</u> Provides writing practice in cursive and also tests knowledge of basic grammar, punctuation, letter format, and spelling.
    <u>Assessment 4</u> Assesses math skills, including numeration, time and money values, addition, subtraction, multiplication, division, word problems, fractions, decimals, and percentages.

The *Bridges* Assessments Include Three Parts:

1. An <u>assessment</u> to test what students already know.
2. A <u>post-assessment</u> to test what students have learned.
3. An <u>assessment analysis</u> to refer you to activity pages in *Bridges* where students can practice specific skills.

Assessment Test Analysis

After you review your child's assessment test, match the problems that contain incorrect answers to the *Bridges* pages below. Pay special attention to these pages and ensure that your student receives supervision and extra help if needed. In this way, your child will strengthen skills in these areas.

Reading Skills
- Reference Books: 4, 6, 8, 17, 26, 61, 82, 93
- Cause & Effect: 12, 13, 72
- Comprehension: 6, 16, 18, 36, 38, 42, 48, 52, 80

Language Skills
- Parts of Speech: 28, 42, 56, 60, 64, 68, 70, 74, 86, 90, 92, 94
- Verb Tense: 46, 54

Writing Skills
- Proofreading/Punctuation: 15, 19, 24, 62, 96

Mathematics
- Numeration: 3, 5, 23, 35, 81
- Addition & Subtraction: 7, 11, 21, 43
- Multiplication & Division: 13, 15, 19, 21, 27, 43, 51, 53, 57, 69, 75, 77
- Word Problems: 9, 17, 63
- Fractions: 39, 41, 55, 83, 85, 91, 93
- Decimals: 25, 87

Assessment 1   Reading Skills

Read the paragraph. Then answer the questions that follow.

The Pyramids of Giza located near Cairo, Egypt, are one of the Seven Wonders of the World. Built over 4,000 years ago, more than 80 pyramids still stand in the deserts of Egypt. Built as burial tombs for ancient pharaohs, some pyramids stand over 400 feet high. The Eiffel Tower is also very tall. Over 2 million blocks of limestone were used to build some of the larger pyramids. The base of a pyramid is either square or triangular, but the sides are always triangular. The pyramids are one of ancient Egypt's legacies to the world.

1. What is the main idea of the paragraph? _____
2. Write 3 sentences from the paragraph that support the main idea.
   _____
   _____
   _____
3. Cross out the sentence that does not belong in the paragraph.
4. Circle the best title for the paragraph.
   A. The Seven Wonders of the World
   B. Pyramids, Egypt's Legacy
   C. Amazing Buildings in Modern Egypt

Choose the reference book you would use to find the answer to the questions. If there is more than one possibility, choose the best answer.

   almanac   atlas   dictionary   encyclopedia   telephone book

5. Where would you find a map of the world? _____
6. Where would you find information about the life of Albert Einstein? _____
7. Where would you find the phone number for an airline? _____
8. Where would you find the definition of *rambunctious*? _____
9. Where would you find information about the U.S. space program? _____
10. Where would you find the average rainfall on May 1st in your area? _____
11. Where would you look to check the spelling of *variety*? _____
12. Where would you look to find the phone number for an auto repair shop? _____

Write the cause and effect in each sentence.

13. My brother forgot to lock his bike, and it was stolen.
    Cause: _____
    Effect: _____
14. Because of the bad storm our electricity went off during the night.
    Cause: _____
    Effect: _____
15. I gave my mother some daisies because I know they are her favorite flowers.
    Cause: _____
    Effect: _____

Level Red   Bridges™

Assessment 2 — Language Skills

Look at the sentence. Then follow the directions.

Mrs. Garcia made our class some tortillas.

1. Draw a line between the subject and the predicate.
2. Underline the proper noun.
3. Circle the common nouns.
4. Draw two lines under the verb.
5. What part of speech is the word *our*? _____

Circle the correct form of the be verb.

6. The boys (was   were) playing ball at the park.
7. We (be   will be) having a test on Friday.
8. The water (has been   been) running all day.
9. My sister (are   is) practicing her piano lesson.
10. They (is   are) going to the movies tonight.

Complete the chart. Use the correct present tense, past tense, & past participle of each verb.

	Present	Past	Past Participle
11.	see		
12.		ate	
13.			written
14.	go		
15.			sung

Circle the correct pronouns in each sentence.

16. My dad asked (me   I) to wash (his   her) car.
17. My brother and (me   I) rode (my   our) bikes to the store.
18. Miss Scriber read the class a book. (Me   We) liked the story a lot.
19. My sister's team won the game. (They   We) played (our   their) best.
20. Allison has two mice. (Its   Their) names are Wilbur and Ralph.

Write the sentences without the double negatives.

21. Our team hasn't never won a game. _____
22. There isn't nothing you can do about that. _____

Circle the adverbs and underline the adjectives in each sentence.

23. The yellow bus pulled slowly away from the curb.
24. The intelligent students spelled the words perfectly.

Assessment 3 — Writing Skills

1. **Rewrite the paragraph in cursive, adding the correct punctuation and capitalization. Look for spelling errors, too.**

   on july 20 1969 neil armstrong became the first man to set foot on the moon. along with buzz aldrin, the two american astronawts spent over 21 hours on the moon's serface armstrong spent 2 hours and 31 minutes walking on the moon aldrin spent almost 2 hours walking on the moon they collikted sampulls of the moon's surface

   _____
   _____
   _____
   _____
   _____

2. **Rewrite the paragraph using apostrophes correctly.**

   At my friends house he always has to help clean the yard on Saturday mornings. He cant play until all of his chores are done. Hes always in trouble for something he didnt finish. Last weekend he couldnt play until after his sisters softball game. My poor friend. He doesnt ever get to play.

   _____
   _____
   _____
   _____

3. **Rewrite this friendly letter. Remember to use the correct letter writing form.**

   983 bonanza court dallas tx 10223 May 8, 2002 dear aunt sally thank you for the money you sent for my birthday i used the money to buy a book about rock collecting i have started my own rock collection so far I have about 30 rocks mom says you have a cool rock collection too i hope i can see it soon thank you again for the money love brett

   _____
   _____
   _____
   _____
   _____

Level Red   Bridges™

Assessment 4 Mathematics—Page 1

Solve the problems.

1.
    2,074   4,763   3998   16,004   22,246
 + 1,985   - 3,329   + 4,190   - 12,061   + 52,077

2.
     25   34   913   371   302
 x 28   x 56   x 72   x 29   x 180

3.
  14$\overline{)732}$ 46$\overline{)307}$ 81$\overline{)419}$ 29$\overline{)5302}$

4.
   18.29   345.2   372.107   435.8
 + 11.3   + 23.32   - 12.08   - 123.03

5.
   5.34   345.2   190.03   345.09
  x 34   x 32   x 48   x 75

6.
   24.3   389.2   348.09   769.02
 x .42   x .33   x 2.31   x .02

Write each number.

7. nine hundred forty-seven thousand, four hundred fifteen _____

8. 500,000 + 30,000 + 7,000 + 200 + 40 + 3 _____

9. 8 hundred thousands, 7 ten thousands, 2 thousands, 3 hundreds, 2 ones _____

10. six hundred sixteen thousand, seven hundred forty-one _____

© Federal Education Publishing   Level Red

Assessment 4

Mathematics—Page 2

Read and solve the problems.

11. What time will it be 2 hours and 15 minutes after 1:45? _____

12. Michael had $47.24. He spent $2.57 on candy and $12.87 on a new CD. How much money does he have left? _____

13. Josh bought 20 candy bars for 30¢ each. He sold the candy bars to his friends and family for 50¢. How much profit did Josh make on the candy bars? _____

14. Rachel's mother gave her $200 to buy clothes for school. She bought two skirts that cost $20.00 each, four tops that were on sale two for $10.00, a sweater that cost $27.00, and a pair of shoes for $35.00. How much money does Rachel have left? _____

Write a decimal and a fraction for each of the following.

15. Five and four hundredths   _____   _____
16. Thirty-six and seven tenths   _____   _____
17. Seventeen and nine tenths   _____   _____
18. Five hundred and five hundredths   _____   _____

Write the equivalent fraction.

19. 3/4 = _____ /8   22. 3/10 = 18/ _____
20. 5/5 = _____ /6   23. 5/12 = 10/ _____
21. 4/6 = _____ /12   24. 2/5 = 8/ _____

Reduce all fractions to lowest terms.

25. 56/5   _____   28. 24/14   _____
26. 45/6   _____   29. 38/8   _____
27. 51/8   _____   30. 17/3   _____

Level Red · xviii · Bridges™

Assessment 4

Mathematics—Page 3

Solve the problems. Write the answer in the simplest terms.

31. 4 3/4 + 3 2/8 _____
32. 5 1/7 + 4 3/14 _____
33. 8 1/2 - 3 1/3 _____
34. 9 3/4 - 2 7/12 _____

35. 3/4 x 7 _____
36. 6/7 x 2/5 _____
37. 3 1/2 x 4 3/4 _____
38. 4 3/5 x 2 7/8 _____

Write each percentage as a fraction and a decimal.

39. 35% _____ _____
40. 8% _____ _____
41. 49% _____ _____
42. 92% _____ _____

Find the following percentage of each number.

43. 40% of 35 _____
44. 7% of 83 _____

45. 12% of 70 _____
46. 90% of 87 _____

© Federal Education Publishing

Level Red

Post-Assessment 1 — Reading Skills—Page 1

Read the paragraph. Then answers the questions that follow.

The Great Wall of China is one of man's most amazing building projects. The Golden Gate Bridge is another amazing building project. Construction of the wall began over 2,000 years ago. It took over 200 years to complete. The Wall is actually made up of several walls built to keep invaders out of China. The exact length of the wall is disputed, but it is about 1,500 to 2,000 miles long. The wall reaches 39 feet high in some places. It is 15 to 25 feet wide across the top.

1. What is the main idea of the paragraph? _____
2. Write 3 sentences from the paragraph that support the main idea.
   _____
   _____
   _____
3. Cross out the sentence that does not belong in the paragraph.
4. Circle the best title for the paragraph.
   A. Amazing Projects
   B. China Keeps Out Invaders
   C. The Great Wall, An Amazing Structure

Choose the reference book you would use to find the answer to the questions. If there is more than one possibility, choose the best answer.

   almanac   atlas   dictionary   encyclopedia   telephone book

5. Where would you find a phone number of a dentist? _____
6. Where would you find the most information about the life of Louisa May Alcott? _____
7. Where would you find the average snowfall in January in the Rockie Mountains? _____
8. Where would you find the definition of *prognosis*? _____
9. Where would you find information about volcanoes? _____
10. Where would you find unusual facts about animals or athletes? _____
11. Where would you look to check the spelling of *necessary*? _____
12. Where would you look to find out how to pronounce *sanguine*? _____

Write the cause and effect in each sentence.

13. I did not study my spelling words so I did poorly on the test.
    Cause: _____
    Effect: _____
14. My sister fell off her bike and scraped her elbow.
    Cause: _____
    Effect: _____
15. Jennifer earned free time by reading five books.
    Cause: _____
    Effect: _____

Level Red — Bridges™

Post-Assessment 2 — Language Skills

Look at the sentence. Then follow the directions.

I fed my horses some hay.

1. Draw a line between the subject and the predicate.
2. Underline the proper noun.
3. Circle the common nouns.
4. Draw two lines under the verb.
5. What part of speech are the words *I* and *my*?_____

Circle the correct form of the be verb.

6. The baby (was   were) crying loudly.
7. They (was   will be] going on vacation next week.
8. I (has been   have been) at school all day.
9. Jenna (was   is) riding her bike to school yesterday.
10. My parents (is   are) going out to dinner tonight.

Complete the chart. Use the correct present tense, past tense, & past participle of each verb.

	Present	Past	Past Participle
11.	ring		
12.		ran	
13.			given
14.	throw		
15.			thought

Circle the correct pronouns in each sentence.

16. My sister and (me   I) left (our   their) bikes out in the rain.
17. My family took (his   our) boat to the lake. (We   Us) like to water ski.
18. Please join (us   our) for dinner after the game.
19. (I   me) went to the store for (my   me) mother.
20. Robert watched (his   her) sister play baseball. (Her   His) team won the game.

Write the sentences without the double negatives.

21. I don't like no peas in my casserole. _____
22. He isn't going no where. _____

Circle the adverbs and underline the adjectives in each sentence.

23. The purple flowers grew wildly in the tall grass.
24. Our fabulous new choir sang beautifully.

Post-Assessment 3

Writing Skills

1. Rewrite the paragraph in cursive, adding the correct punctuation and capitalization. Look for spelling errors, too.

my birfday is february 26. i am going to have a slubber party I will invit six of my best freinds. We will paint our nails do each others hair and eat popcorn. my mom is going to rent some movies for us to watch. we will try to stay up all nite.

_____
_____
_____
_____

2. Rewrite the paragraph using apostrophes correctly.

Last summer my brother and I stayed at our grandmothers house. My parents were in Europe because of my dads work. My brother and I didnt want to go. We wanted to stay with my grandmother so we could see our friends and keep up with our music lessons. My brothers football team also started their practices. He didnt want to miss any of the practices. Im glad my parents let us stay with my grandmother.

_____
_____
_____
_____
_____

3. Rewrite this friendly letter. Remember to use the correct letter writing form.

17723 fox run drive springfield il 10015 september 17, 2002 dear mike thank you for your letter it was good to hear from you I'm glad you like school this year i am enjoying my school too. I have a great teacher he makes learning fun our baseball team is playing great we have won all our games. Write again soon. your friend Todd

_____
_____
_____
_____
_____

Level Red

Post-Assessment 4 — Mathematics—Page 1

Solve the problems.

1.
   - 5,067 + 2,894
   - 4,661 − 1,285
   - 3,092 + 8,198
   - 27,007 − 15,071
   - 42,624 + 37,134

2.
   - 25 × 78
   - 43 × 65
   - 610 × 42
   - 284 × 27
   - 203 × 170

3.
   - 24 ⟌ 736
   - 39 ⟌ 805
   - 71 ⟌ 517
   - 27 ⟌ 5320

4.
   - 17.19 + 14.8
   - 305.6 + 24.21
   - 672.208 − 10.01
   - 125.4 − 39.38

5.
   - 4.43 × 83
   - 307.6 × 48
   - 270.06 × 51
   - 126.29 × 77

6.
   - 27.4 × .56
   - 119.3 × .49
   - 871.09 × 4.32
   - 123.04 × .07

Write each number.

7. six hundred fifty-six thousand, two hundred seventeen _____

8. 700,000 + 40,000 + 2,000 + 100 + 90 + 5 _____

9. 4 hundred thousands, 3 ten thousands, 8 thousands, 2 hundreds, 7 ones _____

10. five hundred twenty-two thousand, four hundred thirty-three _____

© Federal Education Publishing — Level Red

Post-Assessment 4 — Mathematics—Page 2

Read and solve the problems.

11. What time will it be 4 hours and 25 minutes after 11:05? _____

12. John had $52.75. He spent $15.29 on a model and $2.85 on some glue. How much money does he have left? _____

13. Nathan bought 45 ice cream bars for 20¢ each. He sold the ice cream bars to his friends and family for 50¢. How much profit did he make on the ice cream bars? _____

14. Veronica had $65.00 to buy Christmas presents for her friends and family. She bought her mother a vase that cost $11.00. She bought 3 of her friends charms that cost $2.50 each. She spent $12.00 on some golf balls for her dad. She bought her two brothers each a CD costing $15.00 each. How much money does Rachel have left? _____

Write a decimal and a fraction for each of the following.

15. Four and five hundredths   _____   _____
16. Seventy-three and two tenths   _____   _____
17. Eighteen and seven tenths   _____   _____
18. One hundred and six hundredths _____   _____

Write the equivalent fraction.

19. 3/4 = _____ /12   22. 3/5 = 6/ _____
20. 4/4 = _____ /8   23. 5/10 = 10/ _____
21. 5/6 = _____ /18   24. 3/5 = 15/ _____

Reduce all fractions to lowest terms.

25. 44/7 _____   28. 22/12 _____
26. 27/5 _____   29. 35/3   _____
27. 67/8 _____   30. 19/3   _____

Level Red

Post-Assessment 4 — Mathematics—Page 3

Solve the problems. Write the answer in the simplest terms.

31. 3 1/4 + 1 1/8 _____
32. 7 5/6 + 3 9/12 _____
33. 4 1/2 - 2 1/3 _____
34. 8 3/4 - 6 7/8 _____

35. 3/5 x 9 _____
36. 6/7 x 3/5 _____
37. 7 1/2 x 4 1/4 _____
38. 2 3/5 x 3 7/9 _____

Write each percentage as a fraction and a decimal.

39. 37% _____ _____
40. 5% _____ _____
41. 52% _____ _____
42. 86% _____ _____

Find the following percentage of each number.

43. 20% of 35 _____
44. 4% of 71 _____

45. 15% of 65 _____
46. 92% of 59 _____

Assessment Answers

Assessment 1 • Reading Skills
1. The Pyramids of Giza are one of the Seven Wonders of the World.
2. Answers may include any of these sentences:
   Built over 4,000 years ago, more than 80 pyramids still stand in the deserts of Egypt.
   Built as burial tombs for ancient pharaohs, some pyramids stand over 400 feet high.
   Over two million blocks of limestone were used to build some of the larger pyramids.
   The base of a pyramid is either square or triangular, but the sides are always triangular.
3. ~~The Eiffel Tower is also very tall.~~
4. B. Pyramids, Egypt's Legacy
5. atlas
6. encyclopedia
7. telephone book
8. dictionary
9. encyclopedia
10. almanac
11. dictionary
12. telephone book
13. Cause: My brother forgot to lock his bike.
    Effect: His bike was stolen.
14. Cause: There was a bad storm.
    Effect: Our electricity went off.
15. Cause: Daisies are my mother's favorite flowers.
    Effect: I gave her some daisies.

Assessment 2 • Language Skills
1–4. Mrs. Garcia / made our (class) some (tortillas).
5. pronoun
6. were
7. will be
8. has been
9. is
10. are
11. see / saw / seen
12. eat / ate / eaten
13. write / wrote / written
14. go / went / gone
15. sing / sang / sung
16. me / his
17. I / our
18. We
19. They / their
20. Their
21. Our team has never won a game.
22. There is nothing you can do about that.
23. The yellow bus pulled (slowly) away from the curb.
24. The intelligent students spelled the words (perfectly).

Assessment 3 • Writing Skills
1. On July 20, 1969, Neil Armstrong became the first man to set foot on the moon. Along with Buzz Aldrin, the two American astronauts spent over 21 hours on the moon's surface. Armstrong spent 2 hours and 31 minutes walking on the moon. Aldrin spent almost 2 hours walking on the moon. They collected samples of the moon's surface.

2. At my friend's house he always has to help clean the yard on Saturday mornings. He can't play until all of his chores are done. He's always in trouble for something he didn't finish. Last weekend he couldn't play until after his sister's softball game. My poor friend. He doesn't ever get to play.

3.
   983 Bonanza Court
   Dallas, TX 10223
   May 8, 2002

   Dear Aunt Sally,

   Thank you for the money you sent for my birthday. I used the money to buy a book about rock collecting. I have started my own rock collection. So far I have about 30 rocks. Mom says you have a cool rock collection, too. I hope I can see it soon.

   Thank you again for the money.

   Love,
   Brett

Assessment 4 • Mathematics
1. 4,059   1,434   8,188   3,943   74,323
2. 700   1,904   65,736   10,759   54,360
3. 52 R4   6 R31   5 R14   182 R 24
4. 29.59   368.52   360.027   312.77
5. 181.56   11,046.4   9,121.44   25,881.75
6. 10.206   128.436   804.0879   15.3804
7. 947,415
8. 537,243
9. 872,302
10. 616,741
11. 4:00
12. $31.80
13. $4.00
14. $78.00
15. 5.04; 5 4/100
16. 36.7; 36 7/10
17. 17.9; 17 9/10
18. 500.05; 500 5/100
19. 6/8
20. 6/6
21. 8/12
22. 18/60
23. 10/24
24. 8/20
25. 11 1/5
26. 7 1/2
27. 6 3/8
28. 1 5/7
29. 4 3/4
30. 5 2/3
31. 8
32. 9 5/14
33. 5 1/6
34. 7 1/6
35. 5 1/4
36. 12/35
37. 16 5/8
38. 13 9/40
39. 35/100; .35
40. 8/100; .08
41. 49/100; .49
42. 92/100; .92
43. 14
44. 5.81
45. 8.4
46. 78.3

Post-Assessment Answers

Post Assessment 1 • Reading Skills
1. The Great Wall of China is one of man's most amazing building projects.
2. Answers may include any of these sentences:
   Construction of the wall began over 2,000 years ago.
   It took over 200 years to complete.
   The wall is about 1,500 to 2,000 miles long.
   The wall reaches 39 feet high is some places.
3. ~~The Golden Gate Bridge is another amazing building project.~~
4. C. The Great Wall, An Amazing Structure
5. telephone book
6. encyclopedia
7. almanac
8. dictionary
9. encyclopedia
10. almanac
11. dictionary
12. dictionary
13. Cause: I did not study my spelling words.
    Effect: I did poorly on the test.
14. Cause: My sister fell off her bike.
    Effect: She scraped her elbow.
15. Cause: Jennifer read five books.
    Effect: She earned free time.

Post Assessment 2 • Language Skills

1–4. I / fed my (horses) some (hay.)
5. pronouns
6. was
7. will be
8. have been
9. was
10. are

11. ring	rang	rung
12. run	ran	run
13. give	gave	given
14. throw	threw	thrown
15. think	thought	thought

16. I	our
17. our	We
18. us	
19. I	my
20. his	Her

21. I don't like peas in my casserole.
22. He isn't going anywhere.
23. The purple flowers grew (wildly) in the tall grass.
24. Our fabulous new choir sang (beautifully.)

Post Assessment 3 • Writing Skills
1. My birthday is February 26. I am going to have a slumber party. I will invite six of my best friends. We will paint our nails, do each other's hair, and eat popcorn. My mom is going to rent some movies for us to watch. We will try to stay up all night.
2. Last summer my brother and I stayed at my grandmother's house. My parents were in Europe because of my dad's work. My brother and I didn't want to go. We wanted to stay with our grandmother so that we could see our friends and keep up with our music lessons. My brother's football team also started their practices. He didn't want to miss any of the practices. I'm glad my parents let us stay with our grandmother.
3.
   11723 Fox Run Drive
   Springfield, IL 10015
   September 17, 2002

   Dear Mike,

   Thank you for your letter. It was good to hear from you. I'm glad you like school this year. I am enjoying my school, too. I have a great teacher. He makes learning fun. Our baseball team is playing great. We have won all our games. Write again soon.

   Your friend,
   Todd

Post Assessment 4 • Mathematics

1. 7,961	3,376	11,290	11,936	79,758
2. 1,950	2,795	25,620	7,668	34,510
3. 30 R16	20 R25	7 R20	197 R1	
4. 31.99	329.81	662.198	86.02	
5. 367.69	14,764.8	13,773.06		9,724.33
6. 15.344	58.457	3,763.1088		8.6128

7. 656,217
8. 742,195
9. 438,207
10. 522,433
11. 3:30
12. $34.61
13. $13.50
14. $4.50
15. 4.05 4 5/100
16. 73.2 73 2/10
17. 18.7 18 7/10
18. 100.06 100 6/100
19. 9/12
20. 8/8
21. 15/18
22. 6/10
23. 10/20
24. 15/25
25. 6 2/7
26. 5 2/5
27. 8 3/8
28. 1 5/6
29. 11 2/3
30. 6 1/3
31. 4 3/8
32. 11 7/12
33. 2 1/6
34. 1 7/8
35. 5 2/5
36. 18/35
37. 31 7/8
38. 9 37/45
39. 37/100 .37
40. 5/100 .05
41. 52/100 .52
42. 86/100 .86
43. 7
44. 2.84
45. 9.75
46. 54.28

© Federal Education Publishing · Level Red

Reading Book List

Adler, C.S.
  Always and Forever Friends
Alexander, Lloyd
  The Black Cauldron
  The Drackenberg Adventure
Armstrong, William Howard
  Sounder
Avi
  Windcatcher
Babbitt, Natalie
  Tuck Everlasting
Banks, Lynne Reid
  The Adventures of King Midas
  Indian in the Cupboard
Bawden, Nina
  Henry
Bellairs, John
  The Lamp from the Warlock's Tomb
Brittain, Bill
  The Wish Giver: Three Tales of Coven Tree
Burch, Robert
  Ida Early Comes over the Mountain
Butterworth, Oliver
  The Enormous Egg
Byars, Betsy Cromer
  The Summer of the Swans
  The Pinballs
Cannon, A. E.
  Amazing Gracie
Cassedy, Sylvia
  Behind the Attic Wall
Conrad, Pam
  Prairie Songs
Cooney, Caroline B.
  The Face on the Milk Carton
Cooper, Susan
  Over Sea, Under Stone
Coville, Bruce
  Jeremy Thatcher, Dragon Hatcher
  The Ghost Wore Gray
Dahl, Roald
  James and the Giant Peach

DeAngeli, Marguerite
  The Door in the Wall
DeFelice, Cynthia C.
  Weasel
De Jong, Meindert
  The Wheel on the School
Drucker, Malka
  Jacob's Rescue: A Holocaust Story
Estes, Eleanor Ruth
  The Hundred Dresses
Ferguson, Alane
  Cricket and the Crackerbox Kid
Fitzhugh, Louise
  Harriet the Spy
Fleischman, Paul
  I Am Phoenix: Poems for Two Voices
Fleischman, Sid
  Bull Run
Gardiner, John Reynolds
  Stone Fox
Gates, Doris
  Blue Willow
George, Jean Craighead
  Julie of the Wolves
Grahame, Kenneth
  The Wind in the Willows
Gray, Elizabeth Janet
  Adam of the Road
Greer, Gery
  Max and Me and the Time Machine
Henry, Marguerite
  King of the Wind
Hahn, Mary Downing
  Stepping on the Cracks
Hesse, Karen
  Letters from Rifka
Hunt, Irene
  Up a Road Slowly
Hobbs, Will
  Bearstone
Hopkins, Lee Bennet
  Dinosaurs

Level Red — xxviii — Bridges™

Irving, Washington
  The Legend of Sleepy Hollow
Juster, Norton
  The Phantom Tollbooth
Keith, Harold
  Rifles for Watie
Konigsburg E.L.
  From the Mixed Up Files of Mrs. Basil E. Frankweiler
Krumgold, Joseph
  … and Now Miguel
L'Engle, Madeline
  A Wrinkle in Time
Lawson, Robert
  Rabbit Hill
Le Guin, Ursula K.
  A Wizard of Earthsea
Lenski, Lois
  Strawberry Girl
Levetin, Soria
  Journey to America
Lewis, C.S.
  Chronicles of Narnia series
Lowry, Lois
  Number The Stars
  The Giver
MacBride, Roger Lea
  Little House on Rocky Ridge
MacLachlan, Patricia
  Sarah, Plain and Tall
McKinley, Robin
  The Blue Sword
Mills, Claudia
  Dinah In Love
  Dynamite Dinah
Moody, Ralph
  Little Britches: Father and I Were Ranchers
Murphy, Jim
  Across America on an Emigrant Train
Naylor, Phyllis Reynolds
  The Agony of Alice
Nixon, Joan Lowery
  Land of Hope
O'Brien, Robert C.
  Mrs. Frisby and the Rats of NIMH

O'Dell, Scott
  Streams to the River, River to the Sea
Park, Barbara
  Operation: Dump the Chump
  Skinnybones
Paterson, Katherine
  The Great Gilly Hopkins
Paulsen, Gary
  Hatchet
Peck, Richard E.
  Voices after Midnight
Peck, Robert Newton
  Soup
  Soup's Goat
Pevsner, Stella
  Me, My Goat, and My Sister's Wedding
Pinkwater, Daniel Manus
  Lizard Music
Pitts, Paul
  The Shadowman's Way
  Racing the Sun
Prelutsky, Jack
  Tyrannosaurus Was a Beast
Raskin, Ellen
  The Westing Game
Rawls, Wilson
  Where the Red Fern Grows
Roberts, Willo Davis
  The Pet-Sitting Peril
  The View from the Cherry Tree
Rinaldi, Ann
  The Fifth of March
Rostkowski, Margaret I.
  After the Dancing Days
Ruckman, Ivy
  Night of the Twisters
  Who Invited the Undertaker?
Rylant, Cynthia
  Every Living Thing
Sachar, Louis
  There's a Boy in the Girls' Bathroom
Seredy, Kate
  The White Stag
Smith, Doris Buchanan
  The Pennywhistle Tree
Smith, Robert Kimmel
  The War with Grandpa

Snyder, Zilpha Keatley
  The Egypt Game
  The Velvet Room
Sorensen, Virginia Eggertsen
  Miracles on Maple Hill
Speare, Elizabeth George
  Calico Captive
  The Witch of Blackbird Pond
Springer, Nancy
  Colt
Sperry, Armstrong
  Call It Courage
Stolz, Mary
  The Dog on Barkham Street
Taylor, Mildred D.
  Roll of Thunder, Hear My Cry
Taylor, Sydney
  All-of-a-Kind Family
Taylor, Theodore
  Timothy of the Cay
Terban, Marvin
  Hey, Hay! A Wagonful of Funny Homonym Riddles
Tolkein, J.R.R.
  The Hobbit
  The Lord of the Rings
Travers, P.L.
  Mary Poppins
Twohill, Maggie
  Valentine Frankenstein
Uchida, Yoshiko
  Journey to Topaz
Ullman, James Ramsey
  Banner in the Sky
Voight, Cynthia
  Wings of a Falcon
Wallace, Bill
  Beauty
  Never Say Quit
White, E. B.
  Trumpet of the Swan
Winthrop, Elizabeth
  The Castle in the Attic
  The Battle for the Castle
Wyss, Johann David
  The Swiss Family Robinson
Yep, Laurence
  Dragonwings
  Dragon's Gate

Ready for Reading

✔ Reading has been around for thousands of years and can open your mind to new ideas by making you think in different ways than television or radio!

✔ The more you read, the smarter you get!

Books I Have Finished Reading

Title	Author	Pages	Date Finished	Evaluation Great	Okay	Bad

Level Red xxx Bridges™

Incentive Contract Calendar

Month (Mes) _____

My parents and I decided that if I complete 15 days of *Bridges*™ and read _____ minutes a day, my incentive/reward will be:

(Si yo completo 15 días de *Bridges*™ y leo _____ minutos al día, mi recompensa será:)

_____

Child's Signature (Firma del Niño) _____

Parent's Signature (Firma del Padre) _____

Day 1 (Día 1)	☐	☐	____	Day 9	☐	☐	____
Day 2	☐	☐	____	Day 10	☐	☐	____
Day 3	☐	☐	____	Day 11	☐	☐	____
Day 4	☐	☐	____	Day 12	☐	☐	____
Day 5	☐	☐	____	Day 13	☐	☐	____
Day 6	☐	☐	____	Day 14	☐	☐	____
Day 7	☐	☐	____	Day 15	☐	☐	____
Day 8	☐	☐	____				

bridges

Parent: Initial the ____ for daily activities and reading your child completes.
Padre: (Marque ____ para las actividades y lectura que su niño complete.)

Child: Put a ✔ in the ☐ for the daily activities 📓 completed.
Pon ✔ en ☐ para las actividades diaria que hayas completado.

Put a ✔ in the ☐ for the daily reading 📘 completed.
Pon ✔ en ☐ para las actividades diarias de lectura que hayas completado.

Fun Activity Ideas

1. Describe what you look like and write it down.
Describe cómo te ves y escríbelo.

2. Make a picnic lunch for two. Invite a friend over for a picnic in your backyard.
Prepara un picnic para el almuerzo para dos personas. Invita a un amigo al picnic en el patio.

3. Feed the birds.
Alimenta a los pájaros.

4. Find some old socks, buttons, yarn, needle, and thread. Make puppets and name them. Then find a cardboard box and paint it. Cut a hole in the front to put the puppets through, and put on a puppet show for younger children.
Busca medias viejas, botones, lana, aguja e hilo. Fabrica títeres y nómbralos. Luego encuentra una caja de cartón y píntala. Hazle un agujero en el frente para pasar los títeres y prepara un espectáculo de títeres para los niños menores.

5. Polish a pair of your mom's or dad's shoes and put a love note in the toe.
Lustra un par de zapatos de tu mamá o papá y colócales una nota de amor en la punta.

6. Visit a sick neighbor, friend, or relative.
Visita a un vecino, amigo o pariente enfermo.

7. Hold a fire drill in your home.
Organiza un simulacro de incendio en tu hogar.

8. Start a diary.
Comienza a escribir un diario.

9. Learn how to do something you have always wanted to do, like play the guitar, cross-stitch, rollerblade, cook pizza, train your dog, etc.
Aprende a hacer algo que siempre hayas deseado hacer, como tocar la guitarra, bordar a punto cruz, patinar, cocinar pizza, entrenar a tu perro, etc.

10. Write a story about your friend.
Escribe una historia sobre un amigo.

11. In the evening, look at the sky. Find the first star and make a wish.
Por la tarde, observa el cielo, encuentra la primera estrella y pide un deseo.

12. Pick one of your favorite foods and learn how to make it.
Elige una de tus comidas favoritas y aprende a hacerla.

13. Make a pitcher of lemonade or tropical Kool-Aid and sell it in front of your house.
Prepara una jarra de limonada o Kool-Aid tropical y véndela en frente de tu casa.

14. Surprise a family member with breakfast in bed.
Sorprende a un miembro de la familia llevándole el desayuno a la cama.

Use the following information to solve these place value problems.

Day 1

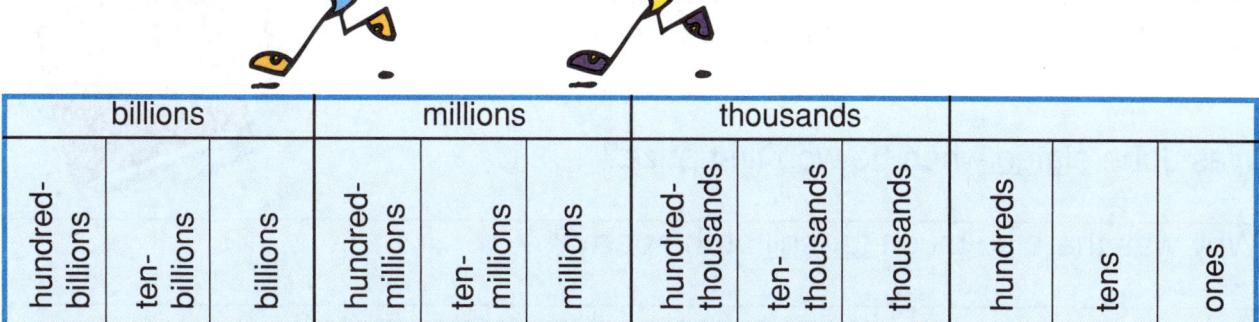

Remember: Commas separate millions, thousands, etc.

Write the following in expanded form.
Escribe estos números en forma expandida.

1. 72,584,361
   70,000,000 + 2,000,000 + 500,000 + 80,000 + 4,000 + 300 + 60 + 1

2. 37,126,489

3. 56,487,320,960

4. 90,675,409,783

Write the following using the correct word form.
Escribe estos números en letras en forma correcta.

5. 826,531,947,683
   Eight hundred twenty-six billion five hundred thirty-one million nine hundred forty-seven thousand six hundred eighty-three

6. 406,723,891,534

7. 861,750,432,971

8. 900,076,580,035

Day 1

Write a sentence showing what the underlined words below mean. Use the underlined word in your answer.

Escribe una oración‡ que muestre lo que significa cada palabra subrayada. Usa la palabra subrayada en tu oración.

1. Was John <u>elated</u> when he won first prize?
2. Why was there so much <u>turmoil</u> at the party?
3. Is it <u>mandatory</u> for you to go to school until you are eighteen?
4. Why is the little boy crying so <u>dolefully</u>?
5. Did the people raise enough money to <u>renovate</u> the old church?
6. Were the Scouts <u>intrepid</u> campers?
7. What was making the kitten <u>quiver</u> so hard?
8. Do you think Mr. Brown is a <u>corpulent</u> man?
9. How <u>palatable</u> are artichokes to you?
10. Were the police <u>inquisitive</u> about the cause of the accident?

Communication skills are very important. Read the sentences below. Rate yourself between 1 (lowest) and 5 (highest) on how well you communicate. Then answer the following questions.

Lee las oraciones. Califícate entre 1 (más bajo) y 5 (más alto) en lo bien que te comunicas. Responde las preguntas.

Your rating: _____

1. I speak clearly and loudly so others can hear what I am saying.   yes   no
2. I express my feelings.   yes   no
3. I try to think before I speak so I will not hurt others' feelings.   yes   no
4. I listen when others are talking.   yes   no
5. I do not share secrets that others have trusted me to keep.   yes   no

- What areas of communication are your strong points? _____
- What areas of communication do you need to improve? _____
- How might you improve in these areas? _____

Level Red   Bridges™

What's in a Number?
Write a definition and some examples of the following terms.
Escribe una definición y da algunos ejemplos de estos términos.

Day 2

Whole numbers	Number integers	Prime numbers	Composite numbers
_____	_____	_____	_____
_____	_____	_____	_____
_____	_____	_____	_____
_____	_____	_____	_____
_____	_____	_____	_____
_____	_____	_____	_____
_____	_____	_____	_____

Label as many states on this map as you can.
Coloca el nombre a la mayor cantidad posible de estados en este mapa.

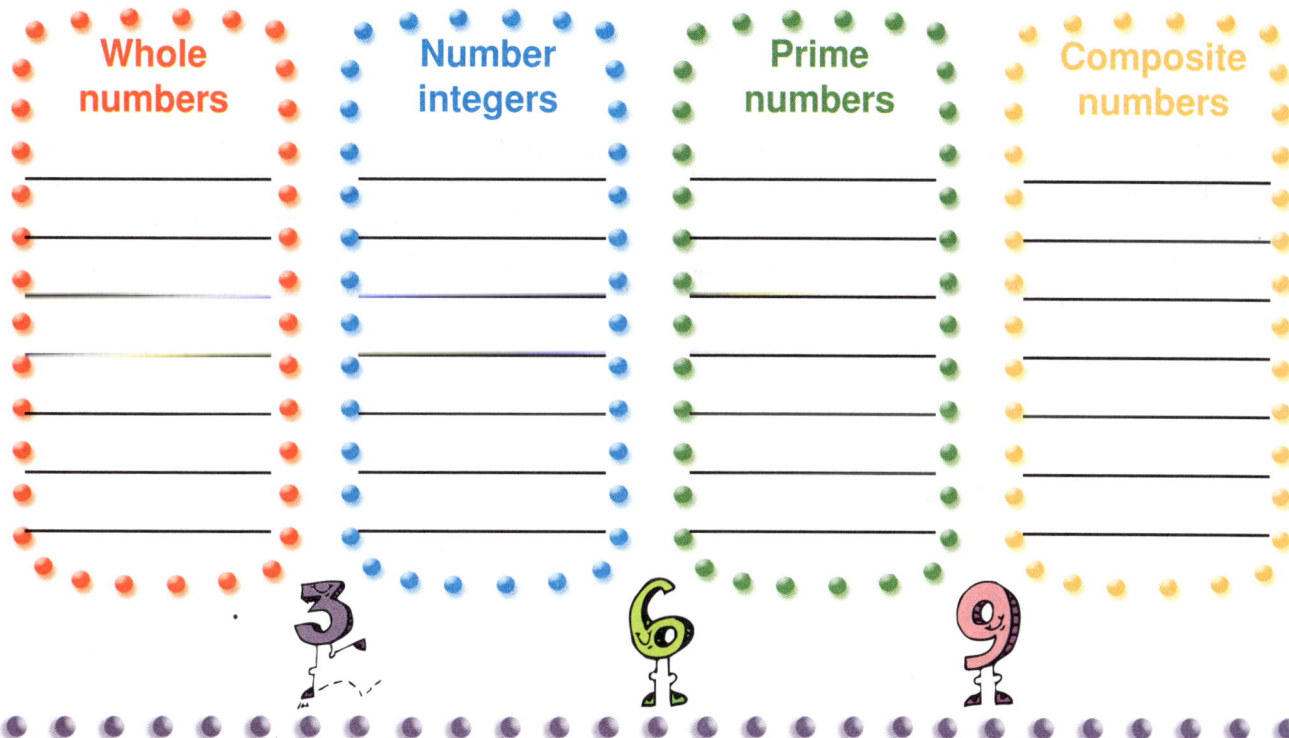

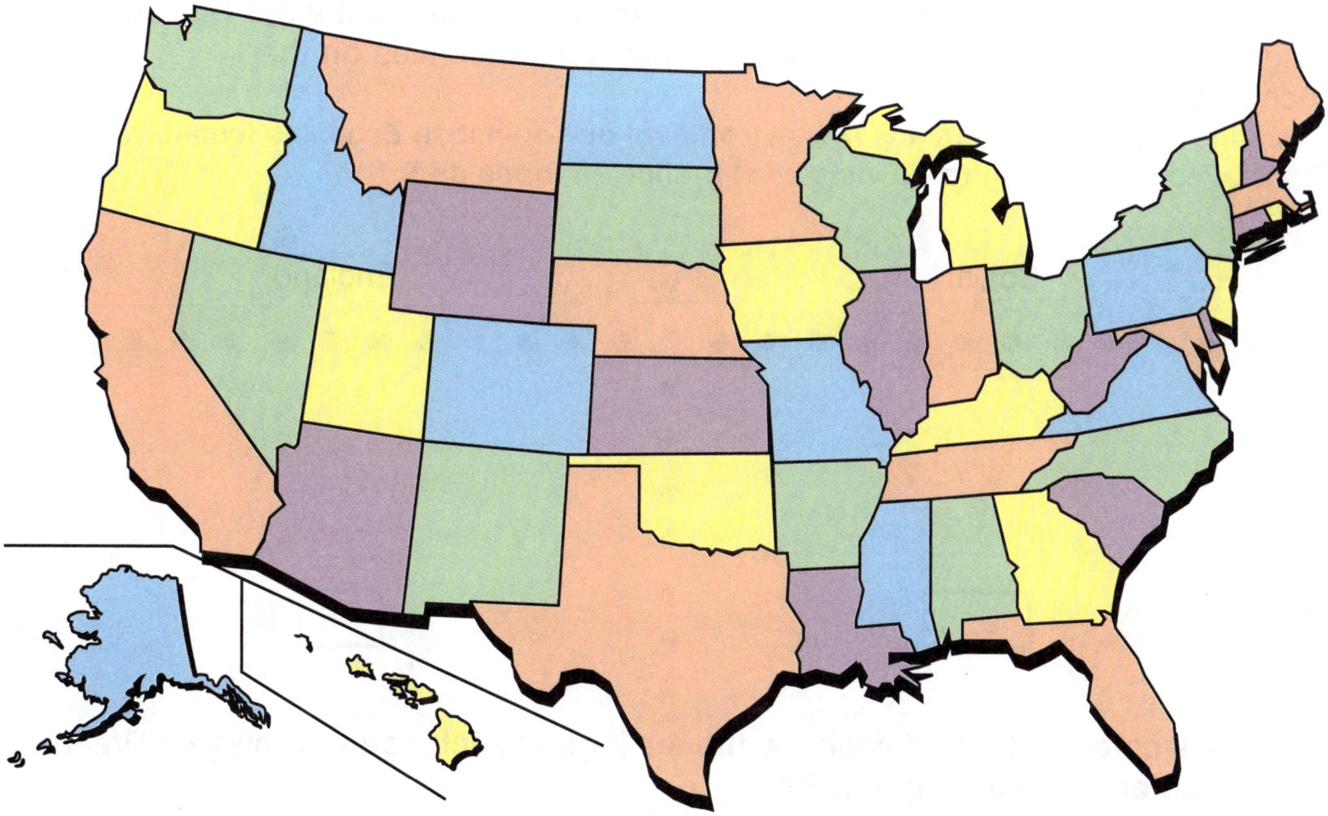

© Federal Education Publishing   5   Level Red

Name _____ Date _____

Day 2

Read the following paragraphs and answer the questions.
Lee estos párrafos y responde las preguntas.

Timbuktu is a small trading town in central Mali. It was established around 1100 A.D. and is located near the southern edge of the Sahara Desert. It was a trading post for products from North and West Africa. Camel caravans from the north traded salt, cloth, cowrie shells, and copper. The dealers in Timbuktu exchanged the goods for gold, kola nuts, ivory, and slaves that they got from the south.

Timbuktu's location left it open to attack, and control of the city changed many times. It has been ruled by the Mali Empire, the Songhai Empire, Morocco, nomads, and others. France controlled it from 1893 until 1960. However, as early as the 1600s it has declined in importance and population. Many of its mud and brick buildings are eroding and are half-buried in the sand.

1. What is the topic of the first paragraph?

2. What is the main idea of the first paragraph?

3. What is the topic of the second paragraph?

4. What is the main idea of the second paragraph?

Investigate the life of Sir Francis Drake. Compare the different ways Spain and England felt about Drake. Write these different perspectives on the T-chart below.
Investiga la vida de Sir Francis Drake. Compara qué opinaban España e Inglaterra sobre Drake. Escribe sus puntos de vista en el gráfico en forma de T.

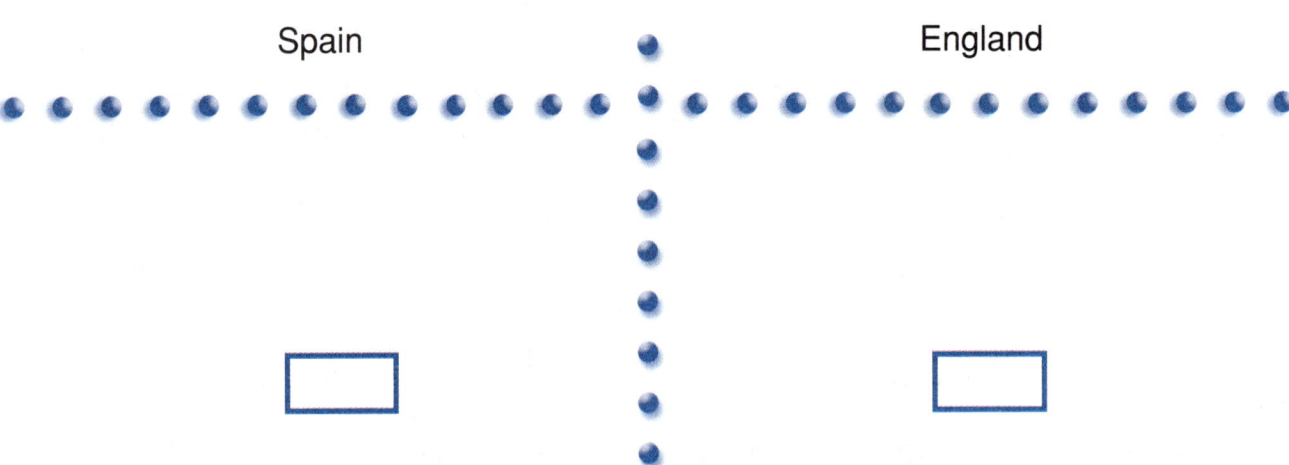

Choose a color that would describe the feelings of each country towards Drake. Put the color in the appropriate box.

Level Red   Bridges™

Front-End Estimation in Addition.
Estimate each sum by using your knowledge of rounding off numbers.
Estima cada suma⁺ redondeando los números.

 **Day 3**

1. 45 + 32   2. 74 + 23   3. 91 + 57   4. 37 + 83

5. 389 + 412   6. 278 + 582   7. 222 + 387   8. 625 + 371

9. 519 + 750   10. 432 + 929   11. 351 + 476   12. 948 + 511

13. 999 + 808   14. 1,243 + 3,569   15. 2,735 + 4,960   16. 5,429 + 2,099

17. 10,364 + 3,910   18. 22,100 + 30,439   19. 7,896 + 49,637   20. 34,433 + 16,377

21. 110,345 + 7,630   22. 205,933 + 460,362   23. 711,393 + 202,501   24. 473,926 + 410,345

Match the correct capital with each state.
Une el estado con la capital correcta.

___ Alabama	___ Nebraska	a. Montpelier	n. Salem
___ Arizona	___ New Hampshire	b. Honolulu	o. Boston
___ California	___ New Mexico	c. Hartford	p. Pierre
___ Connecticut	___ North Carolina	d. Lincoln	q. Sacramento
___ Florida	___ Ohio	e. Columbus	r. Frankfort
___ Hawaii	___ Oregon	f. Madison	s. Montgomery
___ Illinois	___ Rhode Island	g. St. Paul	t. Augusta
___ Iowa	___ South Dakota	h. Springfield	u. Raleigh
___ Kentucky	___ Texas	i. Phoenix	v. Austin
___ Maine	___ Vermont	j. Des Moines	w. Concord
___ Massachusetts	___ Washington	k. Providence	x. Tallahassee
___ Minnesota	___ Wisconsin	l. Olympia	y. Jefferson City
___ Missouri		m. Santa Fe	

© Federal Education Publishing   Level Red

Day 3

Look up the word <u>dramatize</u> in a dictionary and answer the following questions.
Busca la palabra <u>dramatize</u> en el diccionario y contesta las preguntas.

1. What are the guide words on the page?

2. How many meanings are listed for the word?

3. Write the word. Show the special spelling.

4. How many syllables does the word have?

5. What does <u>dramatize</u> mean in this sentence?
   Do you always have to <u>dramatize</u> everything, Annie?

6. Write the other forms of the word given in the dictionary and tell what part of speech they are.

7. List two other words on the same page as dramatize. Show the special spelling.

"I" Messages. A way to share feelings is to use an "I" message. An "I" message includes an action, effect, and feeling. For example, a friend is coming to your house so you can go to a show. He or she is late. You might say to your friend, "Because you were late [action], I thought we would miss the show [effect]. I was angry [feeling]."

Read the scenarios below and write an "I" message.
Lee las situaciones a continuación y escribe un mensaje "I".

1. You find out that a friend is telling lies about you.
   [action]
   [effect]
   [feeling]

2. Your parents have given you a special present.
   [action]
   [effect]
   [feeling]

3. You thought your friend was to meet you at 2:00, but he didn't come until 3:00.
   [action]
   [effect]
   [feeling]

4. Your friend tells you that you have hurt her/his feelings.
   [action]
   [effect]
   [feeling]

Day 4

Field Trip.

Lee el párrafo y responde las preguntas.

The students at Franklin Elementary School are going on a field trip to the Museum of Natural History. 3,068 students are going on Wednesday, and 2,864 are going on Thursday. Mr. Rand, the principal, wants to order special school name tags that come in packs of 1,000. Each package cost $5.25.

How many packages does Mr. Rand need to order? _____

What steps did you use to solve the problem?

Could you have used any of these ways or a combination of ways to find the answer?

- **a.** mental math
- **b.** estimation
- **c.** addition
- **d.** subtraction
- **e.** place value
- **f.** guessed

What information was essential to know before you solved the problem?

What information was not necessary to know?

Restate the problem, changing one or more of the facts without altering the solution or outcome of the problem.

Match the correct capital with each state.

Une el estado con la capital correcta.

State		State			Capital			Capital
____ Alaska		____ Nevada		**a.**	Salt Lake City	**n.**	Helena
____ Arkansas		____ New Jersey		**b.**	Lansing	**o.**	Cheyenne
____ Colorado		____ New York		**c.**	Bismarck	**p.**	Topeka
____ Delaware		____ North Dakota		**d.**	Annapolis	**q.**	Richmond
____ Georgia		____ Oklahoma		**e.**	Nashville	**r.**	Trenton
____ Idaho		____ Pennsylvania		**f.**	Juneau	**s.**	Boise
____ Indiana		____ South Carolina		**g.**	Harrisburg	**t.**	Albany
____ Kansas		____ Tennessee		**h.**	Dover	**u.**	Jackson
____ Louisiana		____ Utah		**i.**	Carson City	**v.**	Columbia
____ Maryland		____ Virginia		**j.**	Little Rock	**w.**	Baton Rouge
____ Michigan		____ West Virginia		**k.**	Indianapolis	**x.**	Atlanta
____ Mississippi		____ Wyoming		**l.**	Denver	**y.**	Charleston
____ Montana				**m.**	Oklahoma City		

© Federal Education Publishing — Level Red

Day 4

Write a sentence for each compound word below.
Escribe una oración‡ con cada palabra compuesta‡ a continuación.

- levelheaded
- hand-me-downs
- halfhearted
- lifesaver
- sightseers
- well-balanced
- self-addressed
- wholesale

1. _____
2. _____
3. _____
4. _____
5. _____
6. _____
7. _____
8. _____

• •

Study the chart of the skeletal system below. Go outside with a partner. Lie flat on the sidewalk and have your partner outline your body. Draw the skeletal system in the outline of your body. Label as many bones as you can.
Estudia el esquema del esqueleto y luego realiza esta actividad.

femur
humerus
scapula
radius
ulna
phalanges
metatarsals
fibula
tibia
phalanges
rib
clavicle
vertebrae
ilium
skull
patella
tarsals
sternum

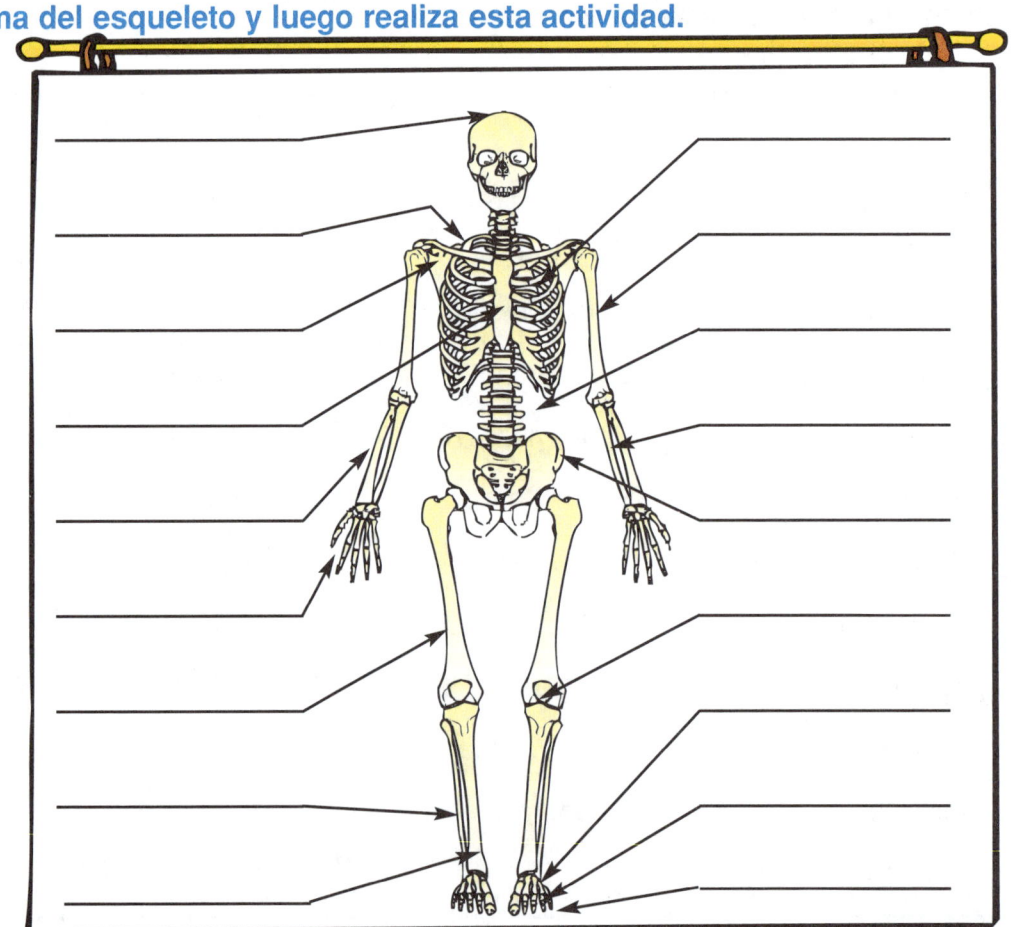

Level Red

Bridges™

Day 5

Estimation with Sums and Differences.
Estimate the sum or difference first; then find the actual sum or difference.
Estima la suma‡ o la diferencia‡ y luego encuentra la suma o diferencia correspondiente.

1. 8,666 +9,346 estimate_____ actual_____	2. 7,543 +2,396 estimate_____ actual_____	3. 3,693 +1,690 estimate_____ actual_____	4. 54,561 +36,287 estimate_____ actual_____
5. 34,865 +62,444 estimate_____ actual_____	6. 47,267 +55,085 estimate_____ actual_____	7. 65,639 +53,263 estimate_____ actual_____	8. 28,790 +83,964 estimate_____ actual_____
9. 5,394 -2,587 estimate_____ actual_____	10. 3,368 -2,139 estimate_____ actual_____	11. 69,293 -22,887 estimate_____ actual_____	12. 125,394 -69,831 estimate_____ actual_____
13. 25,689 -13,798 estimate_____ actual_____	14. 417,937 -409,986 estimate_____ actual_____	15. 709,723 -337,251 estimate_____ actual_____	16. 876,259 -395,828 estimate_____ actual_____

Below are the stressed syllables of some spelling words. Write the other syllables and then write the words in cursive. Each blank stands for a letter.
A continuación se encuentran las sílabas‡ tónicas de algunas palabras. Escribe las otras sílabas y luego escribe las palabras. Cada espacio en blanco representa una letra.

practice   purchaser   glamorous   trillion
measure   refund   ~~January~~   appearance
improvement   magazine   diamond   manager
amazement   chosen   attention   causing

1. Jan´ **u a r y**   *January*   9. di´ _ _ _ _ _ _ _   _____
2. ___ ten´ _ _ _ _ _ _   10. mag´ _ _ _ _ _ _   _____
3. pur´ _ _ _ _ _ _ _   11. man´ _ _ _ _ _   _____
4. re´ _ _ _ _ _   12. caus´ _ _ _ _   _____
5. tril´ _ _ _ _ _   13. __maze´ _ _ _ _   _____
6. mea´ _ _ _ _ _   14. glam´ _ _ _ _ _ _   _____
7. ___ pear´ _ _ _ _ _   15. prac´ _ _ _ _ _   _____
8. cho´ _ _ _ _   16. ___ prove´ _ _ _ _ _   _____

Day 5

Some sentences have a clue word to help show the cause-effect relationship. Fill in the blanks with clue words. Then write the cause and effect.
Completa los espacios en blanco con palabras que muestren la relación causa-efecto. Luego escribe la causa y el efecto.

Our school was closed today <u>because</u> of the bad snowstorm we had last night.
Cause: *Bad snowstorm.*
Effect: *School was closed.*

1. It snowed all day, _____ the ground was white.
   Cause: _____
   Effect: _____

2. Our electricity went off last night, _____ we went out to dinner.
   Cause: _____
   Effect: _____

3. _____ Joe left the gate unlatched, all the cattle were out in the road.
   Cause: _____
   Effect: _____

4. Scott woke up with the flu today; _____ , he had to miss school.
   Cause: _____
   Effect: _____

5. _____ I know how much Judy loves to read, I got her a set of books for her birthday.
   Cause: _____
   Effect: _____

Science–Structure of the Earth. Label the different layers of the earth with the terms below. Use the same terms to complete the sentences below.
Usa estos términos para colocar los nombres a los estratos de la tierra y para completar las oraciones.

center of the earth   crust   inner core
lithosphere   mantle   outer core

1. The core of the earth has two parts.
   The _____ is liquid.
   The _____ is solid.

2. One reason the crust and _____ are brittle is because they are the outermost and coldest layers of the earth.

3. The top layer of the earth is the _____.

4. The _____ is extremely hot and is the thickest layer.

5. As the _____ is approached, pressure and temperature increase.

Level Red   12   Bridges™

Day 6

Mental Math for Multiples of 10, 100, and 1,000. Remember to use mental math!
Usa el cálculo mental para resolver estos problemas.

1. 7 x 10 = _____
2. 16 x 10 = _____
3. 10 x 92 = _____
4. 100 x 8 = _____
5. 50 x 50 = _____
6. 7 x 600 = _____
7. 500 x 200 = _____
8. 5 x 900 = _____
9. 70 x 60 = _____
10. 30 x 400 = _____
11. 200 x 300 = _____
12. 400 x 600 = _____
13. 8 x 1,000 = _____
14. 9 x 3,000 = _____
15. 30 x 5,000 = _____
16. 900 x 200 = _____
17. 800 x 600 = _____
18. 10 x 1,800 = _____
19. 9,000 x 700 = _____
20. 7,000 x 50 = _____
21. 60 x 8,000 = _____
22. 700 x 800 = _____
23. 900 x 900 = _____
24. 1,000 x 19 = _____
25. 52 x 2,000 = _____
26. 400 x 300 = _____
27. 5,000 x 50 = _____
28. 250 x 200 = _____
29. 15,000 x 30 = _____
30. 200,000 x 40 = _____

Healthy Lifestyles. Fill in the chart of acts and consequences. Using the last two lines, fill in two acts that you may do in a day and what consequences follow.
Completa el cuadro de actos y consecuencias. Completa las últimas dos líneas con dos ejemplos propios.

Acts	Consequences
1. Do not eat breakfast	
2. Cheat on test	
3.	Get an A in spelling
4. Comfort a friend	
5.	Feel good about yourself
6.	You have a lot of energy
7. Take a shower every day	
8. Adult catches your friend smoking	
9.	Get sick
10. Visit the elderly	
11. Say NO to drugs	
12.	
13.	

Day 6

Show the syllables by leaving a space between them. Then write <u>long</u>, <u>short</u>, <u>schwa</u>, or <u>silent</u> for the vowel sound in each syllable. The schwa sound is usually heard in the unstressed syllable.

Separa en sílabas‡ dejando un espacio entre ellas. Luego escribe <u>larga</u>, <u>breve</u>, <u>schwa</u>‡ o <u>sorda</u> para el sonido vocal de cada sílaba.

EXAMPLE: terrific   ter   ri   fic   schwa   short   short

1. jackal
2. liable
3. volcano
4. that
5. attraction
6. billow
7. paralysis
8. identify
9. mold
10. victory
11. lesson
12. referee

The Muscular System and Nervous System. Fill in the blanks with the correct word.

Completa los espacios en blanco con la palabra correcta.

cerebrum	involuntary muscles	medulla
nervous system	voluntary muscles	cerebellum
contracts	spinal cord	

1. Muscles you can control are called _____.

2. When one muscle in a pair _____, or shortens, the other muscle relaxes.

3. _____ are muscles that work automatically, such as the heart.

4. The _____ is the network of cells that receive and send messages to and from the brain and spinal cord to every part of your body.

5. The part of your brain that controls your learning and memory is the _____.

6. The _____ controls how your muscles work together.

7. The part of your brain that controls your heart rate and breathing is the _____.

8. The _____ extends from the base of the brain down your back and is involved with all senses.

Day 7

Multiplying by 2- and 3-Digit Numbers.
Multiplica.

Remember:

```
    218          429           293
 x   36       x  375        x  704
  1308         2145          1172
   654         3003           000
  7848         1287          2051
              160875        206272
```

1. 826 x 47	2. 584 x 29	3. 249 x 63	4. 973 x 51
5. 670 x 94	6. 776 x 68	7. 845 x 77	8. 392 x 82
9. 628 x 274	10. 831 x 347	11. 609 x 149	12. 586 x 781
13. 196 x 175	14. 594 x 739	15. 854 x 837	16. 697 x 507

Possessive and plural forms of many nouns sound alike but are different. An s can make the base word noun become a singular possessive. For example: All the <u>players'</u> (plural) coats looked the same, but one <u>player's</u> (singular possessive) coat was ripped in the back. In the following sentences, cross out the plurals and possessives that are incorrect. Write them correctly at the right of the sentences. If they are right, just write "correct."

Tacha los plurales‡ y posesivos incorrectos. Escríbelos correctamente en los espacios en blanco. Escribe OK si no hay errores.

1. All the news <u>reporter's</u> decided to stay at the Brookgreen Inn. _____
2. Ten <u>driver's</u> went out on the job this morning, but only nine returned on time. _____
3. One <u>drivers</u> truck was stuck in a huge snowdrift. _____
4. The <u>announcer's</u> voice sounded awful this morning. _____
5. Many <u>authors</u> had a convention last year to come up with
   new ideas for books. _____
6. The <u>authors</u> new book sold 1,000 copies in four hours. _____
7. The <u>organizer's</u> of this party can be proud of themselves. _____

Day 7

Sequence.
Read this paragraph; then write the main points in the correct order.
Lee y luego escribe los puntos principales en el orden correcto.

Traveling Spiders

The baby wolf spider rides on its mother's back. Jumping spiders travel by ballooning. They raise their abdomens so the wind can pull silk threads from their spinnerets. The wind then lifts the little spiders into the air like balloons on strings. Fisher spiders are very lightweight, so they can travel by walking on water. Crab spiders walk backwards and sidewards. All spiders can make and travel on a dragline (a silk thread).

1. _____
2. _____
3. *Fisher spiders can walk on water.*
4. _____
5. _____

Digestive System.
Put the steps of the digestive process in the proper sequence.
Ordena las fases del proceso digestivo en la secuencia correcta.

_____ Food moves to the small intestine.

_____ The tongue pushes food down the esophagus.

_____ Undigested food passes out of the body through the anus.

_____ Villi in the small intestine absorb digested food into the bloodstream.

_____ Teeth and saliva start to change food.

_____ Undigested food moves to the large intestine, or colon.

_____ Food goes to the stomach where it is further broken down.

Level Red

Day 8

Add, subtract, or multiply. Find the answer to each of the following story problems and tell which operation you used to solve the problem.
Suma, resta o multiplica para resolver los problemas.
Escribe qué operación utilizaste en el espacio en blanco.

1. A person can make 36 single-dipped ice cream cones out of one gallon of ice cream. If you have 12 different flavors of one-gallon ice cream containers, how many cones do you need to use all of the ice cream? _____

2. Mrs. Stone hand-dipped 425 chocolates the first of May, 592 the middle of May, and 143 the last part of May. How many chocolates did she make in May? _____

3. Farmer Tim sold 4,987 pounds of potatoes last year and 12,709 pounds this year. Next year he hopes to do even better. How many more pounds of potatoes did he sell this year than last year? _____

4. Denim shorts sell for $27.59 a pair at Lornet Department Store. Its regular denim jeans sell for $12.18 more than its denim shorts. How much do the store's regular denim jeans cost? _____

5. Mirror Park has 73 ducks on its lake. An average of 670 people visit the ducks each day. If each person fed the ducks 3 pieces of bread each day, how many pieces of bread would each duck get each day? _____

6. If each person in the United States drank 42 gallons of milk a year, and each gallon cost $1.98, how much would each person spend on milk a year? _____

7. Vicki planted 136 red tulip bulbs, 734 white bulbs, and 400 yellow bulbs. How many flowers will she have if each bulb blooms? _____

8. Gloria bought 25 pairs of socks at $5.80 a pair. If her mother gave her $500, would she have enough money left to buy 6 pairs of shoes at $30.00 each? _____

9. Griffin came home with 12 popsicles that cost him $3.00 a dozen. He sold 2 popsicles to his sister, Brynn, at 50¢ each and 4 popsicles to his brother, Tyler, at 50¢ each. How much profit will Griffin make after he sells the rest to his Grandma Dorene at 50¢ each? _____

Look in an atlas. Which states contain the following latitude and longitude?
Busca en un atlas. ¿Qué estados contienen estas latitudes y longitudes?

1. 40° N, 110° W _____
2. 35° N, 110° W _____
3. 35° N, 120° W _____
4. 40° N, 83° W _____
5. 33° N, 87° W _____
6. What is the latitude and longitude of one corner of your state? _____
7. What is the latitude and longitude of your city or town? _____

© Federal Education Publishing   Level Red

Day 8

Context clues help you learn new words and their meanings. Use the context clues in the following sentences to tell what the underlined words mean.
Utiliza las pistas del contexto de la oración‡ para determinar qué significan las palabras subrayadas. Escribe el significado.

1. Mary feigned surprise when her friends had a birthday party for her.

    feigned– _____

2. My colleagues and I work together on many new projects.

    colleagues– _____

3. Maurice looks at his watch often to make sure he is always punctual.

    punctual– _____

4. Joseph, a philatelist, has a large collection of stamps.

    philatelist– _____

5. The pig napping in the mud was hardly able to bestir itself for its dinner.

    bestir– _____

Read the following passage and answer the questions below.
Lee los párrafos y responde las preguntas.

    Englishman Sir Walter Raleigh wanted to start a colony in the New World (North America). In 1585, Raleigh sent colonists to what is now North Carolina. The colonists did not want to work and almost starved to death. They were taken back to England. Two years later a second group of colonists sailed over to the same place as the previous colonists. They worked very hard to survive.

    Because of a war involving England, Raleigh lost track of the colonists. In 1591, a ship from England finally arrived to check on the colonists, but the colonists had disappeared! There was no sign of life. All the sailors found were some empty trunks, rotted maps, and the word CROATOAN carved on the doorpost of the fort. Croatoan was an island 100 miles south of The Lost Colony. No one knows if the colonists were attacked by the Croatoan Indians or if the settlers went to live on Croatoan Island. The Lost Colony has been a great mystery in American history.

1. How many years has it been since the first colony settled in North Carolina?

2. What year did Raleigh send the second set of colonists to North Carolina?

3. How many years did it take Raleigh to send a ship to check on the second set of colonists?

4. Why was this colony called The Lost Colony?

5. State what you think might have happened to The Lost Colony.

6. Think of a title that would be appropriate for this passage.

Level Red   Bridges™

Day 9

Find the quotient when dividing whole numbers.
Encuentra el cociente‡ y el resto.

EXAMPLE:

$$9 \overline{)829} \quad \begin{array}{r} 92 \text{ R } 1 \\ \underline{81} \\ 19 \\ \underline{18} \\ 1 \end{array}$$

829 ÷ 9 = 92 with the remainder of 1

Use mental math or scratch paper if needed.

1. 8)231
2. 4)394
3. 9)894
4. 5)3,305
5. 6)56,707

6. 7)6,845
7. 90)270
8. 60)480
9. 20)1,900
10. 42)336

11. 75)675
12. 63)315
13. 52)4,173
14. 70)5,844
15. 83)4,978

16. 59)4,538
17. 94)2,980
18. 41)3,613
19. 27)6,641
20. 52)9,385

21. 44)9,599
22. 57)92,831
23. 40)73,847
24. 62)79,365
25. 31)62,620

Spelling.
Find the word that is misspelled in each row and spell it correctly.
Encuentra la palabra escrita incorrectamente en cada línea y escríbela de manera correcta.

1.	refund	remodel	decode	previw
2.	deposet	pretend	deflate	pace
3.	mold	respond	brutel	revise
4.	fiction	grieff	unsafe	equip
5.	transfer	defend	truthful	penlty
6.	prdict	decide	gossip	fragile
7.	beware	precice	porches	capital
8.	leashes	cipher	volt	climack
9.	month	friendly	wrench	businiss
10.	jiant	angle	guest	greet
11.	surgery	magnit	usually	bearish
12.	slogan	gigantck	beast	galley

© Federal Education Publishing   19   Level Red

Day 9

Prefixes are added to the beginning of base words. Add prefixes to these base words. Use as many prefixes as you can with the base words and see how many you can make. Use prefixes mis-, re-, un-, non-, and pre-.

Agrega los prefijos‡ mis-, re-, un-, non- y pre- a estas palabras base. Trata de formar la mayor cantidad posible de palabras.

EXAMPLE: view – preview   review

Base words:

join _____	trace _____
name _____	heat _____
spell _____	cut _____
treat _____	turn _____
stop _____	read _____
sure _____	fit _____
call _____	place _____

Choose one word for each of the prefixes and write a sentence with it.

Elige una palabra para cada uno de los prefijos y escribe una oración‡ con la misma.

mis 1._____

re   2._____

un   3._____

non 4._____

pre 5._____

Circulatory System. Label the different parts of the heart with the terms listed. Color the side of the heart that has oxygen-rich blood red. Color the side of the heart where the blood is lacking oxygen blue.

Coloca el nombre a las partes del corazón. Colorea de rojo el lado del corazón con sangre rica en oxígeno. Colorea el otro lado de azul.

- aorta
- left ventricle
- tricuspid valve
- cardiac septum
- left atrium
- aortic valve
- pulmonary valve
- right ventricle
- right atrium
- bicuspid valve
- pulmonary artery
- pulmonary vein

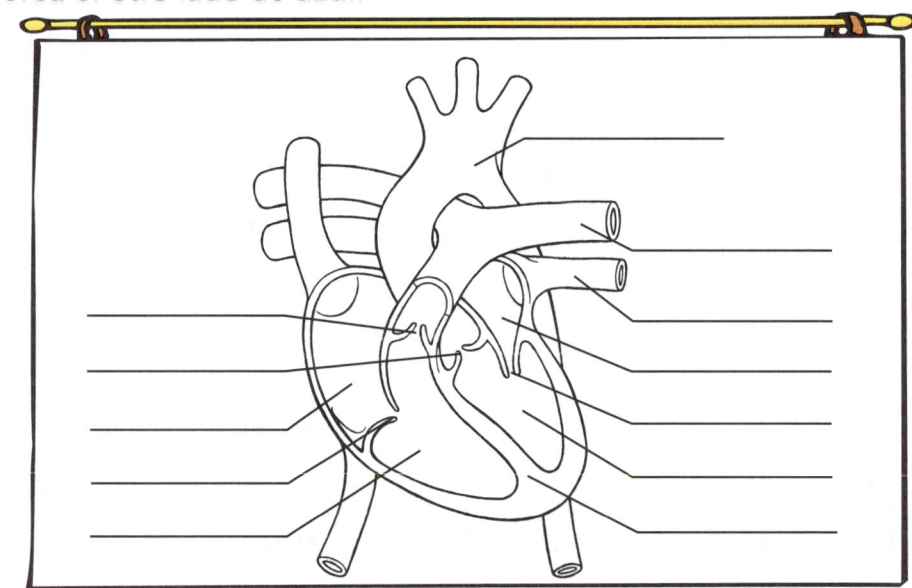

Level Red

Bridges™

Day 10

Mixed Practice. Be sure to watch the signs. You can use mental math or a piece of scratch paper if needed.
Práctica matemática.

1. 684 ÷ 9 = _____
2. 356 ÷ 8 = _____
3. 793 x 27 = _____
4. 469 ÷ 7 = _____
5. 7,133 ÷ 8 = _____
6. 4,036 x 9 = _____
7. 143 + 973 = _____
8. 72,483 + 56,774 = _____
9. 8)9,696 = _____
10. 63,459 - 21,365 = _____
11. 90)48,713 = _____
12. 569,040 ÷ 8 = _____
13. 53,907 x 6 = _____
14. 483 x 175 = _____
15. 763,947 - 244,398 = _____
16. 45)29,705 = _____
17. 14,008 ÷ 60 = _____
18. $678.14 + $990.27 = _____
19. 297 x 47 = _____
20. 3,046 x 70 = _____
21. 34,148 + 95,228 = _____
22. 49,375 ÷ 71 = _____
23. 573 + 4,935 + 7,340 = _____
24. 75)566,212 = _____
25. 456,350 ÷ 32 = _____
26. 3,804 x 43 = _____

Matter. Matter exists in three states: solid, liquid, and gas. Put the following words in the appropriate categories.
La materia existe en estado sólido, líquido o gaseoso. Coloca estas palabras en la categoría correcta.

butter   lava   oxygen   water
box   dust   ice   radon
milk   juice   nitrogen vapor

Solid	Liquid	Gas

Water can be in three different states: liquid-water, solid-ice, gas-vapor. See if you can come up with some items in your home that can be in more than one state.
Piensa en ítems de tu hogar que puedan presentarse en más de un estado.

Solid	Liquid	Gas

© Federal Education Publishing — Level Red

Day 10

You have taken two kinds of tests in the past year: <u>essay</u> and <u>objective</u> tests. When you take an <u>essay</u> test you write out the answers. When you take an an <u>objective</u> test you have multiple-choice, true-false, matching, and completion questions. When you take a test, read the directions carefully before you begin. Think about how much time you should take for each question and then begin. Answer the following questions and tell what kind of test they would be on. Also, if the question is from an objective test, write the type of question.

Responde estas preguntas e identifica si pertenecen a un examen objetivo‡ o a un examen de desarrollo‡. Si la pregunta pertenece a un examen objetivo, escribe qué tipo de pregunta es: verdadero-falso, selección múltiple, etc.

1. Match the words below to their meaning.

equip	confused noise
clatter	to make whiter
penalty	to ask for advice
bleach	furnish
consult	punishment

   Kind of test _____   Kind of question _____

2. Write a paragraph about the produce grown in the state where you live.

   _____
   _____
   _____

   Kind of test _____   Kind of question _____

3. Fill in the blanks.

   a. Most cars run on a fuel called _____.

   b. _____ is candy made with milk, sugar, chocolate, and butter.

   c. _____ _____ is famous for his animated movies.

   d. This state does not border any other state or nation. It is _____.

   e. A sombrero is a kind of _____.

   Kind of test _____   Kind of question _____

4. Write F for false, T for true.

   a. All mammals live on land. _____

   b. After the Industrial Revolution, many people moved to the cities. _____

   c. Eli Whitney invented the cotton gin. _____

   d. A census worker helps find out how many people live in the United States. _____

   Kind of test _____   Kind of question _____

Level Red   Bridges™

Multiples and Common Multiples.

Day 11

Remember: A <u>multiple</u> is a number exactly divisible by another number.
   6 12 18 24 30 are multiples of 6.
Remember: The <u>common multiples</u> for 2 and 4 are 4, 8, 12, or other "numbers in common."

List five or six multiples for the following numbers.
Enumera cinco o seis múltiplos‡ de estos números.

1. 5 _____
2. 9 _____
3. 7 _____
4. 2 _____
5. 10 _____
6. 12 _____
7. 3 _____
8. 8 _____

List three common multiples for these numbers.
Enumera tres múltiplos comunes para estos números.

9. 3 and 4 _____
10. 5 and 10 _____
11. 8 and 12 _____
12. 2 and 9 _____
13. 4 and 7 _____
14. 6 and 8 _____
15. 8 and 10 _____
16. 5 and 6 _____

17. What is the least common multiple for 2 and 9? _____
18. For 5 and 6? _____   19. For 3 and 4? _____   20. For 8 and 10? _____

Refusal skills help a person say No to risky behaviors and situations. Here are some refusal skills you can use:

- Say No firmly and clearly.
- Walk away if a person continues to pressure you.
- Suggest an alternative activity.
- Tell an adult you trust if you are continually pressured.
- Explain the consequences.

Read the following situations below. How would you respond to each situation? Use some of the refusal skills listed above.
Lee las siguientes situaciones. ¿Cómo responderías? Utiliza algunas de las negaciones enumeradas arriba.

1. Your friend's older sister has a pack of cigarettes in her bedroom. Your friend dares you to try one.
2. While at the store, you see a video that your really want to watch. A friend suggests you hide the video in your coat and take it home.
3. Your friend didn't study for the test today. He wants you to let him look at your paper during the test.
4. A group of friends tell you that to be in their club, you need to make fun of other students.

© Federal Education Publishing — Level Red

Day 11

Writing Complete Sentences. <u>Remember</u>: A complete sentence expresses a complete thought. If it does not express a complete thought it is called a sentence fragment. A complete sentence needs to tell whom or what the sentence is about and what happened to the whom or what.

Match the sentence fragments to make complete sentences.
Une los fragmentos de las oraciones para formar oraciones‡ completas.

1. Folklore is passed
2. The early cattle ranchers
3. Jodie rides her
4. The snake in the science corner
5. Can you balance a book

on your head?
escaped from its cage.
drove their cattle to the market.
from generation to generation.
bike to school most days.

For each of the following, write <u>F</u> if it is a sentence fragment or <u>S</u> if it is a complete sentence.
En el espacio en blanco, escribe <u>F</u> si la oración es un fragmento o <u>S</u> si la oración está completa.

1. All of my friends like spaghetti. _____
2. Went camping last summer. _____
3. A turkey buzzard is a dark-colored vulture. _____
4. Collects signatures for the P.T.A. _____
5. Answered the most questions. _____
6. Mr. Able turned on the lights. _____
7. Is Dr. Gold going to put? _____
8. Rummy is the name of a card game. _____

Colonies in the New World.

Many colonists came over by boat to settle in the New World. Make a list of the supplies these adventuresome colonists would need. Write them on the scroll. Try to write as many items as you can!

Analyze the list you made. Circle in red the most important supplies one would need. Underline in blue the supplies that are of medium importance. Cross out in green the supplies that would not be necessary.

Haz una lista de provisiones que necesitarías para colonizar una nueva tierra.

Level Red   Bridges™

Day 12

Adding and Subtracting with Decimals.
Remember: The first step when adding or subtracting decimals is to line up the decimals. If the number of decimal places is not the same, you can attach zeros to the end of a number to make it easier.
Suma‡ o resta. Recuerda alinear los decimales.

EXAMPLE: 3.45 + 5.923 =   3.450
                          + 5.923
                            9.373

Solve the problems.

1. 18.91 + 11.5 = _____
2. 3.806 + 5.29 = _____
3. 5.619 + 3.041 = _____
4. 76.453 + 82.5 = _____
5. 437.7 + 13.906 = _____
6. 42.881 + 8.96 = _____
7. 49.07 - 36.05 = _____
8. 65.007 - 6.3 = _____
9. 34.09 - 9.407 = _____
10. 185.04 - 165.9 = _____
11. 379.76 - 37.435 = _____
12. $224.00 - $116.98 = _____
13. 49.071 + 23.015 = _____
14. 85.089 - 34.12 = _____
15. 377.76 + 59.94 = _____
16. 365.50 - 54.935 = _____

Analogies. Analogies show relationships between words, such as <u>preview</u> is to <u>previewed</u> as <u>decide</u> is to <u>decided</u>, or <u>hear</u> is to <u>ear</u> as <u>talk</u> is to <u>mouth</u>.

Write an analogy for each of the following comparisons.
Escribe una analogía‡ para cada una de las siguientes comparaciones.

1. <u>Blue</u> is to <u>color</u> as <u>nutmeg</u> is to _____.
2. <u>Griddle</u> is to <u>pancake</u> as <u>pot</u> is to _____.
3. <u>Author</u> is to <u>book</u> as <u>artist</u> is to _____.
4. <u>Business</u> is to <u>businesses</u> as <u>address</u> is to _____.
5. <u>Research</u> is to <u>researcher</u> as <u>garden</u> is to _____.
6. <u>Breakfast</u> is to <u>lunch</u> as <u>morning</u> is to _____.
7. <u>Control</u> is to <u>controllable</u> as <u>reason</u> is to _____.
8. <u>TV</u> is to <u>commercial</u> as <u>magazine</u> is to _____.
9. <u>Sad</u> is to <u>cry</u> as <u>shout</u> is to _____.
10. <u>Manager</u> is to <u>store</u> as <u>principal</u> is to _____.
11. <u>Chair</u> is to <u>table</u> as <u>mattress</u> is to _____.

 is to

 as

 is to

© Federal Education Publishing   Level Red

Day 12

Complete Subjects and Predicates. The subject tells what or whom the sentence is about. The predicate tells about the subject.

Listed below are some complete predicates. Write a complete subject to go with them.

Escribe un sujeto‡ completo que coincida con estos predicados‡ completos.

1. _____ know how to operate the computers.
2. _____ fascinated Megan.
3. _____ misplaced his new pocket knife.
4. _____ need water.
5. _____ collapsed suddenly.
6. _____ crashed into the ditch.

Listed below are some complete subjects. Write a complete predicate to go with them.

Escribe un predicado completo que coincida con estos sujetos completos.

7. The package _____.
8. A team of horses _____.
9. The famous actor _____.
10. Sarah and Julie _____.
11. Anthills _____.
12. Nobody _____.

Research the settling of the Puritans and Pilgrims in the New World. Fill in the Venn diagram with their similarities and differences.

Investiga sobre los Puritanos y Colonizadores. Anota semejanzas y diferencias‡ en el diagrama de Venn.

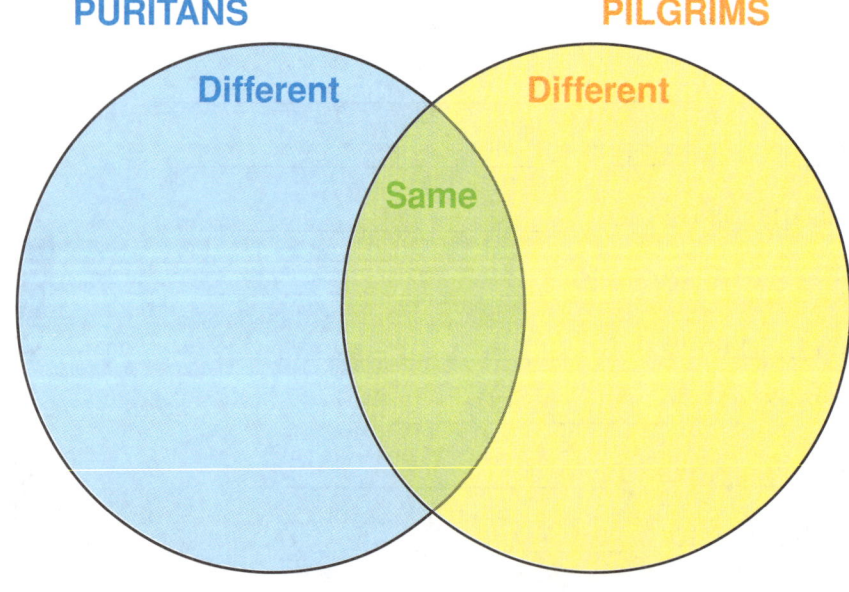

A good book to read about this period in American history is The Witch of Blackbird Pond by Elizabeth George Speare. It is the story of a young girl who lives in a Puritan settlement.

Level Red 26 Bridges™

Multiplying Whole Numbers and Decimals.
Remember to put the decimal point in the correct place in the product.
Multiplica. Recuerda ubicar el decimal en el lugar correcto del producto‡.

1.	0.12 × 6	2.	0.08 × 7	3.	4.6 × 3	4.	5.05 × 8	5.	2.9 × 5	6.	2.71 × 4
7.	6.5 × 13	8.	1.906 × 28	9.	7.0216 × 52	10.	6.65 × 77	11.	5.364 × 93	12.	0.0352 × 49
13.	3.613 × 84	14.	40.35 × 38	15.	7.735 × 47	16.	9.546 × 68	17.	7.263 × 87	18.	9.634 × 54
19.	359.073 × 24	20.	5.9081 × 71	21.	12.504 × 99	22.	8.709 × 56	23.	27.035 × 93	24.	7.893 × 32

25. Jan works delivering pizza and gets paid $37.40 a night. She works 23 nights each month. How much does Jan earn each month? _____

26. Jake works at a grocery store. He gets paid $8.65 an hour for each hour he works. He usually works 37 hours a week. How much does he earn in a week? How much would he earn in a 4 weeks? _____

Chemical Change. With chemical change, two or more substances are combined to form a completely new substance. For example, iron plus oxygen makes rust. Physical change occurs when a substance changes but no new substance is formed (e.g., water to ice).

Read the list below. Determine if a physical change and/or chemical change has occurred. Then come up with some of your own ideas!
Lee la lista a continuación. Determina si ocurre un cambio físico‡ y/o un cambio químico‡. ¡Luego da tus propias ideas!

Activity	Physical Change	Chemical Change	Own Ideas
Chopping wood			
Baking cookies			
Burning wood			
Painting a door			
Making ice cubes			
Cutting tomatoes			
Making ice cream			

Day 13 — Two Kinds of Verbs: Action Verbs and State-of-Being Verbs.

Action verbs tell about an action you can see (ran) or an action you cannot see (hear).

State-of-being verbs tell what something or someone is (is, are, am, appear, look, etc.).

Make a design by coloring the action verbs orange and the state-of-being verbs green. Color the empty spaces any color you like, except orange or green.

Colorea los verbos‡ activos de naranja y los verbos copulativos‡ de verde. Colorea los espacios vacíos de cualquier otro color.

				walk	has been			
				sound	call			
				dance	are			
				will be	sit			
	caught			laugh	been		honked	
				smell	plays			
see				wore	feel			seem
	being			will	gather		were	
			dive	jump	won	dive		
asking	rolled	wiggled		be	is	wiggled	read	eat
writing	cheer	buzzing		are	am	buzzing	barking	selling
		climbs		skiing	paint	cry		
	become			built	have been		was	
remain				has	carried			has had
				bake	felt			
	practice			became	blew		clapped	
				watched	wants			
				have	mopped			
				cooking	had			
				had been	hit			

Level Red 28 Bridges™

Day 14

Measuring with Metrics.

1 centimeter = 10 millimeters   1 meter = 10 decimeters

1 decimeter = 10 centimeters   1 meter = 100 centimeters

1 decimeter = 100 millimeters   1 meter = 1,000 millimeters

1 kilometer = 1,000 meters

Estimate and then measure the following using the metric system.
Estima y luego mide las siguientes cosas utilizando el sistema métrico.

	Estimation	Measurement (Use more than one term of measurement.)
a book		
a toaster		
width of a drawer		
your little finger		
a can of soup		
a necklace		
a spatula		
an eraser		
the bathroom floor		
a garbage can		
a flashlight		

Choose things that you would like to measure.

Level Red

Day 14

Pronunciation and Spelling.

Do you remember that **g** and **c** both have a hard and soft sound? **G** as in su**g**ar (hard) and **g** as in **g**iant (soft), **c** as in **c**amel (hard) and **c** as in **c**ity (soft). In the first column of blanks, put **S** or **H** after each word to tell if the **c** or **g** is soft or hard. In the second column, match the hard or soft **c** and **g** words to another word or words that mean about the same.

En la primera columna de espacios en blanco, coloca S o H luego de cada palabra para indicar si el sonido de c o g es suave (S) o fuerte (H). En la segunda columna, une las palabras que sean sinónimos[‡].

EXAMPLE:

#	Word	S/H	Synonym	Match
1.	geyser	H	attracting	
2.	music		writing instrument	
3.	cyclone		produce	
4.	generate		schedule	
5.	slogan		operation	
6.	calico		melody, harmony	
7.	pencil		violent contact	
8.	regulate		grain	
9.	picture		refusal, not positive	
10.	magnet		painting	
11.	country		hot spring	1
12.	gelatin		motto	
13.	pillage		without pretense	
14.	process		recommendation	
15.	surgery		messenger	
16.	against		jelly-like substance	
17.	collide		territory/land	
18.	angel		hurricane	
19.	calendar		adjust	
20.	sincere		illusions	
21.	magic		cloth	
22.	cereal		transform	
23.	negative		in contact with	
24.	advice		looting	

Level Red

Day 15

Equal Metric Measures. Use the metric measure information on page 29 if you need help to do this activity.

Change each measurement to millimeters.
Transforma a milímetros.

1. 25 cm _____ mm
2. 3 m _____ mm
3. 9 dm _____ mm
4. 10 dm _____ mm
5. 12 m _____ mm
6. 17 cm _____ mm

Change each measurement to centimeters.
Transforma a centímetros.

7. 8 m _____ cm
8. 50 mm _____ cm
9. 100 m _____ cm
10. 4 km _____ cm
11. 400 mm _____ cm
12. 5 km _____ cm

Use greater than (>), less than (<), and equal (=) signs.
Utiliza los signos mayor que (>), menor que (<) o igual (=).

13. 37 m ☐ 370 cm
14. 51 m ☐ 5 dm
15. 216 cm ☐ 216 mm
16. 40 cm ☐ 400 mm
17. 5 m ☐ 15 km
18. 80 km ☐ 80,000 m

An Experiment with Chemical and Physical Change.
Intenta este experimento con cambio químico‡ y físico.

Materials: 5 pennies, 1 nickel, 1 dime, and 1 quarter
salt
vinegar, water, milk
aluminum foil

Directions: Fold foil into a pan with sides turned up.
Place coins in pan.
Pour salt (about 1 tsp.) over coins.
Pour vinegar over each coin.
Observe.

Questions:

1. What happened to each coin?
2. Why did this happen?
3. Predict what would happen if you did this experiment with water or milk.

   Water:

   Milk:

4. Repeat the experiment with the water and milk.
5. Was your prediction right?
6. Which experiment demonstrates chemical change?

   Which experiment demonstrates physical change?

7. Experiment with different liquids to determine if they cause a physical or chemical change.

Day 15

The six sentences below tell the sequence of events in a story. They are in order. Write a story to go with them. Make sure the events in your story are in this order. Give your story a title. Write in cursive.

Las seis oraciones a continuación indican la secuencia de acontecimientos de una historia. Escribe una historia que coincida con ellos.

1. On Saturday, Mom and I went to a professional basketball game.
2. We rode the crowded subway to the game.
3. The Coliseum was even more crowded than the subway.
4. Mom and I traded seats because I couldn't see very well!
5. We both wanted our home team to win.
6. Because we were so tired after the game, we took a taxi home.

Title:

Incentive Contract Calendar

Month (Mes) _____

My parents and I decided that if I complete 15 days of *Bridges*™ and read _____ minutes a day, my incentive/reward will be:

(Si yo completo 15 días de *Bridges*™ y leo _____ minutos al día, mi recompensa será:)

_____

Child's Signature (Firma del Niño) _____
Parent's Signature (Firma del Padre) _____

	📓	📘			📓	📘	
Day 1 (Día 1)	☐	☐	____	Day 9	☐	☐	____
Day 2	☐	☐	____	Day 10	☐	☐	____
Day 3	☐	☐	____	Day 11	☐	☐	____
Day 4	☐	☐	____	Day 12	☐	☐	____
Day 5	☐	☐	____	Day 13	☐	☐	____
Day 6	☐	☐	____	Day 14	☐	☐	____
Day 7	☐	☐	____	Day 15	☐	☐	____
Day 8	☐	☐					

bridges

Parent: Initial the ____ for daily activities and reading your child completes.
Padre: (Marque ____ para las actividades y lectura que su niño complete.)

Child: Put a ✔ in the ☐ for the daily activities 📓 completed.
Pon ✔ en ☐ para las actividades diaria que hayas completado.

Put a ✔ in the ☐ for the daily reading 📘 completed.
Pon ✔ en ☐ para las actividades diarias de lectura que hayas completado.

Try Something New
Fun Activity Ideas

1. Get a piece of paper that is as long and as wide as you. Lie down on it and have someone outline you with a marker. Then color in the details—eyes, ears, mouth, clothes, arms, hands, etc.
   Consigue un pedazo de papel que sea tan largo y ancho como tú. Acuéstate sobre él y pídele a alguien que trace tu contorno con un marcador. Luego colorea los detalles: ojos, oídos, boca, vestimenta, brazos, manos, etc.

2. Invite your friends over for popcorn and vote on your favorite movie. Watch the winning movie; then choose parts and act out the movie in your own way.
   Invita a tus amigos a comer palomitas y voten por su película favorita. Miren la película ganadora y luego elijan partes y actúen la película a su manera.

3. Visit the library and attend story time.
   Visita la biblioteca y asiste a los relatos de cuentos.

4. With bright colored markers, draw a picture of your favorite place to go. Paste it to a piece of posterboard and cut it into pieces for a jigsaw puzzle.
   Haz un dibujo con marcadores de colores brillantes del lugar al que más te gustaría ir. Pégalo a un pedazo de cartón y córtalo en pedacitos para hacer un rompecabezas.

5. Give your dog a bath, or ask your neighbor or friend if you can give their dog a bath.
   Baña a tu perro o pregúntale a un vecino o amigo si puedes bañar el suyo.

6. Pack a lunch and go to the park.
   Prepara un almuerzo y vé al parque.

7. Roast marshmallows over a fire or barbecue.
   Tuesta malvaviscos en el fuego o en una barbacoa.

8. Draw the shape of your state and put a star where you live. Draw your state flower, motto, and bird.
   Dibuja la forma de tu estado y coloca una estrella donde vives. Dibuja la flor, el lema y el pájaro de tu estado.

9. Make a batch of cookies and take them to a sick friend, neighbor, or relative.
   Cocina galletas y llévaselas a un amigo, vecino o pariente enfermo.

10. Plant some flower or vegetable seeds in a pot and watch them grow.
    Planta semillas de flores o verduras en una maceta y observa cómo crecen.

11. Organize an earthquake drill for your family.
    Organiza un simulacro de terremoto para tu familia.

12. Pick one of your favorite foods and learn how to make it.
    Elige una de tus comidas favoritas y aprende a hacerla.

13. Invent a new game and play it with your friends.
    Inventa un juego y juégalo con tus amigos.

Day 1

A negative number has a quantity less than zero. A positive number, on the other hand, is a number greater than zero.

Illustrate and/or explain positive and negative numbers using a number line, a countdown at Cape Canaveral, and a thermometer.
Ilustra y/o explica los números positivos y negativos utilizando una línea de números, una cuenta regresiva en Cabo Cañaveral y un termómetro.

Write a story problem to go with one of the illustrations and/or explanations you used above.
Escribe una situación problemática que coincida con uno de tus ejemplos.

• •

Facts from the Colonies in the 1600s and 1700s.
Responde estas preguntas sobre las trece colonias norteamericanas.

The Southern Colonies. From the list below, choose the word that means almost the same as the underlined word or phrase in the sentences.

    indigo   indentured servants   proprietor
    slaves   cash crops

_____ 1. George Calvert was the first <u>owner</u> of a colony.

_____ 2. A lot of Southern farmers grew <u>crops that they could sell for money</u>.

_____ 3. In the 1740s, Eliza Lucas developed <u>a blue dye made from a plant</u>.

_____ 4. <u>Originally people who agreed to work five or seven years to pay their passage to America</u> labored on Southern farms. These people were eventually replaced by <u>men, women, and children captured from Africa who were forced to work for nothing</u>.

The Middle Colonies. Circle all the colonies considered to be the Middle Colonies.

    New Jersey   Georgia   Rhode Island
    Delaware   New York   Pennsylvania

The New England Colonies. Circle the correct answer to complete each statement.

1. A person who wanted to purify the church was called a
    a. Programmer   **b.** Puritan   **c.** Convert
2. A person whose expertise is shipbuilding is called a
    a. carpenter   **b.** cartwright   **c.** shipwright
3. Usually in the center of town was a grassy area called a
    a. field   **b.** common   **c.** meadow

© Federal Education Publishing   Level Red

Day 1

Word Meanings. Fill in the blanks from the word list below.
Completa los espacios en blanco con las palabras de la lista.

> inland   suspicious   desert   escorts   conduct
> frank   allergy   knead   margin   impression
> inlets   stethoscope appalled subscribe owing

1. All the _____ around the lake were crowded with boats.
2. Everyone in the class had a chance to listen to my heart through the _____.
3. The night watchman became _____ of the two men parked near the back door of the building.
4. We _____ to at least four different newspapers.
5. Did you leave a _____ on both sides of your paper?
6. Ted spends too much money. He is always _____ for something.
7. She was _____ in telling me she did not like my new dress.
8. Use both hands when you _____ the bread dough.
9. My _____ acts up every time I go to the theater because I'm allergic to perfume.
10. Toby's _____ at the party was rude and inexcusable.

You should know how to spell these words. Put the words in alphabetical order.
Ordena estas palabras alfabéticamente.

> stranger   pottery   individual   journey   rely
> toiletry   reunite   robbery   adventure   delay
> subscription alleys   cemetery   identify   unnecessary
> announcement celery   victorious   enemy   grocery
> hurried   deciding   toil   misplaced

1. _____
2. _____
3. _____
4. _____
5. _____
6. _____
7. _____
8. _____
9. _____
10. _____
11. _____
12. _____
13. _____
14. _____
15. _____
16. _____
17. _____
18. _____
19. _____
20. _____
21. _____
22. _____
23. _____
24. _____

Level Red

Deposits and Deductions.

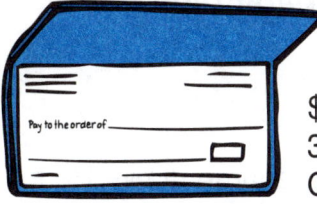

Amanda opened a checking account on May 15th with $500.25. On May 31st she deposited another $496.80. On June 4th she withdrew $145.00 to buy a bicycle. On June 15th she deposited $435.20. On June 30th she deposited $600.00. On July 1st she withdrew $400.00 to go to Camp Rockland, plus she also needed $63.00 for a sleeping bag. On July 15th she deposited $110.00. On July 24th she withdrew $900.00 to buy a compact TV with a built-in VCR.

Day 2

Use the chart below to record Amanda's checking account record.
Utiliza la información del párrafo para completar los cuadros.

DATE	DEPOSITED	WITHDREW	TOTAL $
May 15	$500.25		$500.25
May 31			
June 4			
June 15			
June 30			
July 1			
July 15			
July 24			

Remember, when you deposit money you add, and when you withdraw money you subtract.

Use Amanda's checking account record to graph the total dollar amounts.

	May 15	May 31	June 4	June 15	June 30	July 1	July 15	July 24
$2,000.00								
$1,800.00								
$1,600.00								
$1,400.00								
$1,200.00								
$1,000.00								
$800.00								
$600.00								
$500.00								
$400.00								

Name____ Date____

© Federal Education Publishing — Level Red

Day 2 — Topic Sentences.

Remember: The topic sentence expresses the main idea of the paragraph.

Underline the topic sentences of these paragraphs.
Subraya las oraciones‡ principales de estos párrafos.

1. The beginning of his life was very unusual. He was born in Texas into a large family. He fell out of a covered wagon and was not missed for many days because he had so many brothers and sisters. His parents couldn't find him, so he was raised by coyotes. He thought he was a coyote until he discovered he didn't have four feet and a tail.

2. Nuclear energy is the most awesome power that exists. It produces tremendous heat and light. It has been used to produce hydrogen and atomic bombs. It results from changes in the core of atoms. One important use of nuclear energy is in producing electricity. Scientists believe that if it were fully developed, nuclear energy could produce all the world's electricity for millions of years.

Now it's your turn! Write a topic sentence for these two paragraphs. Try to make it interesting so others will want to read the paragraph.
Escribe una oración principal‡ para estos dos párrafos.

3. _____
They are among the world's oldest and largest living things. Some are thousands of years old and over 200 feet tall. Some of them are about 100 feet around at the base. You can see them in California and Oregon. They are the giant sequoia and redwood trees.

4. _____
It ranges from great works like Michelangelo's carvings to African masks. A piece of sculpture can be very large, like the Statue of Liberty, or small enough to sit on a table or hold in your hand. It has always played an important part in the history of man. Sculpture is an excellent way to express your own ideas and feelings.

Fill in the vowels for these words. Write each word three times in cursive.
Completa estas palabras con las vocales. Escribe cada palabra en cursiva‡ tres veces.

1. r h __ n __ c __ r __ s
2. c h __ m __ c __ l
3. s t __ m __ c h
4. r h __ b __ r b
5. s c h __ l __ s t __ c
6. r h __ t h m
7. l __ g g __ g __
8. r __ m __ __ n d __ r
9. __ m __ t t __ d
10. m __ l __ t __ r __

Level Red

Bridges™

Fractions. <u>Remember</u>: When talking about fractions, the denominator names the number of equal parts of a whole amount, and the numerator names the number of parts being taken from the whole.

Write the fraction that tells what part is shaded.
Escribe la fracción‡ que indica cuánto está sombreado.

1.
2.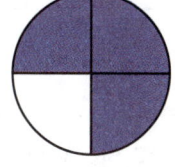
3.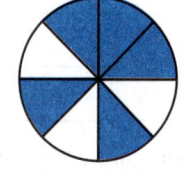
4.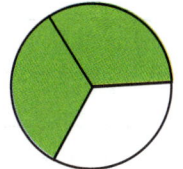

5.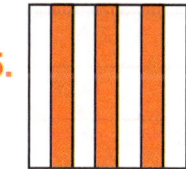
6.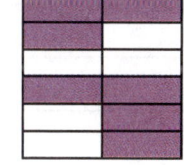
7.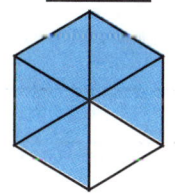
8.

Write the fractions on the number line.
Escribe las fracciones en la línea de números.

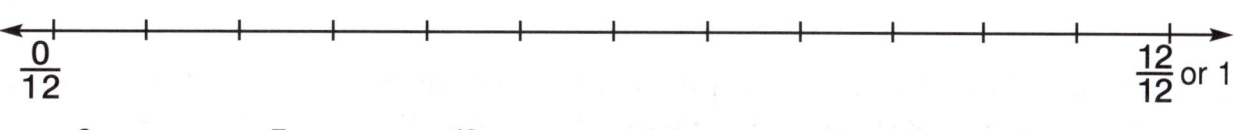

9. $\frac{3}{12}$ 10. $\frac{7}{12}$ 11. $\frac{10}{12}$ 12. $\frac{1}{12}$ 13. $\frac{5}{12}$ 14. $\frac{9}{12}$

Use < (less than), > (greater than), and = (equal to) to compare these fractions.
Usa <, > e = para comparar estas fracciones.

15. $\frac{7}{15} \square \frac{9}{15}$ 16. $\frac{3}{4} \square \frac{6}{8}$ 17. $\frac{4}{6} \square \frac{1}{3}$ 18. $\frac{5}{9} \square \frac{5}{8}$

19. $\frac{7}{8} \square \frac{14}{16}$ 20. $\frac{9}{9} \square \frac{8}{8}$ 21. $\frac{1}{10} \square \frac{1}{5}$ 22. $\frac{14}{20} \square \frac{9}{10}$

1700s Communication. Improved roads, mail service, and newspapers improved communication between the Colonies in the 1700s. Fill in the chart below. List some things that have helped present-day communications. Predict what types of communication we might have in the next 100 years.
Completa el cuadro con información sobre cómo la comunicación ha cambiado y todavía puede cambiar.

1700s	Present Day	100 Years
mail service		
improved roads for coaches		
newspapers		

Day 3

Read a book or story of your choice and do the following.
Elige un libro o una historia para leer y luego haz lo siguiente.

1. Write the names of four characters and tell why they were important to the story.
   a. _____
   b. _____
   c. _____
   d. _____

2. What are some important details or events of the story you read? List at least three.
   a. _____
   b. _____
   c. _____
   d. _____

3. How did the story end?

4. Would you like it to end differently? If so, how would you have it end?

Plate Tectonics. Circle the seven major plates of the earth's surface. On the world map below, divide the earth into the seven plates. See if you can label them correctly. Check the answers in the back to see how close you came!

Encierra en un círculo los nombres de las siete placas tectónicas más importantes de la superficie de la tierra. Marca y coloca el nombre a las placas en el mapa.

Alaska
North America
Australia-India
China
Atlantic
Arctic
Eurasia
Pacific
North Pole
South America
Japan
India
African
Canada-USA
Antarctic
Western

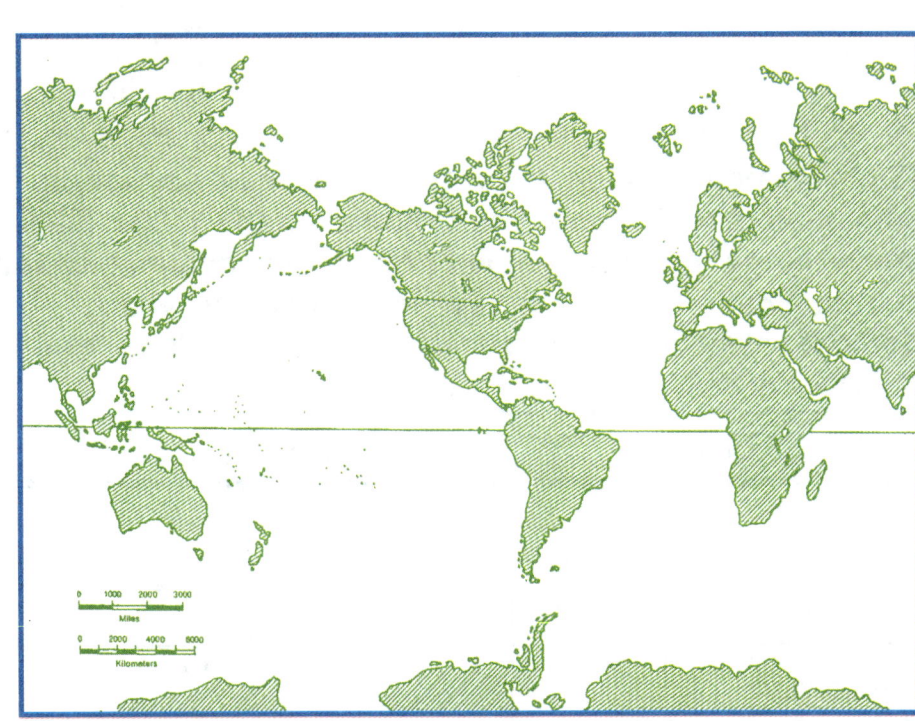

Level Red   40   Bridges™

Day 4

Divide to find the fraction of a number. Divide para encontrar la fracción‡.

1. $\frac{1}{2}$ of 10 = ____
2. $\frac{1}{8}$ of 24 = ____
3. $\frac{1}{6}$ of 48 = ____
4. $\frac{1}{5}$ of 45 = ____
5. $\frac{1}{4}$ of 32 = ____
6. $\frac{1}{3}$ of 60 = ____
7. $\frac{1}{7}$ of 56 = ____
8. $\frac{1}{12}$ of 36 = ____

Divide to find the equivalent fractions. Divide para encontrar las fracciones equivalentes.

9. $\frac{3}{4} = \frac{}{8}$
10. $\frac{5}{8} = \frac{}{16}$
11. $\frac{10}{25} = \frac{2}{}$
12. $\frac{4}{9} = \frac{}{36}$
13. $\frac{7}{12} = \frac{28}{}$
14. $\frac{6}{6} = \frac{12}{}$
15. $\frac{3}{4} = \frac{}{20}$
16. $\frac{7}{15} = \frac{}{45}$

Multiply to find the equivalent fractions. Multiplica para encontrar las fracciones equivalentes.

17. $\frac{9}{12} = \frac{36}{}$
18. $\frac{2}{3} = \frac{10}{}$
19. $\frac{3}{10} = \frac{18}{}$
20. $\frac{1}{3} = \frac{3}{}$
21. $\frac{5}{8} = \frac{}{72}$
22. $\frac{2}{5} = \frac{8}{}$
23. $\frac{5}{12} = \frac{}{36}$
24. $\frac{11}{24} = \frac{44}{}$

Reduce the fractions to the lowest terms that make whole or mixed numbers. Simplifica las fracciones.

25. $\frac{56}{6} =$
26. $\frac{14}{4} =$
27. $\frac{38}{8} =$
28. $\frac{51}{8} =$
29. $\frac{17}{2} =$
30. $\frac{35}{5} =$
31. $\frac{14}{6} =$
32. $\frac{10}{8} =$

Health—Communicable Diseases. Answer <u>T</u> for true or <u>F</u> for false to the following statements. If false, correct the sentence so it is true.
Contesta T para verdadero y F para falso. Si es falso corrige las oraciones para convertirlas en verdaderas.

____ 1. Pathogens are people who build roads.
____ 2. Communicable diseases are spread by contact with an infected person.
____ 3. The common cold, flu, and sore throat are considered communicable diseases.
____ 4. Pathogens cannot spread by touch or through the air.
____ 5. Washing hands does not reduce the risk of pathogens entering the body.
____ 6. Medicines that kill some pathogens are called antibiotics.

Imagine you are principal of your school. As principal, you must write some rules that would help the school be free from the spread of pathogens that can cause communicable diseases. Write five rules you would enforce.
Imagina que eres el director de una escuela. Escribe cinco reglas para evitar la diseminación de agentes patógenos que puedan causar enfermedades contagiosas.

Day 4

Main Verbs and Helping Verbs. Remember: The verb in a sentence may be one word or a few words. Some words can be either a helping verb or a main verb. Underline the complete verb in these sentences.

Subraya los verbos‡ completos en estas oraciones. Incluye los verbos auxiliares‡.

EXAMPLE: Jack <u>was</u> in town. Or, Jack <u>was working</u> in town.

1. Joseph is walking to the park with his friends.
2. My mother has been working at Sears for many years.
3. I might have called if I had known you were home.
4. The snowstorm yesterday buried all the beautiful flowers.
5. Jim does enjoy sports.
6. Mark is playing outdoors with Sam.
7. David does his homework every day.
8. Misty and Courtney are watching television.
9. The hikers were thirsty and hungry.
10. I have been thinking about the play all day.

Liberty Bell. Read the following report on the Liberty Bell and correct the ten facts that are inaccurate.

Lee este informe sobre Liberty Bell y corrige diez hechos incorrectos.

    The Liberty Bell was rung at noon on July 4, 1776, to announce the adoption and signing of the Bill of Rights. Its inscription, "Proclaim Liberty throughout all the land unto all the inhabitants thereof," is from Shakespeare (1564–1616). The bell originally had a different name. It was first called Independence Bell. The province of Pennsylvania paid about $300 for it in 1752. The Liberty Bell weighs more than 2,080 tons. The Liberty Bell was cast in Spain. It broke in ringing after its arrival and was recast in New York City from the same metal but with a different inscription in 1753. It rang at each successive anniversary of the Adoption of the Declaration of Independence until 1935. The Liberty Bell is no longer rung, since it broke, but it has been struck on special occasions. On June 6, 1944, when the Allied forces landed in France, Philadelphia officials struck the bell. Special sound equipment picked up the tone and broadcast it to all parts of the United States. Officials rang a larger bell in the steeple of Independence Hall to announce America's entry into World War III.

Corrections:

1.	6.
2.	7.
3.	8.
4.	9.
5.	10.

Day 5

Mixed Practice.
Estimate first, then solve the problem to see how close you got.
Haz primero una estimación y luego resuelve el problema.

EXAMPLE:

		Est.						
1.	6,525	7,000	2.	1,236	3.	74,652	4.	28,746
	3,910	4,000		4,253		75,843		93,009
	+2,335	2,000		+7,237		+18,284		+88,537
actual	12,770			_____		_____		_____
estimate	13,000	13,000		_____		_____		_____

5.	365,244	6.	866,533	7.	904,568	8.	350,859
	-79,087		-278,184		-578,179		-126,388
actual _____		_____		_____		_____
estimate _____		_____		_____		_____

9.	533	10.	975	11.	4,675	12.	342,250
	x 24		x 53		x 85		x 27
actual _____		_____		_____		_____
estimate _____		_____		_____		_____

13.	24)164	14.	80)286	15.	62)190	16.	73)1,494
actual _____		_____		_____		_____
estimate _____		_____		_____		_____

George Washington. Below are some sentences about our first president, George Washington. Read the sentences and put them in the correct chronological order.
Lee las oraciones y colócalas en el orden cronológico correcto.

____ When his father died in 1743, Washington went to live on a plantation known as Mount Vernon.
____ George Washington was born in 1732 in Virginia.
____ Washington married Martha Dandridge Custis in 1759.
____ After the Revolutionary War, Washington was elected first president of the United States in 1789.
____ During his childhood years, Washington enjoyed reading about battles and war heroes.
____ In 1758 Washington became a member of the Virginia House of Burgesses.
____ George Washington died in 1799.
____ Beginning his military career at age 21, Washington served in the French and Indian War from 1754–1758.
____ During the Revolutionary War, Washington won victories at Trenton in 1776 and Yorktown in 1778.
____ Washington believed America needed independence from England. In 1778, he was chosen to lead the Continental Army against the British soldiers.

"Washington" is the name of our nation's capital, a state, 31 counties and at least 16 cities. Why do you think so many places are named after George Washington?
¿Por qué crees que tantos lugares llevan el nombre de George Washington?

Day 5

Syllables. Write your telephone number down the side of the paper. Include your area code. For each digit, write a word that has that number of syllables. If you have numerals over 5 you can use two words to total the number. If your phone number has a zero, leave the line blank.

Utiliza tu número telefónico para practicar escribir palabras multi-silábicas.

The following words are names of birds. Some are water birds, some are land birds, and some are tropical birds. Some can't even fly! If you want to be a birdwatcher, you will need to know the names of birds. Unscramble these bird names. The first letter is underlined.

Ordena estos nombres de pájaros. La primera letra está subrayada.

1. aayr<u>c</u>n _____
2. wii<u>k</u> _____
3. dirnaal<u>c</u> _____
4. eon<u>hr</u> _____
5. rle<u>k</u>elid _____
6. un<u>p</u>iegn _____
7. h<u>g</u>ldinocf _____
8. <u>h</u>bdrmuimgni _____
9. ono<u>l</u> _____
10. idn<u>m</u>cgkriob _____
11. nacuo<u>t</u> _____
12. ic<u>o</u>srht _____
13. dkhea<u>c</u>iec _____
14. n<u>f</u>oacl _____
15. tsnaha<u>p</u>e _____
16. <u>p</u>eatreak _____
17. g<u>e</u>ela _____
18. maio<u>f</u>gln _____
19. prwora<u>s</u> _____
20. elehov<u>sr</u> _____

Level Red   Bridges™

Grocery Store Estimation in Weight and Cost.
Before you go to the grocery store, estimate how much you think certain produce will weigh. Make a chart showing your results; then go to the grocery store and actually weigh the produce. Chart these results. <u>Remember</u>: Most scales in the United States will be in pounds and ounces, whereas other countries use grams and kilograms.

Haz una estimación de lo que crees que un producto‡ puede pesar. Ve al negocio y averigua el peso verdadero. Haz una tabla con tus resultados.

EXAMPLE:

produce	estimated weight	actual weight	estimated cost	actual cost
6 apples	3 pounds	2 pounds 3 oz	$3.00	$3.15

Precursors to the Revolutionary War.
Answer the following questions. Use the time line.
Usa la línea del tiempo para responder las siguientes preguntas.

1754	1763	1765	1770	1773	1774	1775
French and Indian War	King George III gives proclamation to limit western settlement	Stamp Act	Boston Massacre	Boston Tea Party	Intolerable Acts	Battles fought at Lexington and Concord

1. How many years after the French and Indian War did the Boston Massacre occur? _____

2. Which events occurred in Boston? _____, _____

3. Which occurred first—the Stamp Act or the Intolerable Acts? How many years are there between these events? _____, _____

4. Choose four events on the time line. Draw and color four pictures in the rectangles below that show the sequence of those events.

Level Red

Day 6

Verbs. Circle the correct form of the be verb.
Encierra en un círculo la forma correcta del verbo‡ to be.

1. I (be, am) guessing the number of pennies in the jar.
2. What (is, be) your favorite month of the year?
3. The workmen (been, were) repairing the road in front of our house.
4. Carla (was, were) laughing very loud.
5. (Is, Are) you the team leader?
6. My Uncle Clint (been, has been, have been) an astronaut, an explorer, and is now a teacher.
7. The haunted house (is being, are being) torn down.
8. We (be, will be) playing in the orchestra on Saturday night.

Now write a sentence for each of these words. Make sure your sentences are different from the ones above.
Escribe una oración‡ con cada una de estas palabras.

9. were _____
10. has been _____
11. was being _____
12. are _____

Plate Movement. Match the type of plate boundary with the correct synonyms and definitions.
Une el tipo de límite de placas tectónicas con el sinónimo‡ y la definición correctos.

Synonyms	Definitions
1. sliding	a. plates push against each other
2. spreading	b. plates move away from each other
3. colliding	c. plates slide by each other

Synonyms	Definitions	Type of Plate Boundary
_____	_____	divergent boundary
_____	_____	convergent boundary
_____	_____	transform boundary

Look at the pictures below. Determine which picture represents each type of plate boundary listed above.
¿Qué dibujo representa cada tipo de límite de placas tectónicas?

Level Red 46 Bridges™

Geometric Lines. Match the terms with their definitions.
Une los términos con sus definiciones.

____ segment
____ ray
____ angles
____ perpendicular lines
____ parallel lines
____ congruent
____ symmetric
____ congruent segments
____ circumference
____ radius
____ diameter
____ AB or BA

a. A figure that can be folded and both parts fit perfectly.
b. Lines that never meet.
c. Has an end point or a starting point and can go from there in one direction.
d. A part of a line that can be named by its endpoints.
e. Lines that intersect to form right angles of 90 degrees.
f. Rays with the same endpoint.
g. Ways of labeling endpoints on a segment.
h. Figures having the same shape and size.
i. Segment that passes through the center of a circle and has both endpoints on the circle.
j. A line connecting the center of a circle to a point on the outside of a circle.
k. The distance around a circle.
l. Have equal lengths.

Illustrate each of these geometric terms.
Ilustra estos términos geométricos.

1. segment
2. ray
3. angles
4. perpendicular lines
5. parallel lines
6. congruent
7. symmetric
8. congruent segments
9. circumference
10. radius
11. diameter
12. AB or BA

Fill in the blanks. Writing is a process of steps.
Completa los espacios en blanco.

Step one:	Prewriting should include these activities: _____ ideas that you want to write about, _____ a topic, _____ ideas, and _____ ideas.
Step two:	Write some paragraphs about your topic.
Step three:	Kinds of information you can include about the topic are _____, _____, _____, _____, and _____.
Step four:	Describe things about the topic in the _____ order.
Step five:	Proofread and check for mistakes in _____, _____, and _____.
Step six:	Rewrite and _____.

Day 7

© Federal Education Publishing

Level Red

Day 7

Read this part of the Declaration of Independence and answer the questions.

Lee esta parte de la Declaración de la Independencia y responde las preguntas.

> We hold these truths to be self-evident, that all men are created equal, that they are endowed by their Creator with certain unalienable Rights, that among these are Life, Liberty and the pursuit of Happiness.
>
> That to secure these rights, Governments are instituted among Men, deriving their just powers from the consent of the governed.
>
> That whenever any Form of Government becomes destructive of these ends, it is the Right of the People to alter or to abolish it, and to institute new Government, laying its foundation on such principles and organizing its powers in such form, as to them shall seem most likely to effect their Safety and Happiness.

1. What are the basic rights of all people in accordance to the Declaration of Independence?
2. Why are governments "instituted," or created?
3. If people feel the government is not acting in their best interest, what should they do?
4. On what principles will the new American government be founded?
5. Draw and color a flag below that expresses the feelings and beliefs of the Declaration of Independence.

Earth's Magnetic Field. Read the following passage and answer the questions below.

Lee el párrafo y responde las preguntas.

The earth is like a huge magnet. It has a magnetic field. Its magnetism is the strongest at the North and South Poles. When rock forms, any magnetic particles will align themselves with the earth's magnetic field. They will point towards either the North or South Poles. There are some rocks that do not point to the current North and South Poles. Scientists conclude that either the North and South Poles have moved, or the rocks themselves have moved since they were formed. Most feel the rocks and continents have moved. Geologists use this information to determine how the continents have moved over time.

1. Why is the earth compared to a magnet?
2. Where are the earth's strongest points of magnetism?
3. How can geologists study the movements of the continents?
4. How might the magnetism of the earth affect a compass?
5. What would happen to a ship and its compass if the earth's magnetic strong area became the western part of the earth and NOT the North Pole?

Level Red   Bridges™

Find the Perimeter.
Remember: To find the perimeter, you have to add the lengths of each side.
Encuentra el perímetro‡.

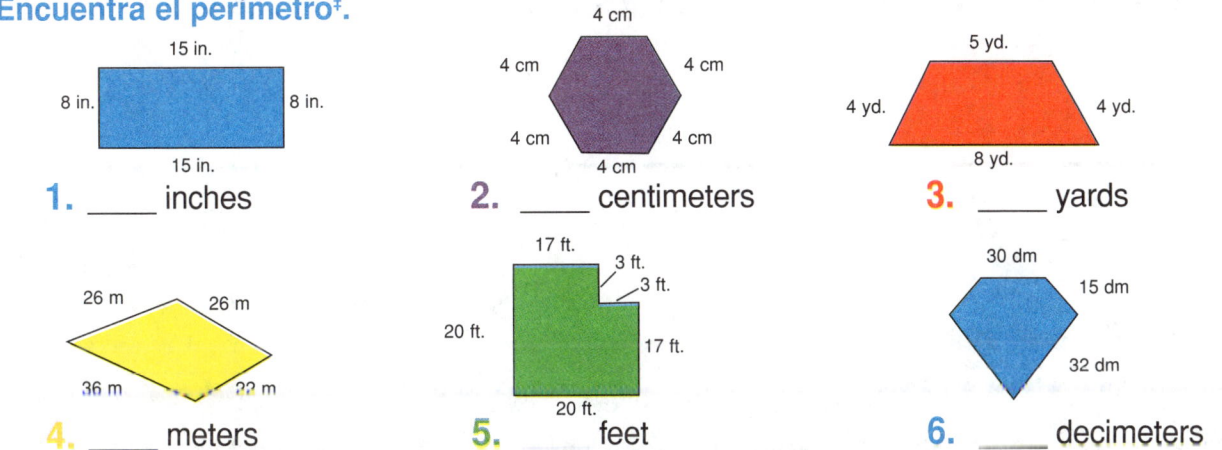

1. _____ inches
2. _____ centimeters
3. _____ yards
4. _____ meters
5. _____ feet
6. _____ decimeters

Find the Area. Remember: Area is measured in square units. Area = length x width.
Encuentra el área‡.

Remember:
1/2 x base x height for triangles

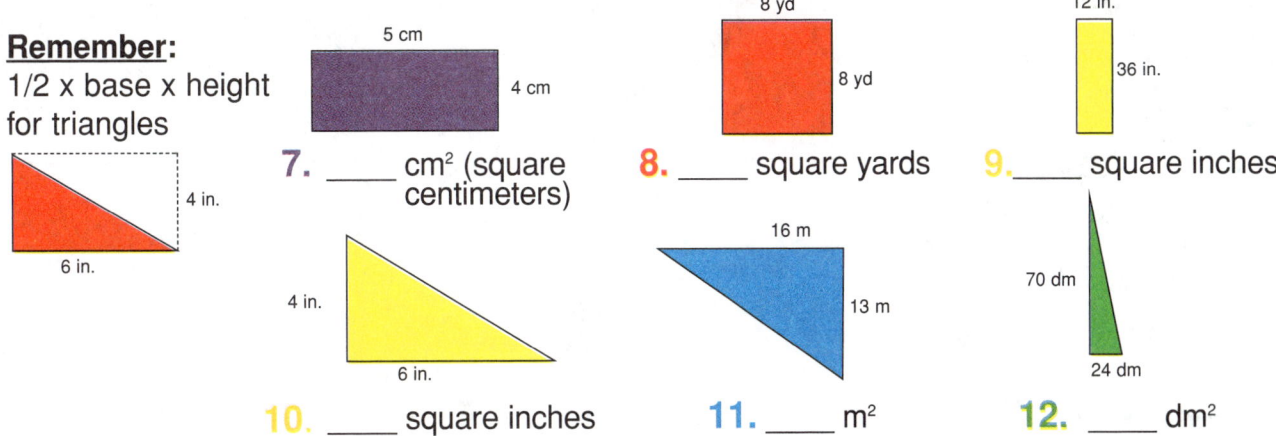

7. _____ cm² (square centimeters)
8. _____ square yards
9. _____ square inches
10. _____ square inches
11. _____ m²
12. _____ dm²

The Revolutionary War. Answer **T** for true or **F** for false to the following statements. If false, correct the statement so it will be true.
Responde T para verdadero o F para falso. Si es falso, corrige la oración‡ para convertirla en verdadera.

____ 1. Loyalists supported the colonists.

____ 2. Thomas Paine convinced many colonists to break from Great Britain with his pamphlet Common Sense.

____ 3. The British had no struggle in taking Breed's Hill, known as the Battle of Bunker Hill.

____ 4. The Declaration of Independence was written by John Adams on July 4, 1775.

____ 5. The patriots had support from many American women when fighting their battles.

____ 6. Mary Ludwig Hays, known as Molly Pitcher, carried pitchers of water to men who were fighting in battles.

Day 8

Earthquakes. Many earthquakes occur at the plate boundaries. Study the map of earthquake epicenters and answer the questions below.
Estudia el mapa de los epicentros de terremotos y responde las preguntas.

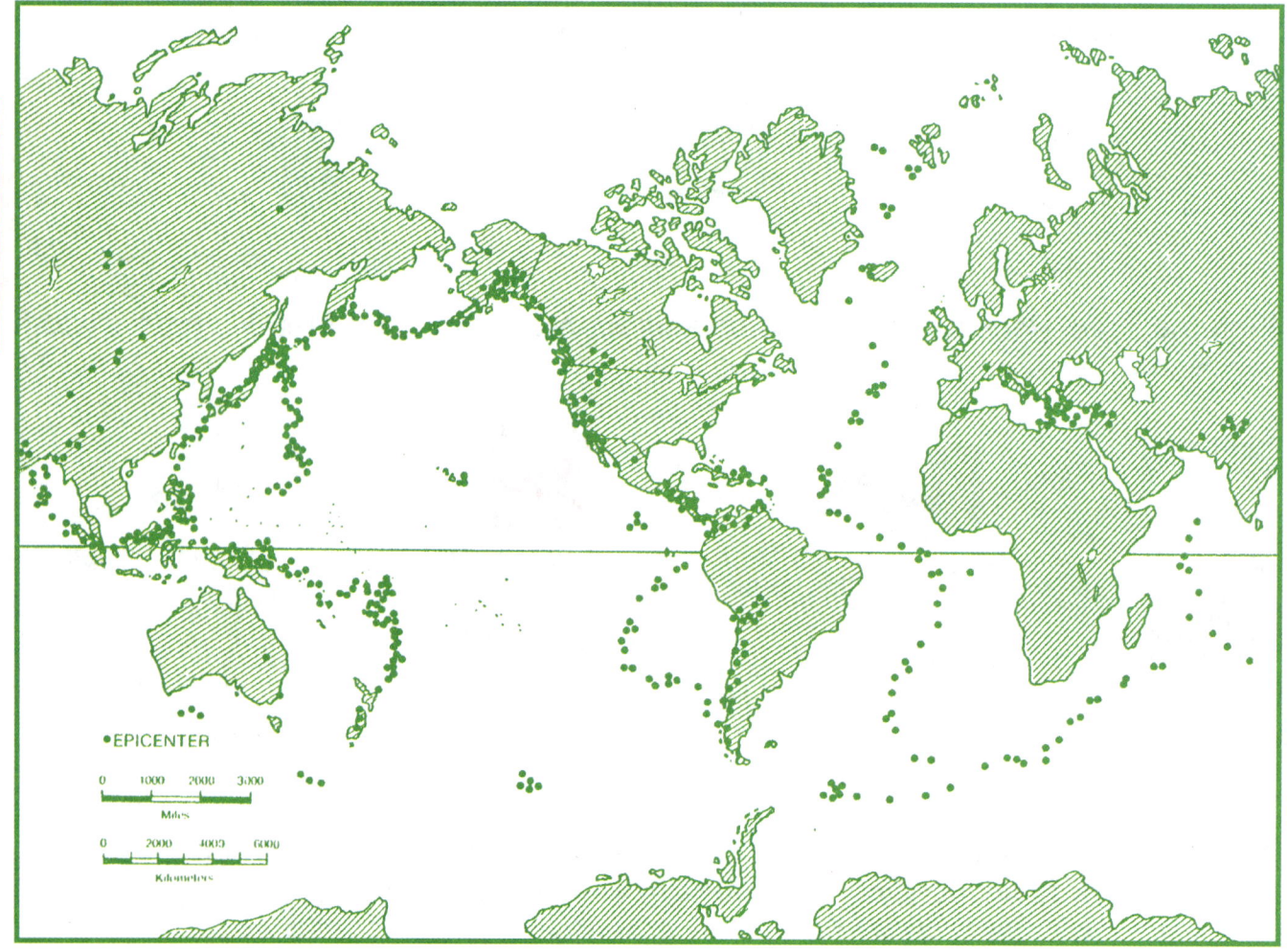

1. Color the areas with the most earthquake activity. What pattern do you see?

2. Review the map on plate boundaries on page 40. What is similar about these boundaries and earthquake activity?

3. Explain how you came up with your answer for question 2.

4. Observe the earthquakes that occur in the interior of the plates (e.g., China, U.S., and Australia). How is the distribution of these earthquakes different from that of earthquakes along the plate boundaries?

Level Red   Bridges™

Write the rest of the number families.
Escribe el resto de las familias de números.

Day 9

1. 78 x 42 = 3,276
   42 x 78 = 3,276
   3,276 ÷ 42 = 78
   3,276 ÷ 78 = 42

2. 39 x 56 = 2,184

3. 95 x 37 = 3,515

4. 49 x 76 =

5. 141 x 27 =

6. 3,762 ÷ 38 =

7. 26,320 ÷ 47 =

8. 48,306 ÷ 83 =

9. 194 x 92 =

10. 16,019 ÷ 83 =

11. 2,650 x 54 =

12. 876,600 ÷ 360 =

Respiratory System. There are a lot of ways you can take care of your respiratory system. Some ways are exercising regularly, not smoking, and not inhaling chemicals produced by products such as paint or glue.

Look at some old magazines and ask your parents if you can cut out pictures of people caring for their respiratory system. If you don't have any old magazines, draw and color pictures.

Recorta de revistas viejas fotos de personas que se preocupan por su sistema respiratorio o haz y colorea dibujos.

© Federal Education Publishing   51   Level Red

Day 9

Read these paragraphs. Remember to ask yourself:

1. Does the paragraph have one main idea?
2. Do all the sentences in the paragraph tell about the main idea?
3. Is every sentence in the paragraph a complete sentence?

Cross out any sentences that do not belong in the paragraph. Tell why.
Tacha las oraciones que no pertenezcan al párrafo. Explica por qué no pertenecen.

1. Water in the ocean never stops moving. The most well-known movements are waves. Waves are set in motion by earthquakes, winds, and the gravitational pull of the sun and moon. Ocean water is also very salty. On shore, we see waves caused by the wind. Their size depends on whether they come from far across the ocean or are caused by winds from nearby storms.

2. The beaver is a furry animal with a flat, wide tail that looks like a paddle. There are more beavers in the U.S. and Canada than anywhere else. The beaver's strong front teeth are used for cutting down trees. They use the branches to build dams and homes, but they eat the bark from them first. Beavers almost always seem. We often call people who work hard "eager beavers."

3. Write a paragraph. Try to remember the three rules as you write.

Earthquakes. Read the paragraph and fill in the blanks with the words listed.
Lee el párrafo. Completa los espacios en blanco con las palabras de la lista.

seismologists	earthquake	seismic waves	energy
epicenter	fault	above	fracture
focus			beneath

An _____ is sudden shaking of the ground that happens when _____ stored in rock is released. A _____ is a break, or _____, in the Earth's crust. As rock breaks, stored energy moves along the fault. The hypocenter, or _____, is where an earthquake begins. This occurs _____ the Earth's surface. The point on the Earth's crust which is directly _____ the focus is called the _____. _____, or shock waves, move out from the focus and cause the ground to shake. _____ study and record these shock waves and determine the size of the earthquake.

Level Red

Mixed Practice. Find the missing factors.
Encuentra los factores que faltan.

Day 10

1. 67 x ____ = 536
2. 96 x ____ = 864
3. ____ x 77 = 385
4. ____ x 84 = 924
5. 2,210 ÷ ____ = 85
6. 5,518 ÷ ____ = 62
7. 29 x ____ = 1,972
8. 19,347 - ____ = 18,470
9. 23,432 + ____ = 24,089
10. 32 x ____ = 6,400
11. ____ x 75 = 11,250
12. 4,905 ÷ ____ = 327
13. 56,993 - ____ = 55,598
14. 4,266 ÷ ____ = 711
15. 33 x ____ = 17,886
16. ____ + 34,561 = 40,090
17. 307 x ____ = 18,113
18. 741 x ____ = 61,503
19. 50,000 ÷ ____ = 1,250
20. ____ x 56 = 16,016
21. 40,572 ÷ ____ = 126
22. 19,263 + ____ = 66,390
23. 73,477 - ____ = 62,305
24. ____ - 80,399 = 110,099
25. ____ x 48 = 64,800
26. 83,037 ÷ ____ = 933
27. ____ ÷ 19 = 773
28. ____ ÷ 49 = 192
29. 932 x ____ = 355,092
30. 5,396 + 3,217 + ____ = 10,990

Endocrine System. Read the phrases below. Determine whether the pituitary gland or thyroid gland is responsible. Write **P** for pituitary and **T** for thyroid.
Lee las frases a continuación. Determina si la responsable es la glándula pituitaria o la glándula tiroidea. Escribe P para pituitaria o T para tiroidea.

1. _____ A person's height
2. _____ Influences the reproductive system
3. _____ Rate at which the body uses food
4. _____ Helps control growth rate
5. _____ May affect the weight of a person

© Federal Education Publishing   Level Red

Day 10

Irregular Verbs. Change the present form of the verb at the first of the sentence to the past form. Write the past form in the blank.

Cambia el verbo‡ en presente por la forma en pasado. Escríbelo en el espacio en blanco.

EXAMPLE: wear I ___wore___ an old coat to school.

ring   1. The telephone _____ ten times before she answered it.

build   2. The contractor _____ a new apartment building every year for five years.

feed   3. Aunt Dawn _____ her cats three times a day.

choose   4. We each _____ a friend to go with us to Disneyland.

spend   5. My brother _____ all of his allowance on ice cream.

spin   6. The top _____ for five minutes.

run   7. Our family _____ in a marathon two summers ago.

eat   8. The monkey _____ four bananas.

shake   9. I was so afraid of the dark that I _____ all over when the lights went out.

hold   10. Kit _____ his breath for one minute.

bleed   11. My nose _____ for half an hour last night.

draw   12. The class _____ pictures showing what they did on their field trip.

ride   13. Alexander _____ his Shetland pony in the rodeo parade last summer.

teach   14. Julie's mother _____ us how to jump double dutch with our new jump ropes.

fight   15. My sisters and I _____ a lot when we were children.

Quotes.
Make a list of favorite or frequently used quotes among your family and friends. Have your family and friends help you compile your list.

Haz una lista de las frases que se utilizan entre tu familia y amigos.

EXAMPLE: If wishes were fishes we'd all take a swim.

Day 11

Simplify the fractions down to the lowest term possible.
Simplifica las fracciones.

EXAMPLE:

1. $\frac{5}{10} = \frac{1}{2}$
2. $\frac{8}{12} =$ —
3. $\frac{6}{9} =$ —
4. $\frac{15}{25} =$ —
5. $\frac{9}{27} =$ —

6. $\frac{50}{75} =$ —
7. $\frac{16}{20} =$ —
8. $\frac{9}{72} =$ —
9. $\frac{18}{45} =$ —
10. $\frac{60}{100} =$ —

11. $\frac{24}{32} =$ —
12. $\frac{75}{100} =$ —
13. $\frac{36}{45} =$ —
14. $\frac{16}{24} =$ —
15. $\frac{16}{72} =$ —

16. $\frac{30}{80} =$ —
17. $\frac{8}{64} =$ —
18. $\frac{15}{40} =$ —
19. $\frac{27}{45} =$ —
20. $\frac{18}{24} =$ —

21. $\frac{10}{35} =$ —
22. $\frac{4}{18} =$ —
23. $\frac{9}{15} =$ —
24. $\frac{14}{21} =$ —
25. $\frac{21}{28} =$ —

26. $\frac{8}{40} =$ —
27. $\frac{45}{120} =$ —
28. $\frac{32}{48} =$ —
29. $\frac{144}{180} =$ —
30. $\frac{18}{144} =$ —

31. $\frac{150}{200} =$ —
32. $\frac{32}{40} =$ —
33. $\frac{81}{135} =$ —
34. $\frac{280}{420} =$ —
35. $\frac{72}{96} =$ —

Heroes in America. Match these people with the important contributions they made during America's fight for independence.
Une estas personas con la contribución que realizaron para la independencia de los Estados Unidos.

____ George Washington
____ Thomas Jefferson
____ Patrick Henry
____ Benjamin Franklin
____ Thomas Paine
____ John Paul Jones
____ Mary Ludwig Hays
____ Francis Marion
____ Deborah Sampson

a. "Swamp Fox," guerrilla warfare
b. commander of American ship *Bonhomme Richard*
c. dressed in men's clothing and joined the army
d. crossed the Delaware River on Christmas Eve
e. "Gentlemen, we must all hang together, or most assuredly we shall all hang separately."
f. carried pitchers of water to soldiers
g. "Give me liberty or give me death!"
h. Common Sense
i. wrote the Declaration of Independence

Choose one of these people and do a small report on him/her. After giving so much of themselves to gain independence for America, how do you think they would feel if they saw America today? What do you think they would say?
Realiza un breve informe sobre una de estas personas.

© Federal Education Publishing — Level Red

Day 11

Direct objects are nouns or pronouns that complete or receive the action of the verb. They follow action verbs only. Circle the verb and underline the direct objects in these sentences. Use the direct objects to complete the puzzle.

Encierra en un círculo el verbo‡ y subraya los objetos directos de estas oraciones.

EXAMPLE:

1. John Smith (guided) the <u>colonists</u> in the new world.
2. The robber threw the jewels into the bag and ran.
3. Sarah bought some groceries at the supermarket.
4. The crowd begged the musicians to play more.
5. We captured the tarantula in an old glass jar.
6. The sun melted the icicles that were on the house.
7. My brother, the quarterback, made a touchdown.
8. The movers loaded the furniture into the truck.
9. Loryn watches movies with her friends.
10. Trenton sold fifty tickets for the drawing.
11. Julia cut the watermelon into a dozen pieces.
12. The tangled string ruined my kite.
13. Allison borrowed my new umbrella.

Complete the puzzle.
Usa los objetos directos para completar el crucigrama.

Level Red

Bridges™

Day 12

Mysterious Division Power. Choose any 2-digit number. Write it 3 times to make a 6-digit number. Divide it by 13; then divide the answer by 21, and divide that answer by 37.
Intenta este truco matemático.

EXAMPLE: 14   141,414 ÷ 13 = 10,878 ÷ 21 = 518 ÷ 37 = 14 MAGIC!

1. 56   565,656 ÷ 13 = _____ ÷ 21 = ____ ÷ 37 = ___
2. 35   353,535 ÷ 13 = _____ ÷ 21 = ____ ÷ 37 = ___
3. 73   737,373 ÷ 13 = _____ ÷ 21 = ____ ÷ 37 = ___
4. 29   292,929 ÷ 13 = _____ ÷ 21 = ____ ÷ 37 =
5. 80   808,080 ÷ 13 = _____ ÷ 21 = ____ ÷ 37 = ___

Now use your own 2-digit numbers. *Ahora usa tus propios números de dos dígitos.*

6. ____   _____ ÷ 13 = _____ ÷ 21 = ____ ÷ 37 = ___
7. ____   _____ ÷ 13 = _____ ÷ 21 = ____ ÷ 37 = ___
8. ____   _____ ÷ 13 = _____ ÷ 21 = ____ ÷ 37 = ___
9. ____   _____ ÷ 13 = _____ ÷ 21 = ____ ÷ 37 = ___
10. ____   _____ ÷ 13 = _____ ÷ 21 = ____ ÷ 37 = ___
11. ____   _____ ÷ 13 = _____ ÷ 21 = ____ ÷ 37 = ___
12. ____   _____ ÷ 13 = _____ ÷ 21 = ____ ÷ 37 = ___

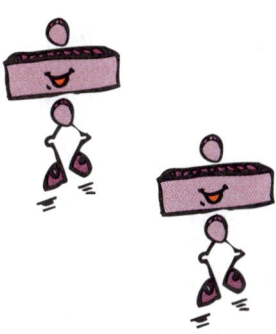

Teeth. Match the appropriate term and definition.
Une el término con su definición.

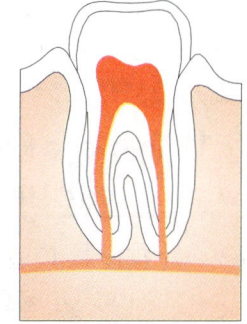

____ crown
____ root
____ enamel
____ dentin
____ pulp
____ cementum

a. soft tissue that contains nerves and blood vessels in center of tooth
b. part of tooth above the gum
c. hard tissue that covers the root
d. part of tooth that holds it in the jawbone
e. hard tissue that forms body of tooth
f. hard tissue that covers the crown of tooth

Write a short story titled "The Tale of Tooth City." Have a villain whose name might be "Wicked Wizard Plaque." Be creative with your story. Have a happy ending with healthy teeth.
Escribe una historia breve.

_____
_____
_____
_____

Day 12

Syllables. Read these sentences; then write the underlined word on the line, leaving a space between the syllables.
Escribe la palabra subrayada en la línea. Deja un espacio entre las sílabas‡.

1. We used some old <u>wicker</u> chairs on our patio. _____
2. <u>Lavender</u> is a shade of the color purple. _____
3. My brother, who is six feet six inches tall, has <u>enormous</u> feet. _____
4. In the spring, my favorite flowering bush is the <u>lilac</u>. _____
5. We use <u>natural</u> gas to heat our house. _____
6. If you want to be a doctor of <u>dermatology</u>, you would study about skin diseases. _____
7. I could hear a <u>whispering</u> voice behind me. _____
8. Have you ever been to <u>San Francisco</u>? _____
9. The <u>coauthor</u> of my new book is Carla Powers. _____
10. We think it's fun to visit cities that have <u>cobblestone</u> streets. _____
11. How old were you when you learned the <u>alphabet</u>? _____
12. Allen acted like a <u>zombie</u> after being up all night. _____
13. The comedian's <u>originality</u> was amusing. _____
14. Jay was in <u>misery</u> for a long time after the accident. _____

Analogies. Analogies are similar relationships between two pairs of words. Write an analogy to finish each sentence.
Escribe una analogía‡ para finalizar cada oración‡.

EXAMPLE:

1. <u>Tree</u> is to <u>lumber</u> as <u>wheat</u> is to **flour**.
2. <u>Page</u> is to <u>book</u> as _____ is to the <u>United States</u>.
3. <u>Brake</u> is to <u>stop</u> as <u>engine</u> is to _____.
4. <u>Mechanic</u> is to <u>motors</u> as <u>plumber</u> is to _____.
5. <u>Bird</u> is to <u>nest</u> as _____ is to <u>den</u>.
6. <u>Bricks</u> are to a <u>wall</u> as <u>fingers</u> are to _____.
7. <u>Finger</u> is to <u>hand</u> as <u>toe</u> is to _____.
8. <u>Penny</u> is to <u>dime</u> as <u>inch</u> is to _____.
9. <u>Space</u> is to <u>rocket</u> as _____ is to <u>boat</u>.
10. <u>Stage</u> is to <u>actor</u> as <u>pit</u> is to _____.
11. <u>Diamond</u> is to <u>jewel</u> as <u>steel</u> is to _____.
12. <u>Fame</u> is to <u>famous</u> as <u>study</u> is to _____.

Level Red

Chart the graph point by point. The first number tells how far to go to the right. The second number tells how far to move up. The distance between the grid lines represents 2 units.

Navega por el gráfico punto por punto. El primer número indica cuánto debes moverte hacia la derecha. El segundo número indica cuánto debes moverte hacia arriba.

1. Place the dot and letter on the point called for. The first one is done for you.

(2, 2) dot A
(12, 16) dot H
(16, 12) dot J
(6, 4) dot P
(14, 10) dot K
(10, 14) dot G
(4, 6) dot B
(8, 12) dot F
(8, 6) dot O
(12, 8) dot L
(8, 10) dot D
(10, 8) dot N
(13, 13) dot I
(6, 8) dot C
(10, 11) dot E
(11, 10) dot M
(16, 4) draw a ★
(4, 14) draw a ★
(2, 18) draw a ★
(16, 8) draw a ●
(2, 10) draw a ●
(10, 18) draw a ●

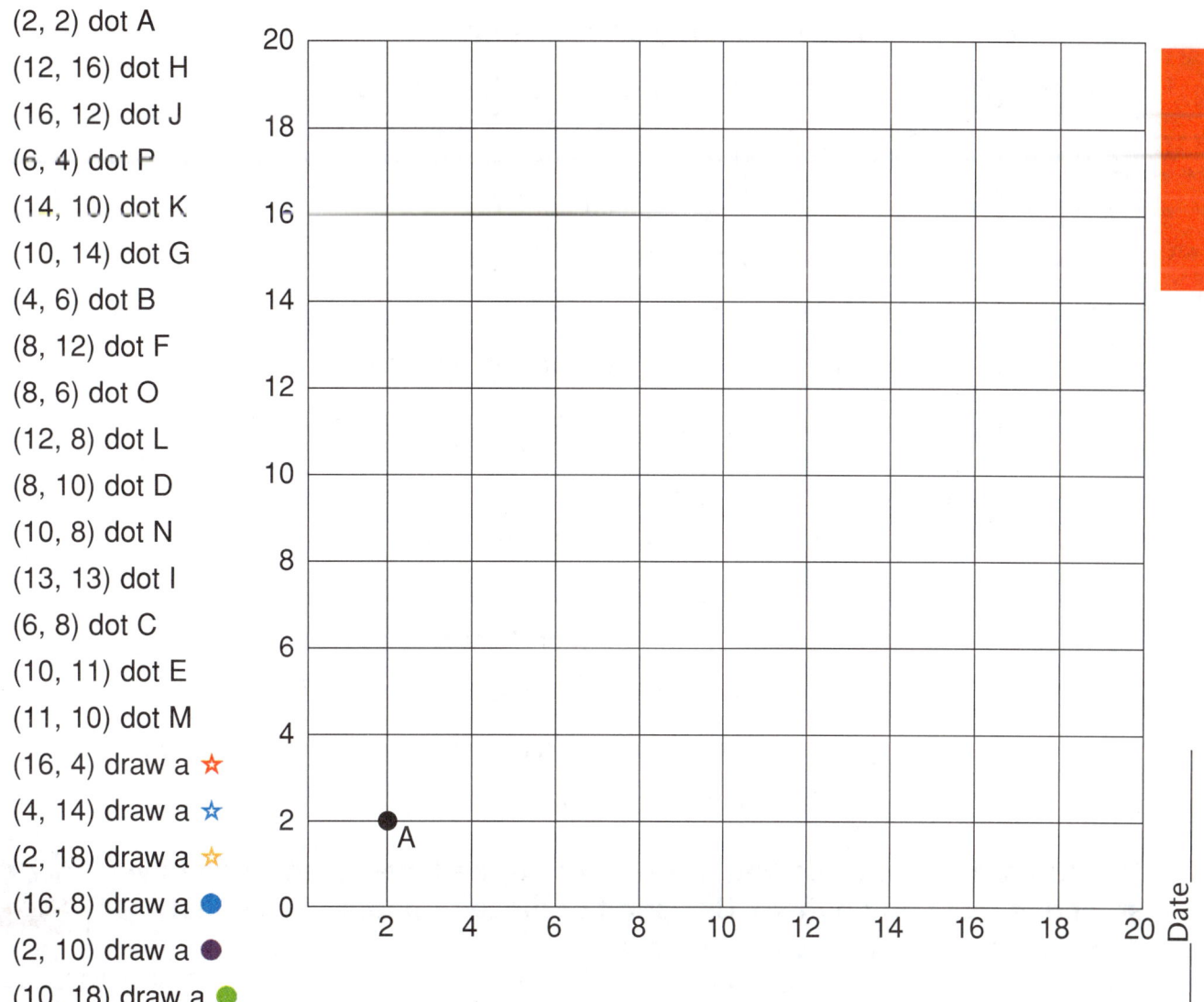

2. Connect dots A through P in alphabetical order.

3. Connect dot P to A.

4. Connect dots E to I and I to M.

Make a "point by point" direction course and have a friend or family member see if they can graph it. You could make a design, picture, or map. Use your imagination and have fun.

Inventa un curso "punto por punto" e intenta que un amigo lo une.

Day 13

Circle the correct noun.
Encierra en un círculo el sustantivo‡ correcto.

1. The (Farmers', Farmers) Market was only open on Friday.
2. That (mountain, mountains) peak is too hard for me to climb.
3. (Ed White's, Ed White) was the first astronaut to walk in space.
4. We saw a herd of (deer, deers) along the side of the road.
5. Why do (goose, geese) have webbed (foot, feet)?

Write the plural form of each noun to fill in the blanks.
Escribe en el espacio en blanco el plural‡ del sustantivo.

| potato |
| man |
| trout |
| party |
| elf |

6. The _____ on our farm were the best!
7. The nurse took the pulses of the _____.
8. My father caught ten rainbow _____ that day.
9. The _____ we went to were all fun.
10. Many _____ worked on the shoes for the queen.

Fill in the blanks with proper nouns.
Completa los espacios en blanco con sustantivos propios.

11. We live very close to the _____ Mountains.
12. _____ comes in the month of October.
13. The _____ Islands are very beautiful.
14. Judge _____ went on vacation as soon as the trial was over.
15. _____ favorite basketball team is the _____.

Practice writing and spelling these words three times each. Then have someone test you on them. Use another piece of paper for the test.
Escribe estas palabras tres veces cada una.
Luego pídele a alguien que te evalúe.

1. practicing _____
2. guesses _____
3. manufacture _____
4. poisonous _____
5. loafer _____
6. vigorous _____
7. boundary _____
8. prejudice _____

Level Red
Bridges™

Day 14

Exchange and Share $906.00. You have $906.00 to share among 7 family members. Find out if you can share it equally. To begin with, you have nine $100 bills, no $10 bills, and six $1 bills. Share and exchange down.

Intenta repartir $906.00 en partes iguales entre siete miembros de una familia.

1. You have nine $100 bills. How many $100 bills does each family member get? _____ How many are left? _____
2. Exchange the $100 bills you have left for _____ $10 bills.
3. Each family member gets _____ $10 bills. How many are left? _____
4. Exchange your $10 bills for _____ $1 bills. How many $1 bills do you have altogether? _____
5. Each family member gets _____ $1 bills. How many are left? _____
6. Each family member gets _____ $100 bills, _____ $10 bills, and _____ $1 bills.
7. How much money does each family member get? _____
8. What could you do with the amount left over? _____
9. Is there another way to share the money equally? Show us!

Make up your own "Exchange and Share" situation or use the following: $504 among 21 people. Use the above method.

• •

The Bill of Rights is the name given to the first ten amendments added to the Constitution. Other amendments also have been added. Read the passages below and determine which situations are constitutional or unconstitutional. Then write down which amendment would support your decision.

Lee los pasajes y determina si las situaciones son constitucionales o no. Escribe la enmienda que respalde tu decisión.

1. In the 1960s, a group of black students walked around with signs that said "Down with segregation!"
2. A city police department would not allow women to join the police force.
3. A person accused of a serious crime refuses to give evidence against himself.
4. A town does not like the religious beliefs of a particular group, so it forbids that group to build a place where they can worship.
5. A woman accused of a serious crime wants a trial with a jury. The government says she doesn't have enough money for this type of trial.
6. A group of students who just turned eighteen want to vote for whom they would like as the next president of the United States.
7. The president of the United States wants to run for office again. This would be his/her third term.

Day 14

Contractions. Words like **let's** (let us), **you'll** (you will), etc., are contractions. Contractions that have the word **not** in them are called negatives. The rule is NEVER use double negatives when you write or speak. Other words like **nothing**, **never**, and **nobody** are also negatives. In these sentences, find the double negatives and rewrite the sentence in cursive, using the correct word.

Vuelve a escribir estas oraciones para eliminar la doble negación‡.

EXAMPLE: The fight didn't solve nothing. *The fight didn't solve anything.*

1. The team didn't want no trouble.

2. Haven't you never seen Yellowstone Park?

3. There weren't no eggs left in the carton.

4. I haven't never been happier to finish a school year.

5. This path doesn't lead nowhere.

6. Can't no one in this class solve the puzzle?

7. Richard didn't have nothing to read.

8. Nanette said that she hadn't never thought of that idea.

9. Don't spill none of the juice on the carpet.

10. There isn't nothing you can do about the weather.

11. Thad doesn't know nobody in his algebra class.

12. The bus didn't have no empty seats when we got on.

Level Red   62   Bridges™

Day 15

Eggs? What eggs? Chicken eggs! Down through the ages, eggs have been eaten around the world. In America, the most popular eggs to eat are chicken eggs. Chicken eggs are classified primarily by their weight. Small eggs weigh approximately 18 ounces a dozen. Medium eggs weigh 21 ounces a dozen. Large eggs weigh 24 ounces a dozen. Extra large eggs weigh a hefty 27 ounces a dozen. Jumbo eggs, which are classified as the largest sellable eggs, weigh 30 ounces a dozen.

Lee el párrafo y responde las preguntas sobre huevos.

1. 6 dozen _____ eggs weigh a total of 180 ounces.

2. How many eggs are in 6 dozen? ____

3. How many eggs are in 12 dozen? ____ What are two different ways you can use to find the answer to this question? _____, _____

4. Which weighs more—3 dozen jumbo eggs or 5 dozen small eggs? _____

5. If 5 dozen eggs weigh a total of 150 ounces, which eggs would they be? _____

6. If you wanted to boil a total of 120 eggs for an Easter egg hunt and you wanted an equal number of each size of egg, how many of each size would you boil? _____

7. What is the minimum weight you can have if you have 4 dozen eggs? ____ ounces of _____ eggs.

8. If you bought a dozen of each size of egg, what should be the total weight in ounces? _____

9. Jan gathered 4 dozen medium-sized eggs, 3 dozen small eggs, 1 dozen large eggs, 2 dozen extra-large eggs, and 1/2 dozen jumbo eggs. How many eggs did she gather? ____ How many ounces did she have altogether? _____

10. Mother bought 3 dozen eggs, but some broke on the way home. When she got home, she tried to divide them evenly between 2 bowls, but she had 1 left over. With 3 and 4 bowls she again had 1 left over. When she divided them into 5 bowls, they came out exactly even! How many eggs did she have? _____

The Skin. Go to the store or look in a magazine for products used to keep your skin healthy. On the chart below, write the name of the product and its purpose. Then ask yourself if this product is necessary to help keep your skin healthy. If the answer is yes, put a star by the product. If you find that the product will not really help keep your skin healthy, put a moon by the product.

Haz un estudio sobre productos‡ para el cuidado de la piel y anota tus resultados.

Name	Purpose	Star or Moon

© Federal Education Publishing — Level Red

Day 15

Pronouns. Fill in the blanks with pronouns.
Completa los espacios en blanco con pronombres‡.

EXAMPLE: Maggie collects books. <u>She</u> likes old books best.

1. Nancy's parents collect books also; _____ are professors.
2. Mark had a pet wolf. _____ wolf was named Silver.
3. Andrew handed Mary the rock. Mary showed _____ the fossils in _____.
4. Emily washed _____ hair.
5. I asked _____ sister to give _____ a ride home.
6. The cat washed _____ baby kittens.
7. The girls made lunch for _____ family.
8. "Craig, will _____ give _____ _____ phone number?"

The pronouns <u>we</u> and <u>us</u> are sometimes used with nouns. Fill in the blanks with <u>we</u> or <u>us</u>. Use <u>we</u> when the noun is the subject; use <u>us</u> when it is not.
Completa los espacios en blanco con <u>we</u> o <u>us</u>.

9. _____ Americans have a lot of pride in our country.
10. At the dinner party, _____ guests made sandwiches.
11. The stranger made a map for _____ travelers.
12. Will the teacher give _____ students good grades?

Use the letters from these spelling words to make three or four new words. Try to make four- and five-letter words also. Use a letter only once in each word.
Utiliza las letras de estas palabras para formar nuevas palabras.

EXAMPLE: journeys   *our*   *runs*   *yes*   *nose*

1. enemies
2. intermediate
3. vocabulary
4. inscription
5. purpose
6. suspended
7. examiner
8. pendulum
9. luxurious
10. monotonous

Level Red

Incentive Contract Calendar

Month (Mes) _____

My parents and I decided that if I complete 15 days of *Bridges*™ and read _____ minutes a day, my incentive/reward will be:

(Si yo completo 15 días de *Bridges*™ y leo _____ minutos al día, mi recompensa será:)

_____

Child's Signature (Firma del Niño) _____
Parent's Signature (Firma del Padre) _____

	📓	📘			📓	📘	
Day 1 (Día 1)	☐	☐	____	Day 9	☐	☐	____
Day 2	☐	☐	____	Day 10	☐	☐	____
Day 3	☐	☐	____	Day 11	☐	☐	____
Day 4	☐	☐	____	Day 12	☐	☐	____
Day 5	☐	☐	____	Day 13	☐	☐	____
Day 6	☐	☐	____	Day 14	☐	☐	____
Day 7	☐	☐	____	Day 15	☐	☐	____
Day 8	☐	☐	____				

bridges

Parent: Initial the ____ for daily activities and reading your child completes.
Padre: (Marque ____ para las actividades y lectura que su niño complete.)

Child: Put a ✔ in the ☐ for the daily activities 📓 completed.
Pon ✔ en ☐ para las actividades diaria que hayas completado.

Put a ✔ in the ☐ for the daily reading 📘 completed.
Pon ✔ en ☐ para las actividades diarias de lectura que hayas completado.

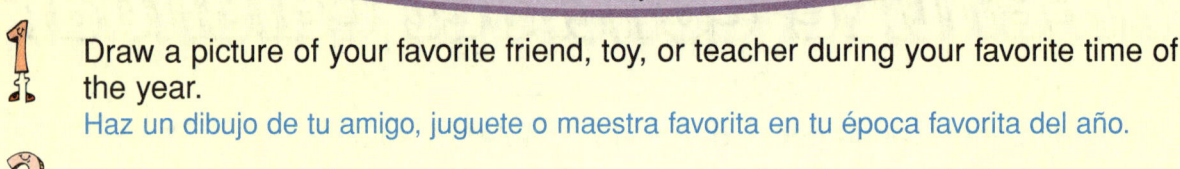

1. Draw a picture of your favorite friend, toy, or teacher during your favorite time of the year.
Haz un dibujo de tu amigo, juguete o maestra favorita en tu época favorita del año.

2. Put together a collection of leaves from your neighborhood and label as many as you can.
Junta hojas de tu vecindario y colócale el nombre a la mayor cantidad posible.

3. Write five questions that you would like to ask the president of the United States.
Escribe cinco preguntas que te gustaría hacerle al presidente de los Estados Unidos.

4. Invent a new ice cream flavor. How is it made? What will you call it?
Inventa un nuevo sabor de helado. ¿Cómo se prepara? ¿Cómo se llama?

5. Play football with a frisbee.
Juega al fútbol con un frisbee.

6. Find out how to recycle in your town; then make and deliver flyers to inform your neighbors.
Averigua cómo se recicla en tu pueblo. Luego fabrica volantes y repártelos para informar a tus vecinos.

7. Use a book on astronomy to help you look for stars and constellations.
Usa un libro de astronomía que te ayude a buscar las estrellas y las constelaciones.

8. Write your answer to the following question: How would the world be different without Alexander Graham Bell?
Escribe tu respuesta a la siguiente pregunta: ¿Cómo sería diferente el mundo si Alexander Graham Bell no hubiera existido?

9. Surprise your parents and weed a flower bed or garden, rake the leaves, do the dishes, etc.
Sorprende a tus padres y desmaleza un macizo de flores o el jardín, rastrilla las hojas, lava los platos, etc.

10. Play flashlight tag, tonight!
¡Juega a la pesca de la luz esta misma noche!

11. Design a comic strip and draw it.
Diseña una tira cómica y dibújala.

12. Paint a mural on butcher paper.
Pinta un mural en papel de carnicería.

13. Set up a miniature golf course in your backyard.
Haz una cancha de mini-golf en tu patio.

14. Play hockey using a broom.
Juega al hockey usando una escoba.

Level Red   Bridges™

Day 1

Let's Go with Division.
Choose a place you would like to go that you can drive to in a few days. Find a map and chart your course. Estimate, then check how many miles it is from your house. Decide how fast you can drive and how many hours you are going to travel each day. Using division, figure out how many days it will take. Make a chart using the information you have. Decide how long you can stay. Remember, you have to save some time to drive home. Try a one-week trip, then a three-week trip. Remember, you have to travel by car. Could you chart your results? Can you estimate the cost of your trip? Involve your parents to help you in this plan!
Lee el párrafo y utiliza la división como ayuda para planear un viaje.

Day 1

More Pronouns.
Use I or me in these sentences. When I is part of a compound subject, use it last.
Utiliza I o me en estas oraciones.

EXAMPLE: She and I made a cake.

1. Mom and ____ went to the store.
2. When will you come to see Kent and ____?
3. Karen asked ____ to answer the door.
4. Ann Marie and ____ ate our lunch outside.
5. Snakes scare ____ to death.
6. The gift was sent by Aunt Jean and ____.
7. Carla and ____ were both born in May.

Possessive pronouns show ownership. Use possessive pronouns in these sentences.
Utiliza pronombres posesivos en estas oraciones.

8. Did you see _____ faces when they saw Santa?
9. _____ handwriting is very neat.
10. The prize is _____ for the asking.
11. The book you gave to Leza was _____.
12. _____ uncle, Clint, is coming for a visit.
13. The prints on the mirror are _____.
14. The elephant stood on _____ drum.

Volcanoes. Answer T for true or F for false to the following statements. If false, correct the sentence so it will be true.
Responde T para verdadero o F para falso. Si es falso, corrige la oración para convertirla en verdadera.

____ 1. A volcano is an opening in the crust of the Earth through which lava, gases, ash, and rocks erupt.

____ 2. In a short time, volcanic material can build up to form mountains.

____ 3. These mountains can form only on land.

____ 4. All magma comes from the Earth's core.

____ 5. Most volcanoes happen underwater.

____ 6. Mid-ocean ridges are formed from underwater volcanoes.

____ 7. Mid-ocean ridges happen when lava builds up under water and creates underwater mountain chains.

____ 8. Most volcanoes on land occur at diverging plate boundaries.

____ 9. Mid-ocean ridges form at convergent boundaries.

____ 10. Volcanoes on land occur on the edge of a continent or on islands.

____ 11. When two plates converge, compression forces some rocks upward to make mountains.

Level Red   Bridges™

Day 2

Sharpen your skills with this timed multiplication test! Estimate how much time you think it will take you to do these problems. _____ Now do the actual test. How long did it take you to do it? _____ What's the difference between the two times? _____

Agudiza tus habilidades haciendo este examen de multiplicación en tiempo limitado.

1. 6 x 7 = ____
2. 12 x 2 = ____
3. 5 x 10 = ____
4. 9 x 6 = ____
5. 7 x 8 = ____
6. 11 x 12 = ____
7. 7 x 5 = ____
8. 11 x 2 = ____
9. 10 x 3 = ____
10. 5 x 6 = ____
11. 9 x 5 = ____
12. 8 x 4 = ____
13. 8 x 0 = ____
14. 6 x 12 = ____
15. 8 x 3 = ____
16. 10 x 2 = ____
17. 6 x 6 = ____
18. 8 x 9 = ____
19. 7 x 2 = ____
20. 8 x 7 = ____
21. 11 x 7 = ____
22. 5 x 2 = ____
23. 10 x 6 = ____
24. 9 x 4 = ____
25. 6 x 3 = ____

26. 8 x 9 = ____
27. 6 x 9 = ____
28. 11 x 10 = ____
29. 10 x 9 = ____
30. 9 x 11 = ____
31. 7 x 3 = ____
32. 12 x 10 = ____
33. 9 x 9 = ____
34. 8 x 8 = ____
35. 7 x 7 = ____
36. 10 x 10 = ____
37. 11 x 3 = ____
38. 6 x 5 = ____
39. 5 x 3 = ____
40. 9 x 2 = ____
41. 12 x 5 = ____
42. 10 x 0 = ____
43. 9 x 10 = ____
44. 8 x 2 = ____
45. 11 x 5 = ____
46. 8 x 8 = ____
47. 7 x 6 = ____
48. 7 x 7 = ____
49. 11 x 9 = ____
50. 5 x 12 = ____

51. 5 x 5 = ____
52. 9 x 0 = ____
53. 9 x 3 = ____
54. 7 x 4 = ____
55. 12 x 4 = ____
56. 9 x 9 = ____
57. 7 x 9 = ____
58. 8 x 5 = ____
59. 10 x 4 = ____
60. 9 x 8 = ____
61. 7 x 6 = ____
62. 10 x 5 = ____
63. 11 x 4 = ____
64. 7 x 8 = ____
65. 12 x 12 = ____
66. 9 x 7 = ____
67. 7 x 11 = ____
68. 5 x 4 = ____
69. 9 x 7 = ____
70. 10 x 8 = ____
71. 9 x 11 = ____
72. 8 x 12 = ____
73. 8 x 6 = ____
74. 12 x 3 = ____
75. 5 x 7 = ____

76. 11 x 5 = ____
77. 9 x 6 = ____
78. 9 x 12 = ____
79. 6 x 8 = ____
80. 7 x 10 = ____
81. 5 x 11 = ____
82. 10 x 10 = ____
83. 6 x 11 = ____
84. 12 x 11 = ____
85. 12 x 9 = ____
86. 8 x 7 = ____
87. 5 x 8 = ____
88. 0 x 8 = ____
89. 8 x 6 = ____
90. 11 x 8 = ____
91. 11 x 12 = ____
92. 10 x 7 = ____
93. 8 x 11 = ____
94. 11 x 6 = ____
95. 6 x 10 = ____
96. 6 x 4 = ____
97. 11 x 8 = ____
98. 12 x 6 = ____
99. 8 x 10 = ____
100. 12 x 12 = ____

101. 8 x 10 = ____
102. 0 x 10 = ____
103. 7 x 9 = ____
104. 10 x 11 = ____
105. 7 x 12 = ____
106. 12 x 12 = ____
107. 11 x 9 = ____
108. 12 x 7 = ____
109. 11 x 6 = ____
110. 9 x 5 = ____
111. 9 x 3 = ____
112. 12 x 9 = ____
113. 11 x 7 = ____
114. 5 x 9 = ____
115. 9 x 10 = ____
116. 9 x 8 = ____
117. 9 x 4 = ____
118. 10 x 12 = ____
119. 8 x 12 = ____
120. 11 x 11 = ____
121. 7 x 12 = ____
122. 8 x 11 = ____
123. 11 x 11 = ____
124. 0 x 9 = ____
125. 12 x 8 = ____

Cover up the answers with another sheet of paper and try it again!

© Federal Education Publishing — Level Red

Day 2

Subject Pronouns and Object Pronouns. If the pronoun is not part of the subject it is an object pronoun. Write SP if the pronoun is a subject pronoun. Write OP if it is an object pronoun.

Si el pronombre‡ no es parte del sujeto‡ es un pronombre objetivo. Escribe SP si el pronombre forma parte del sujeto y OP si el pronombre es objetivo.

_____ 1. The funny story made <u>us</u> laugh.

_____ 2. McCall held the dance trophy in front of <u>her</u> and Ted.

_____ 3. Will <u>we</u> see any sharks at Sea Life Park?

_____ 4. Kathy and <u>I</u> went ice skating with <u>her</u> family.

_____ 5. Don't give <u>her</u> the present until noon.

_____ 6. Did <u>they</u> fly or take the train home?

_____ 7. <u>We</u> are going to Washington D.C. this summer.

_____ 8. Are <u>you</u> a cousin to Hal Tomlyn?

_____ 9. <u>I</u> bought blue gym shoes this year because I like <u>them</u>.

_____ 10. The dog got <u>its</u> paw caught in the bear trap.

Verbs. Regular verbs show action that happened in the past by adding -ed to the base word. But to show past tense for irregular verbs, you have to change the spelling.

EXAMPLE: sit - sat

In the square there are some irregular verbs. Write them under the correct heading below.

En el cuadrado aparecen algunos verbos‡ irregulares. Escríbelos bajo el encabezado correcto.

Remember: The past participle is used with a helping word when in a sentence.

Present	Past	Past Participle

Level Red   70   Bridges™

Day 3

Choices. Clayton's mother bought him some new clothes to go to camp. She bought him 4 pairs of shorts—red, blue, green, and white. She also bought him 8 T-shirts—2 red, 2 blue, 2 green, and 2 white. She bought him 4 long-sleeved sweatshirts—2 white and 2 blue.

Use a tree diagram to organize the data to find out how many different choices of shorts and shirts Clayton can wear. _____ total choices

Lee el párrafo. Usa el diagrama en forma de árbol para determinar cuántas combinaciones de pantalones y camisetas Clayton puede usar.

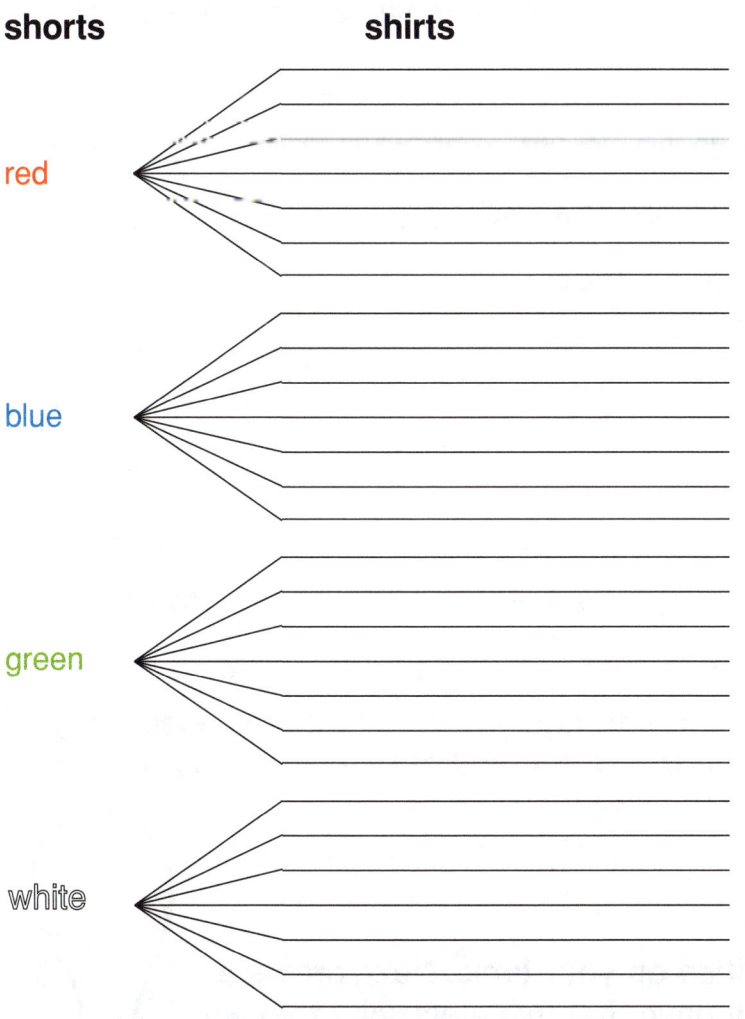

Our government is divided into three branches. Each branch is given different, but equal, powers. In the circle below, write down the branch, the power it has, and draw a picture that could represent each branch.

En el círculo, escribe cada rama del gobierno, qué poder tiene y haz un dibujo para representarla.

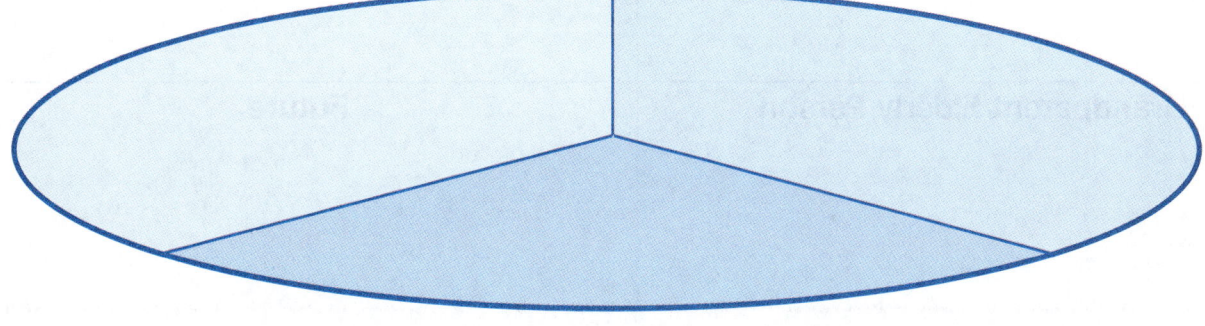

Day 3

Below are some parts of sentences that give the cause. Finish the sentence by writing what the effect might be. Look for clue words.

Estas partes de oraciones establecen una causa. Completa la oración‡ escribiendo cuál puede ser el efecto.

EXAMPLE: (cause) The old house had not been painted for years, (effect) so the first thing we did was paint it. (The clue word is "so.")

1. Our Thanksgiving turkey was burned because _____.

2. _____ because my new shoes were too tight.

3. The wind was blowing hard, so _____.

4. Because I didn't get up early enough this morning, _____.

5. Some children were playing with matches; as a result, _____.

Now it's your turn to write the cause to the effects.

6. The plane crashed due to _____.

7. _____, my stomach hurt.

8. _____, so we decided to celebrate.

9. The drinks were very sweet because _____.

10. _____, there was no fruit on the trees this summer.

● ●

Electricity. In the table below, make a list of things you enjoy that use electricity. Now ask a parent, adult, or grandparent to list things that use electricity that we have now, but they did not have when they were your age.

Haz una lista de cosas que disfrutas y que usen electricidad, cosas que tus padres y abuelos no tenían, y cosas que vayan a existir en el futuro.

Compare the differences and similarities on your table. Next, create a list of things children in 30 years may have that use electricity that we do not have today. Be creative!

You	Parent/Adult
Grandparent/Elderly Person	**Future**

Level Red   Bridges™

Broken Line Graphs, "Using Leisure Time."

Keep track of how much television you watch daily in a two-week period, then graph the results. Do the same with how much time you play computer games or TV games, then graph the results. Now do the same with how much time you spend with your friends, then graph the results. You can use the same graph for all three if you use different colored pens or pencils.

Realiza un gráfico para hacer el seguimiento de tu tiempo libre.

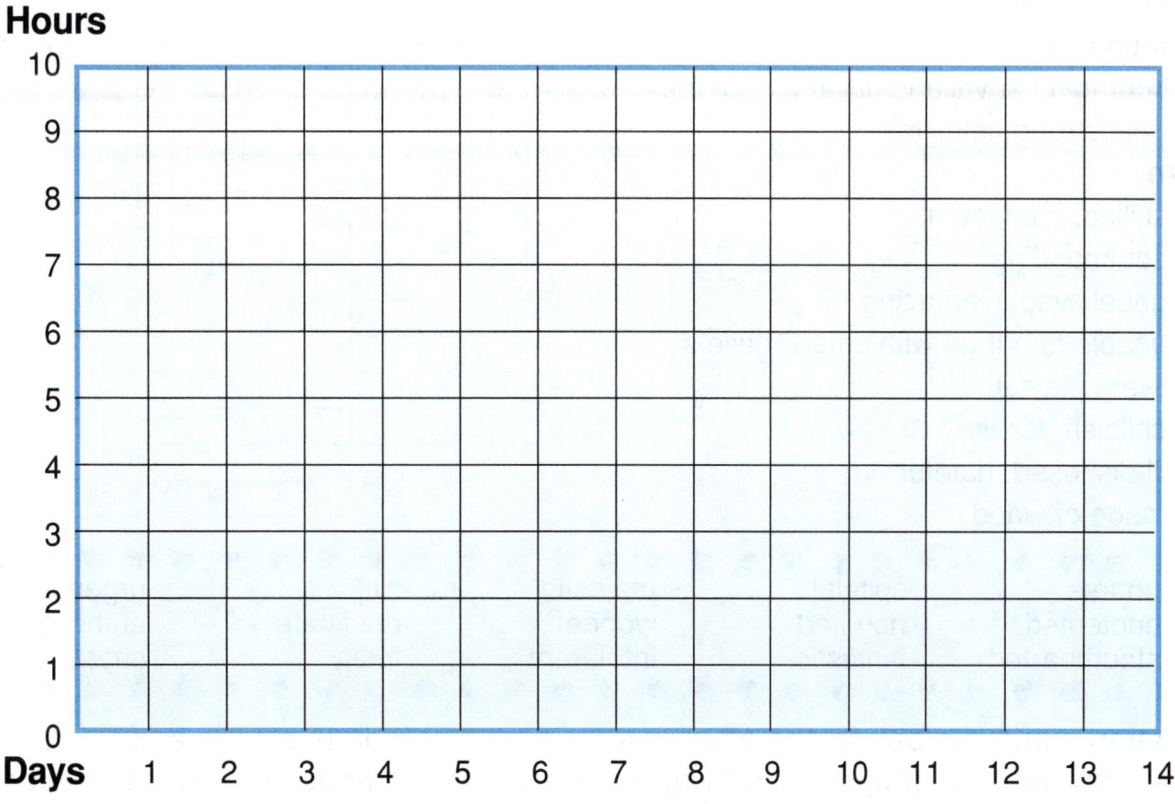

Powers of the Government. Decide which branch of government (legislative, executive, or judicial) that each statement describes.

¿A cuál rama de gobierno (legislativa, ejecutiva o judicial) describe cada oración‡?

_____ 1. Can impeach the president of the United States.

_____ 2. Approves treaties.

_____ 3. Approves or vetoes bills.

_____ 4. Interprets and examines laws and treaties.

_____ 5. Appoints justices.

Day 4

Adjectives make reading more interesting. Adjectives modify or describe nouns and pronouns. Read the clues and do the crossword puzzle. The answers are adjectives that are listed below.

Lee las pistas y completa el crucigrama. Las respuestan son adjetivos[‡] del Recuadro de Palabras.

Across
1. satisfied
4. dignified, lofty, noble
8. filled with fear
11. critical, immediate
12. rough voice
13. courageous, valiant, gallant
14. headstrong, inflexible

Down
1. skilled, competent
2. commanding
3. unbelievable, amazing
5. unable to put up with others' beliefs
6. lively, playful
7. childish, foolish
9. ill-disposed, hateful
10. made of wood

hoarse	spiteful	majestic	silly	urgent
contented	horrified	wooden	obstinate	authoritative
stouthearted	fantastic	intolerant	frisky	capable

Quotation marks go before and after exactly what a person is saying and the titles of stories, poems, and songs. Tell why quotation marks are used in these sentences.

Indica por qué se utilizaron comillas[‡] en estas oraciones.

1. Robert asked, "What are the rules for this game?"
   _____
2. Mother was fixing lunch when David came home. "Please set the table," she said.
   _____
3. Jim gave Lance a copy of "Solving Math Puzzles" to take on his trip.
   _____
4. "What's that terrible noise?" cried Carla.
   _____

Your turn. Put quotation marks in these sentences.

Coloca las comillas en estas oraciones.

5. I don't think I can do this by myself, Marge sighed.
6. Hillary is singing America the Beautiful to her sister.
7. Do you like baseball or football best? Debra asked. I like baseball best.
8. Not me, answered Eleanor. I like basketball best.

Level Red 74 Bridges™

Day 5

Complete this table to see which of these numbers can be divided by 2, 3, 5, 9, and 10 without remainders. After you have finished the chart, see if you can come up with some hypotheses to form some divisibility rules.

¿Qué números de la tabla pueden dividirse por 2, 3, 5, 9 y 10 sin resto? ¿Puedes determinar alguna hipótesis para reglas de división?

y = yes and n = no

Hypotheses of 2, 3, 5, 9, and 10

2 Hypothesis

3 Hypothesis

5 Hypothesis

9 Hypothesis

10 Hypothesis

Divisible by	2	3	5	9	10
3,825	n	y	y	y	n
930					
792					
856					
1,440					
6,825					
1,854					
41,004					
85,010					
314,402					
4,277,133					
10,009,407					
9,617,590					
9,591,314					

Try out your hypotheses on number combinations of your own to see if they really work.

The Expansion West. Write a dialogue that might have happened between the following people during the expansion west: an Indian, a settler, and a soldier. Remember to keep an open mind about their different points of view. Have your parents, brothers, sisters, or friends read the parts in costume!

Escribe un diálogo que pueda haber sucedido entre las siguientes personas durante la expansión hacia el oeste: un Indio, un colono y un soldado.

_____

_____

_____

_____

_____

© Federal Education Publishing Level Red

Day 5

Fill in the blank in each sentence with a synonym of the boxed word.
Completa el espacio en blanco con un sinónimo‡ de la palabra en el recuadro.

EXAMPLE: I had to [finish] _complete_ my work before I could go with my friends.

1. Sarah and Angie go for a [walk] _____ every day except Sunday.
2. It's fun to watch the little colts [play] _____ in the green pastures.
3. The electricians have done [enough] _____ work for this week.
4. I cannot [find] _____ the information I [need] _____ for my report.
5. You will have to [write] _____ all the important events of your [trip] _____.
6. The lost couple had not had any [food] _____ for six days.
7. Will you please [show] _____ how your new invention works?
8. They will [try] _____ to climb Mount Everest again next summer.
9. Tourists [might] _____ be able to travel to the moon by the year 2010.
10. The value of this coin will [grow] _____ over the years.
11. The applicant must [reply] _____ within three weeks.
12. I think your [story] _____ was a little farfetched!

Electric Current. Read each passage on electricity. One sentence in each passage is false. Cross out the false sentence and try to correct it. Then answer the questions after each passage.
Cruza la oración‡ falsa de cada párrafo e intenta corregirla. Luego responde las preguntas.

1. An electrical current is moving energy. You can see electricity at work in lights, motors, computers, and some toys. Any material that allows an electric current to pass through is called a battery.

    Question: How many things can you think of in 1–2 minutes that need electricity? Have a race with someone to see who can think of the most ideas.

2. Material that does not allow an electric current to pass through it is called a circuit. This material covers conducting materials. It stops electricity from escaping and causing harm.

    Question: What are five things you can do to ensure safety in your home with electricity?

    1. _____ 2. _____ 3. _____
    4. _____ 5. _____

Level Red — Bridges™

Day 6

Choose numbers between 10 and 100 and put them in the outer circle. Next, put numbers between 1 and 12 in the following circle. Then multiply the outer circle's number by the second circle's number.

Escribe números entre 10 y 100 en el círculo exterior. Coloca números entre 1 y 12 en el círculo siguiente y luego multiplica ambos números.

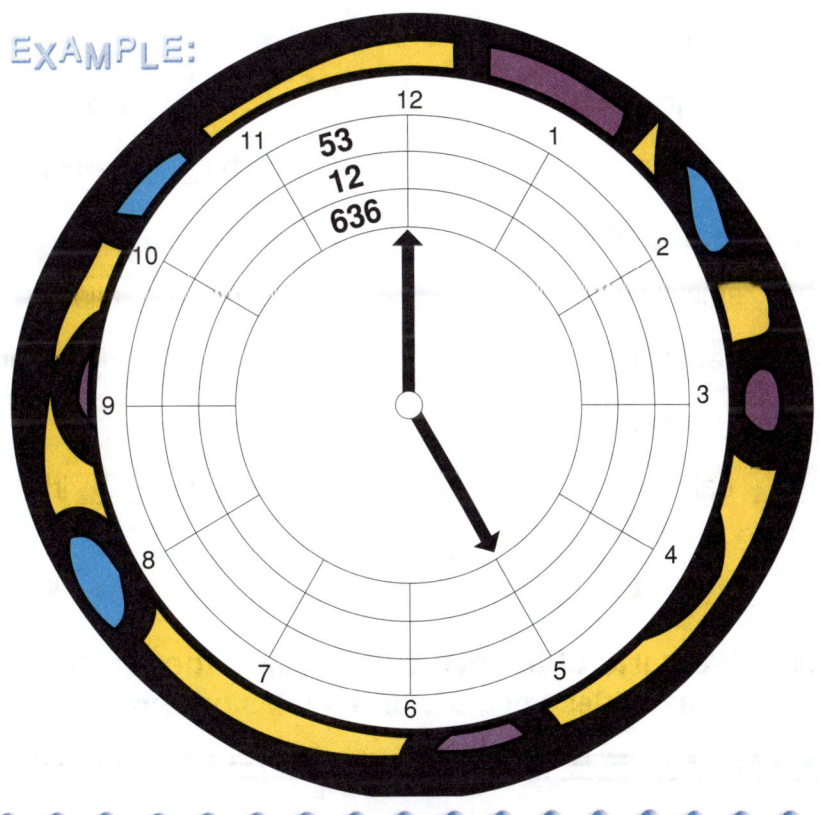

EXAMPLE: 53 × 12 = 636

• •

Hunters, trappers, and pioneers moved west in the 1800s. Brainstorm things you would need for a trip west and make a list. Put the items on your list into categories. For example, one category might be food.

Cazadores, tramperos y pioneros se trasladaron hacia el oeste en la década de 1800. Lanza ideas de cosas que necesitarías para un viaje al oeste. Haz una lista y categoriza los artículos.

Day 6

Spelling. What double consonants go in these spelling words?
¿Qué consonantes dobles van en estas palabras?

1. i __ __ ediately
2. su __ __ ort
3. i __ __ egular
4. a __ __ ribute
5. di __ __ erence
6. a __ __ e __ __ ment
7. i __ __ emovable
8. a __ __ reviation
9. exce __ __ ence
10. a __ __ ual
11. su __ __ osed
12. po __ __ ible
13. inte __ __ igence
14. a __ __ egiance
15. bu __ __ ernut
16. i __ __ ocent
17. di __ __ atisfied
18. a __ __ e __ __ ible
19. scri __ __ le
20. permi __ __ ing

Health—Eyes. Label the parts of the eye below using the following words:
Coloca los nombres de las partes del ojo utilizando las palabras a continuación.

retina
cornea
lens
iris
pupil
vitreous humor
optic nerve

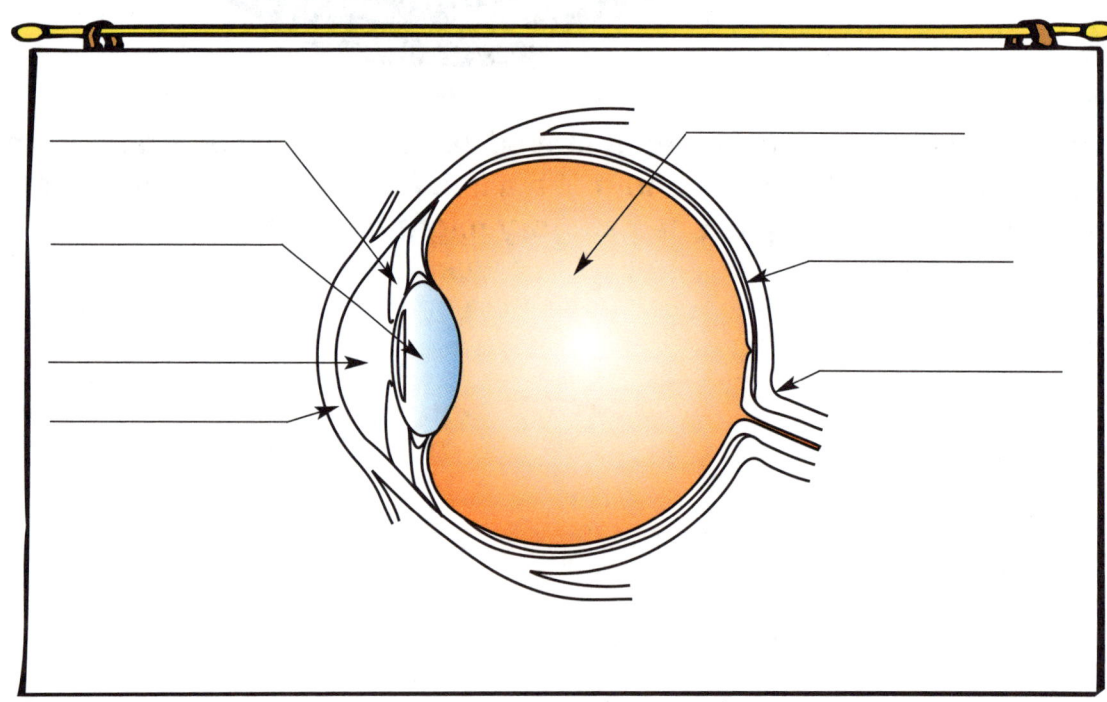

Make a journal of all the activities you do in one day. Look back over the activities at the end of the day. Imagine that you could not see. How would this have affected your day? What would you have needed to do differently?
Imagina que no puedes ver. ¿Cómo afectaría esto tu día?

Level Red   78   Bridges™

Polyominoes.
Responde estas preguntas sobre polimios.

1. These are all polyominoes.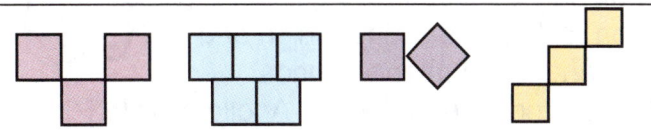

   Why? _____

2. These are not polyominoes.

   Why not? _____

3. Draw some polyominoes of your own using 5 squares.

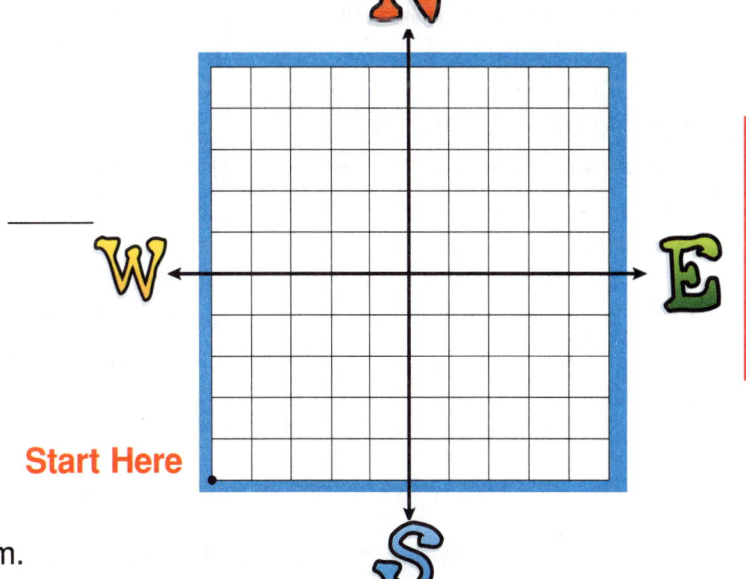

4. Chart the course by following lines according to the instructions below. How many polyominoes did you chart? _____

   east 1, north 3, east 5, north 3,
   east 1, south 5, east 1, north 3,
   west 5, south 4, west 1, north 6,
   west 1, north 3, east 1, south 2,
   east 5, north 1, west 3, north 1,
   east 4, south 1, east 1, south 6,
   west 1, south 2, west 8, and you
   should be back where you started from.

How a Law Is Made. Put into sequence the following steps on how a bill can become a law. Then come up with a bill you think should become a law. Draw a comic strip that shows characters putting these steps into action.
Coloca en la secuencia correcta los pasos para que un proyecto se convierta en ley. Piensa en un proyecto propio. Dibuja una tira cómica mostrando los cuatro pasos.

____ Get the president to approve.

____ Write a bill.

____ Get a majority vote in Congress.

____ If the president vetoes the bill, then it may become a law by 2/3 vote in Congress.

Your own bill: _____

© Federal Education Publishing   79   Level Red

Day 7

"The Eagle has landed."

Lee el párrafo y responde las preguntas.

American astronauts Neil Armstrong and Buzz Aldrin became the first men on the moon on July 20, 1969. The giant Apollo moon rocket was 363 feet high and weighed six and a half million pounds.

The Lunar Module (LM) left the Apollo at 1:45 P.M. "The Eagle has wings," Armstrong stated. At 3:46 the LM emerged from behind the moon. "The burn was on time," reported Armstrong matter-of-factly. At that time, they were at an altitude of about 20 miles, descending toward 50,000 feet. The astronauts had to make the all-important and final decision whether to remain in orbit or to descend to the lunar surface to make the landing.

At approximately 4:07 P.M., Armstrong pressed the button marked "Proceed." Aldrin and Armstrong realized in horror that the computer-controlled guidance system was taking them right down into a football-field-sized crater with a large number of big boulders and rocks. With only precious seconds to spare, Armstrong took manual control of the spacecraft. He searched for and found a clear area amid the menacing rock field below. "Houston," Armstrong radioed, "Tranquility base here. The Eagle has landed."

It was the first time men from earth had touched down on the moon. Armstrong was the first human being to set foot on the lunar surface. As his left foot touched the moon to take the first step, he spoke the now famous words, "That's one small step for man, one giant leap for mankind."

1. What was Armstrong referring to when he said "The Eagle has landed"?

2. The word "lunar" is used several times. What is another word for lunar?

3. What did "all-important and final decision" really mean to the astronauts?

4. What was the real significance of this mission to humankind?

5. What does this report tell you about what type of men Armstrong and Aldrin are?

6. What does this event say to you personally?

Electricity. Two electrical pathways are series circuits and two are parallel circuits. Label the pictures as either a series circuit or parallel circuit.

Indica si los dibujos son circuitos en serie o circuitos en paralelo.

_____   _____   _____   _____

Level Red   Bridges™

Day 8

Relationship between Missing Numbers. Find the missing numbers and then write the rule.
Encuentra los números que faltan y luego escribe la regla.

1.	M	N	2.	M	N	3.	M	N	4.	M	N	5.	M	N
	15	20		25	36		54	45		9	72		8	48
	40	45		19	30		89	80		11	88		4	24
	90	__		57	__		73	__		7	__		10	__
	35	__		__	84		__	61		5	__		6	__

Rule: M + 5 = N   Rule: M + 11 = N   Rule: M −   Rule: M ×   Rule: _____

6.	M	N	7.	M	N	8.	M	N	9.	M	N	10.	M	N
	21	7		48	8		36	24		7	63		10	120
	30	10		12	2		57	45		__	81		__	144
	18	__		__	7		63	__		__	54		9	108
	12	__		24	__		__	78		3	27		__	132

Rule: M ÷   Rule: _____   Rule: _____   Rule: _____   Rule: _____

11.	M	N	12.	M	N	13.	M	N	14.	M	N	15.	M	N
	3.2	5.5		35	50		24	3		4.2	8.4		0.09	0.14
	7.1	__		73	__		56	__		__	18.6		0.13	0.18
	__	7.3		__	42		72	__		8.1	16.2		__	0.10
	4.4	__		100	__		__	8		__	15.0		3.21	__

Rule: _____   Rule: _____   Rule: _____   Rule: _____   Rule: _____

Trail of Tears. Do research on the Trail of Tears. Write a poem about this event using the letters of Trail of Tears at the beginning of each line. Be sure to include the emotions felt at this time. Make a border around the poem with colors and objects you feel would best describe the mood of your poem.
Investiga sobre Trail of Tears. Escribe un poema sobre el tema utilizando las letras de "Trail of Tears" al comienzo de cada línea.

T _____
R _____
A _____
I _____
L _____
O _____
F _____
T _____
E _____
A _____
R _____
S _____

Day 8

Contents and Index. Read this fictitious contents and index from a history book. Then answer the questions below.
Lee la tabla de contenidos y el índice, y luego responde las preguntas.

Contents		Index	
1. The Nation Grows	216	Civil War	250–300
Exploring the West	217	background	254–255
Louisiana Purchase	222	problems after	304–310
War of 1812	229	Economy	97,319,420
Country Growth	236	after American Revolution	97–100
2. The Civil War	250	after Civil War	319
The Beginning	251	of Great Lakes	400
The Two Sides	260	Jackson, Andrew	100–101, 124–130
The First Part of War	270	Louisiana Purchase	222
The Second Part	289	Massasoit	172
The Civil War at Sea	300	Native Americans see American Indians	
Maps	R60		
Glossary	R95	Water	5–6, 12, 21–25, 610

1. What is the difference between the contents and the index in books? _____

2. If you wanted to know if this book had a section on the War of 1812, where would you look? _____

3. If you wanted to see if there was a picture of Andrew Jackson in the book, where would you look? _____

4. Where would you look to find out who fought in the Civil War? _____

5. How many chapters does this book have? _____

6. How many sections are in chapter one? _____

7. On what page would you look to find out about Native Americans? _____

8. On what page could you look to learn who Massasoit was? _____

9. How many sections are there about the Civil War? _____

10. What information is in the glossary of books? _____

Unscramble the syllables to make words. There might be one or two extra syllables in each word. Cross them out. All the words have something to do with transportation.   EXAMPLE: ing merg m̶e̶r̶ **merging**
Ordena las sílabas‡ para formar palabras. Tacha las sílabas extra.

1. fic duc traf _____
2. bred ough thor fare _____
3. pave ved ment pa _____
4. ped tri pe an des _____
5. y per py slip par _____
6. in en state tar ter _____
7. tude struc tion con _____
8. ed ri strict strik re _____
9. jen mer tus e cy gen _____
10. toe a tow way u _____
11. ger dan dap ous dler _____
12. tion sek ter sti sec in _____
13. ex way te pro press _____
14. mum min i ion _____

Level Red   Bridges™

Match the term to the mathematical definition dealing with fractions.
Une el término con la definición correcta.

1. fraction
2. improper fraction
3. quotient
4. mixed number
5. denominator
6. numerator

a. It's the answer you get by dividing one number by another number.
b. It's the number found below the line in a fraction.
c. It's a number that names a part of a set or part of a whole.
d. It's the number found above the line in a fraction.
e. It's a number that has a whole number and a fraction number.
f. It's a fraction whose numerator is greater than its denominator or can be equal to its denominator.

Show your understanding. Sigue las instrucciones.

7. Show $15 \div 7$ as an improper fraction. _____

8. Show $2 \div 9$ as a fraction. _____

9. Show $11 \div 7$ as an improper fraction. _____

10. $82 \div 7$ can be written $\frac{82}{7}$ or $7\overline{)82}$.

    What is the divisor? _____

    What is the remainder? _____

    Write it as a mixed number. _____

11. What kind of fractions are these: $\frac{28}{5}$ $\frac{17}{12}$ $\frac{59}{7}$?

    _____

    Write a mixed fraction for each.

12. Write a mixed fraction for the following:

    $7\overline{)29}$ $8\overline{)143}$ $25\overline{)90}$ $10\overline{)433}$

A Trailblazer. On his expeditions, Meriwether Lewis kept an illustrated journal on things he discovered. Imagine that you are also an explorer. Go outside and study natural objects or look at photographs of plants, animals, and physical features in your area. Write a journal entry on one of the objects you have found. Look at it as though you have never seen it before. Describe the structure of the object and hypothesize its function. After writing the description, draw and label the object.

Imagina que eres explorador. Estudia o mira fotografías de plantas, animales y características físicas de tu área. Describe una de las cosas como si fuera la primera vez que la vieras. Luego haz un dibujo y colócale el nombre a las partes.

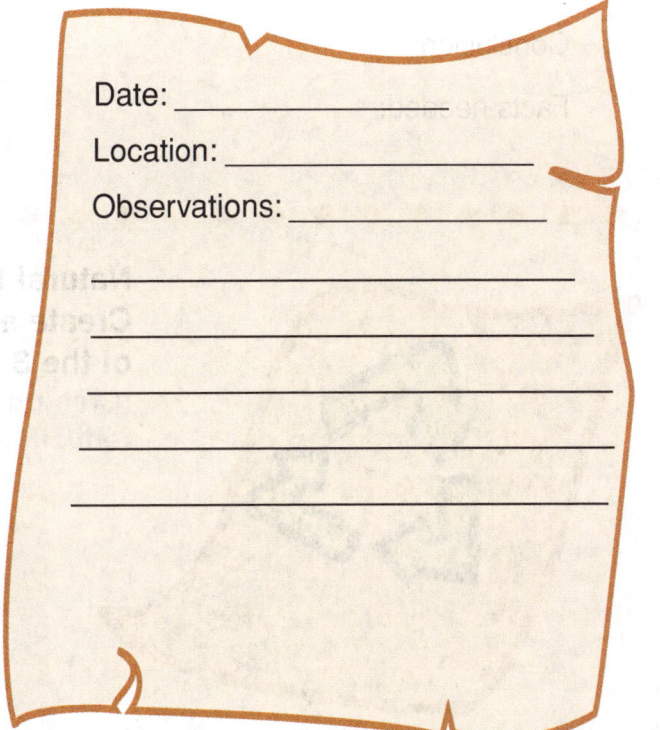

Day 9

Conclusions Versus Facts. People, young and old, often jump to conclusions. They frequently make up their mind without looking for facts or reasons behind a situation. Write a conclusion for each situation given and then think of facts you need to verify your conclusion.

Escribe una conclusión para cada situación dada. Luego piensa hechos necesarios para verificar tu conclusión.

1. There is a large package with your name on it at your doorstep without a note saying who it's from. It's not your birthday.

   Conclusion:

   Facts needed:

2. Your teacher sends a note home with you addressed directly to your parents. He/she tells you to make sure your parents get it.

   Conclusion:

   Facts needed:

3. When you go to the game, no one will speak to you or play with you.

   Conclusion:

   Facts needed:

4. The house is dark and the doors are locked when you get home.

   Conclusion:

   Facts needed:

5. You have looked all through the house and all over the yard, and you cannot find your pet turtle.

   Conclusion:

   Facts needed:

Natural Resources.
Create a poster that reminds us of the importance of the 3 Rs: Reduce, Reuse, and Recycle!
¡Crea un poster que les recuerde a las personas reducir, reusar y reciclar!

Level Red — Bridges™

Add to find the fraction. The sum of each is found in the center.
Suma‡ para encontrar la fracción‡. La suma se encuentra en el centro.

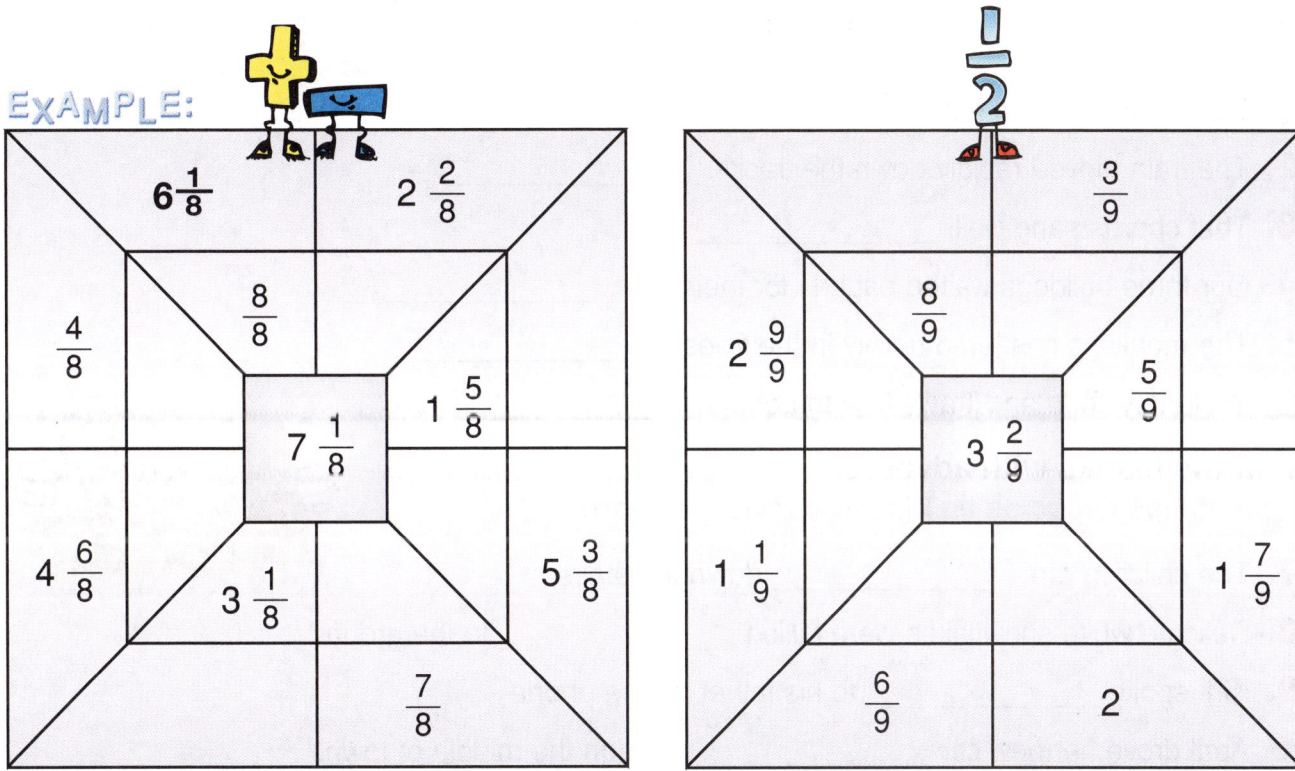

Ears. Label the drawing and fill in the outline below with the terms in the proper sequential order; then explain how sound waves reach the brain through the ears.
Coloca los nombres a las partes del dibujo y completa el resumen a continuación. Luego explica como las ondas sonoras llegan al cerebro a través de los oídos.

cochlea   stirrup   pinna   auditory canal   hammer   anvil   eardrum

I. Outer Ear
  A.
II. Middle Ear
  A.
  B.
  C.
  D.
  E.
III. Inner Ear
  A.

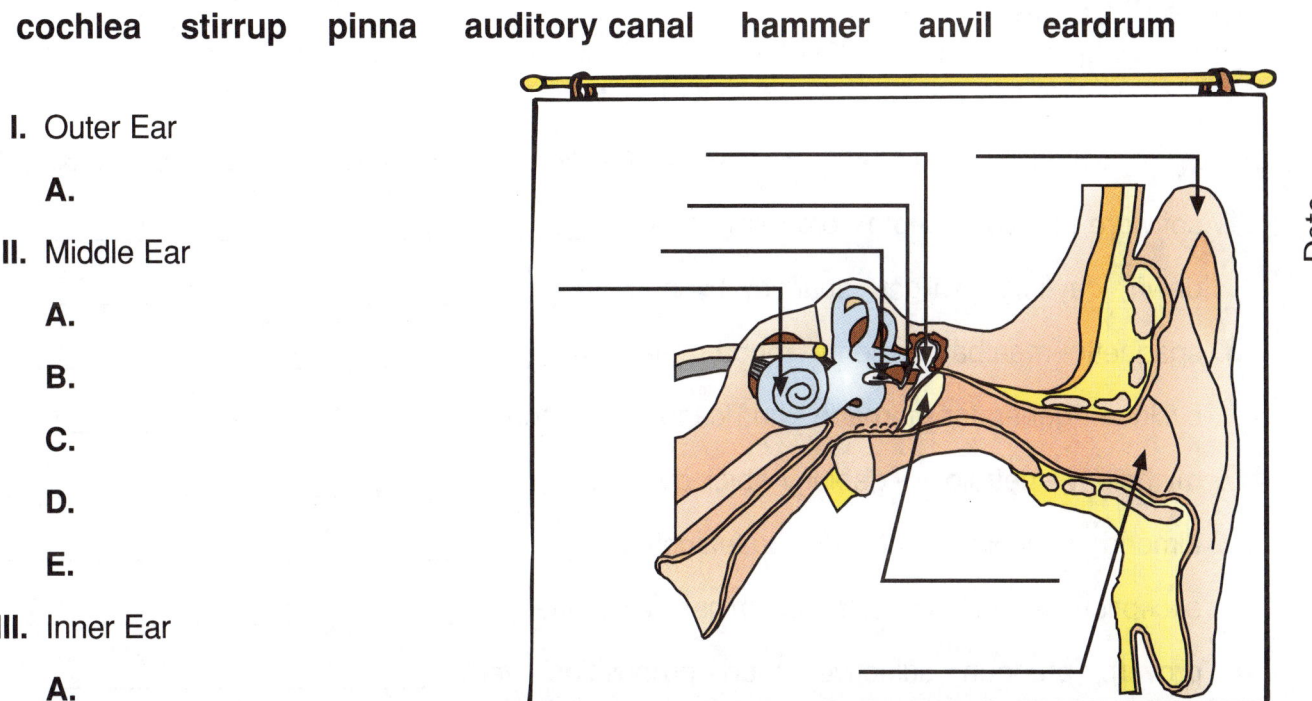

Create a commercial that shows the importance of ear safety. Present it to your family.
Crea un comercial que muestre la importancia de la seguridad de los oídos.

© Federal Education Publishing — 85 — Level Red

Day 10

Adverbs. Underline the adverb in each sentence. At the end of the sentence, write the word it modifies.

Subraya el adverbio‡ de cada oración‡. Luego escribe la palabra a la que modifica.

1. Brent's broken arm hurts badly. _____
2. The train moved rapidly down the tracks. _____
3. That chorus sang well. _____
4. Our three bulldogs waited eagerly for their walk. _____
5. The monkeys chattered noisily in the trees. _____
6. Yesterday Todd and Travis flew to London. _____

Fill in the blanks with adverbs.

Completa los espacios en blanco con adverbios.

7. The children ran _____ down the stairs.
8. Delicate white snowflakes were falling _____ to the ground.
9. Kirk spoke _____ to his father on the phone.
10. April drove her new car _____ through the middle of town.
11. The old windmill worked _____ after he oiled it.
12. Seven baby possums clung _____ to their mother's back

Categories. Find the word that does not belong in the category. Draw a line through it and write a sentence using the word you drew a line through to tell why it doesn't belong.

Tacha la palabra que no pertenezca a la categoría. Escribe una oración usando esa palabra para indicar por qué no pertenece a la categoría.

EXAMPLE: street - road - turnpike - ~~railroad~~ - freeway - highway <u>Cars do not travel on a railroad.</u>

1. software - mouse - depth - program - disk _____
2. dawn - daytime - twilight - sunrise - hyphen _____
3. spaghetti - meatballs - menu - rhubarb - lasagna _____
4. cyclone - generator - tornado - hurricane - monsoon _____
5. mythology - petrology - geology - biology - zoology _____
6. almond - chocolate - caramel - butterscotch _____
7. exception - export - impolite - examiner - excavate _____
8. proverb - pronoun - adjective - noun - preposition - verb _____
9. period - comma - apostrophe - colon - clause _____
10. export - portable - support - importance - medieval _____

Day 11

Zeros with Decimals. Remember the extra zeros when necessary.
Resuelve estos problemas con decimales.

1. 41.5 × 0.17
2. 1.09 × 0.68
3. 3.05 × 85.2
4. 0.003 × 3.9
5. 0.07 × 1.06

6. 0.025 × 0.04
7. 0.59 × 100
8. 347 × 0.06
9. 78.6 × 1,000
10. 7.029 × 0.04

11. 7.4 × 0.07
12. 0.09 × 2.3
13. 0.035 × 0.02
14. 0.005 × 55
15. 3.72 × 0.07

16. 27.5 × 0.91
17. 60 × 0.005
18. 0.92 × 12.5
19. 1.08 × 2.03
20. 0.06 × 0.12

First Aid. Read the following scenarios. After reading each sentence, determine whether proper first aid procedures were being followed. Make a smiley face if they were done correctly. Mark an X if they were not done correctly.
Luego de leer cada oración‡, dibuja una cara sonriente si los procedimientos de primeros auxilios fueron realizados correctamente. Marca con una X si no lo fueron.

Scenario 1: Dallin fell off his bike and could see a big bruise forming on his leg.
____ He immediately put ice on it.
____ Next, he used compression by applying pressure with a cloth on the bruise.
____ Dallin then elevated his leg.

Scenario 2: While Jana and Adam were playing, a dog bit Adam.
____ Jana chased the dog for two blocks trying to capture it.
____ When she came back, Jana called her mom to help Adam.
____ Jana thought they should put butter on the wound.
____ Jana's mom washed the bite with soap and water.
____ They took Adam to the doctor's office.
____ Jana's mom called animal control.

Scenario 3: Linda felt dizzy and fainted.
____ Stephen quickly caught her from falling.
____ He gently put her to the floor and raised her feet.
____ He turned Linda's face to the side in case she vomited.
____ Mac suggested they slap or throw water on Linda to wake her up.
____ Stephen said, "No, let's get an adult to help us."

*As a child, an important thing to remember with first aid is to get emergency help. Make a card of phone numbers you can call in case of an emergency. Put it by your phone.

Level Red

Day 11

Answer T for true or F for false to the following statements about a discussion group. Tell why you think the false statements are false.

Responde T para verdadero y F para falso a estas oraciones sobre grupos de discusión.

____ 1. You talk with others about an idea.

____ 2. The leader of the group should do most of the talking.

____ 3. The leader's only job is to keep things moving.

____ 4. It is important to listen to what is being said.

____ 5. Everyone should have a turn to talk.

____ 6. The people in the group should not ask questions.

____ 7. Questions should be asked by just the leader.

____ 8. Disagreeing is okay in a discussion group.

____ 9. One of the leader's duties is to keep order.

____ 10. All participants should be polite to one another.

____ 11. Anyone in the group can state the problem.

____ 12. The discussion leader should sum up what has been decided or discussed at the end of the session.

Natural Resources. Pollution is a problem that affects all people on the Earth. Match the definition with the correct word. Put a smiley face in the column if this term helps with pollution problems or a sad face if it does not. If it is a sad face, come up with an idea of how we can improve in this area!

Une la definición con el término correcto. Coloca una cara sonriente en la columna si el término ayuda con los problemas de contaminación o una cara triste si no ayuda. ¡Si colocas una cara triste propone una idea para mejorarlo!

1. a tanker runs aground and leaks oil
2. energy generated from falling water
3. food for gardens from leaves and clippings
4. exhaust from cars and pollution from factories that create a layer of pollution; heat rays from the sun cannot go back into the atmosphere
5. energy generated from the inside of the Earth
6. poisonous materials like paint thinner
7. saving
8. smoke and exhaust that mix with water vapor
9. waste taken to a dump that is eventually covered with earth

____ greenhouse effect
____ hazardous waste
____ acid rain
____ compost
____ conservation
____ geothermal energy
____ hydroelectric energy
____ landfill
____ oil spill

Smiley or Sad	Idea

Level Red 88 Bridges™

Finding the Circumference.

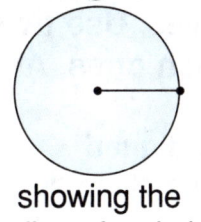
showing the radius of a circle

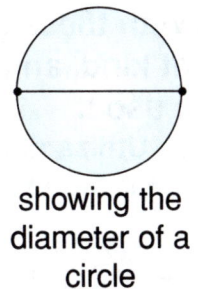
showing the diameter of a circle

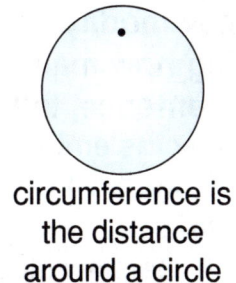
circumference is the distance around a circle

Remember: To find the circumference of a circle, you must multiply the diameter by 3.14. With this information, complete the missing data in the table below.

Encuentra la circunferencia. Completa los datos faltantes de la tabla a continuación.

	Radius of the Circle	Diameter of the Circle	Circumference of the Circle
1.	12 mm	24 mm	75.36 mm
2.	11 inches	22 inches	
3.		18 cm	
4.	10 meters		
5.	13 yards		
6.			150.72 feet
7.		42 inches	
8.	17 cm		
9.			282.60 mm
10.			314 inches
11.		108 yards	
12.			621.72 cm

Because of women such as Lucy Stone, Susan B. Anthony, Lucretia Mott, Elizabeth Cady Stanton, and Sarah and Angelina Grimke, women have many rights today that they didn't have in earlier times. Research one of these women and write of the trials she had to go through because of what she believed.

Investiga y escribe sobre Lucy Stone, Susan B. Anthony, Lucretia Mott, Elizabeth Cady Stanton o Sarah y Angeline Grimke.

Day 12

Adjectives tell how many, what kind, or which one about the nouns or pronouns they modify. Fill in the blanks with these kinds of adjectives. Use two adjectives telling how many, two telling what kind, and one telling which ones. At the end of the sentence, tell which kind you used.
Completa los espacios en blanco con adjetivos‡. Utiliza dos adjetivos que indiquen cuántos, dos que indiquen de qué tipo y uno que indique cuáles. Escribe qué clase de adjetivo utilizaste.

1. _____ cars got stuck in the traffic jam. _____
2. _____ adventure was the most exciting I've ever had. _____
3. The _____ teddy bear cost twenty-five dollars. _____
4. There were _____ camels than lions at the zoo. _____
5. The _____ lizard that came after us was huge. _____

Articles: Special Adjectives (a, an, the). Circle the correct word.
Encierra en un círculo la palabra correcta.

6. Was that (a, an, the) alligator or (a, an) crocodile we saw back there?
7. The student gave her teacher (a, an) crisp, red apple.
8. (A, An, The) excited child was playing with (a, an) fluffy kitten.
9. After (a, an) rainstorm (a, an, the) sun glistens on (a, an, the) puddles.
10. If March comes in like (a, an, the) lion, it should go out like (a, an, the) lamb.

Compound Words. Take a word from list A and a word from list B to make compound words. Write the compound word in the middle. A word in list B could be the first word in the compound. Toma una palabra de la lista A y una de la lista B para formar palabras compuestas. Escribe la palabra compuesta‡ en el centro.

A		B
weather	blood	speaker	news
craft	guard	silver	sight
loud	clip	wrist	wreck
ship	moon	man	writer
vine	mint	walk	board
anchor	turtle	yard	pepper
watch	man	neck	woman
type	frost	space	bite
print	in	hound	life
ware		watch	

1. _____
2. _____
3. _____
4. _____
5. _____
6. _____
7. _____
8. _____
9. _____
10. _____
11. _____
12. _____
13. _____
14. _____
15. _____
16. _____
17. _____
18. _____
19. _____

Level Red

Day 13

Multiplying Fractions Pictures.

Question: How do you picture what 1/2 of 1/2 is?

Picture 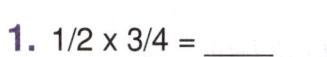 1/2 of a box as 1/2 of 1. Now picture what 1/2 of 1/2 is.
So 1/2 of 1/2 = 1/4, or 1 ÷ 2 ÷ 2 = 1/4.

With the above information, illustrate and answer the following multiplication problems. Reduce to the simplest terms.
(**Hint**: Remember, when you multiply fractions, the product gets <u>smaller</u>.)

Ilustra y responde estos problemas de multiplicación. Simplifica.

1. 1/2 x 3/4 = ____
2. 1/4 x 1/2 = ____
3. 1/2 x 1/3 = ____
4. 1/3 x 2/3 = ____
5. 2/3 x 1/6 = ____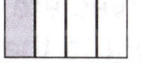
6. 1/3 x 1/4 = ____
7. 2/3 x 4/5 = ____
8. 2/3 x 2/3 = ____
9. 1/4 x 2/3 = ____
10. 3/4 x 2/5 = ____
11. 5/8 x 2/3 = ____
12. 4/5 x 3/5 = ____

● ●

Early Inventions in America. Match the inventor with his invention. Then sketch an invention of your own and explain in detail how it would work and why it would be a good idea.

Une el inventor con el invento. Bosqueja un nuevo invento y explica cómo funcionaría.

____ Eli Whitney   **a.** telegraph

____ Elias Howe   **b.** phonograph

____ Levi Strauss   **c.** sewing machine

____ Cyrus McCormick   **d.** cotton gin

____ Samuel F. B. Morse   **e.** telephone

____ Thomas Edison   **f.** reaper

____ Alexander G. Bell   **g.** blue jeans

© Federal Education Publishing — Level Red

Day 13

More than one adjective can be used to modify the same noun.
Underline the adjectives in the sentences. Circle the word they modify.
Subraya los adjetivos‡ de las oraciones. Encierra en un círculo la palabra a la que modifiquen.

1. The wild, eerie wind frightened the animals.
2. A fuzzy, brown caterpillar was creeping down the sidewalk.
3. Staci splashed some fresh, cool water on her face.
4. The hot, tired explorers swam in a large, clear lake.
5. The spicy aroma of apple cider filled Jason's small, warm tent.
6. I found a wee, puny puppy on my doorstep this morning.

Some adjectives are used to compare.
Add -er or -est to these adjectives to complete the sentences.
Agrega –er o –est a estos adjetivos.

7. The (rainy) _____ spot in the world is in Hawaii.
8. Our back door is (wide) _____ than our front door.
9. Mozart was one of the world's (young) _____ composers.
10. I think the gorilla is one of the (ugly) _____ of all the apes.
11. New Jersey is one of the (small) _____ states.
12. The swan egg was (large) _____ than the duck egg.

Answer these questions Yes or No.
Responde a estas preguntas con Yes o No.

1. Is a gizzard a kind of bird? ____
2. Would the boy wear his mukluk? ____
3. Could you work as a gofer? ____
4. Do you wear a goatee on your head? ____
5. Could you play with a googol? ____
6. Would you sit on a cloy? ____
7. Is a truffle a rich chocolate candy? ____
8. Could you plant a vetch? ____
9. Can a little girl wear aarf? ____
10. Does yep mean yes? ____
11. Is a yeti mysterious? ____
12. Could animals be kept in a sedge? ____
13. Is an orlop part of a ship? ____
14. Can you live in a yurt? ____
15. Would you chop wood with an italic? ____
16. Is an albatross a large sea serpent? ____
17. Could you have a huffy on your shirt? ____
18. Would you eat a mango? ____
19. Can you drive an osier? ____
20. Is a lilt a song or tune? ____

Level Red   Bridges™

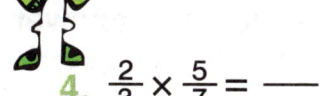

Day 14

Practice Multiplying Fractions. Remember to multiply the numerators, then multiply the denominators.
Practica multiplicar estas fracciones.

1. $\frac{1}{2} \times \frac{3}{4} =$ ___
2. $\frac{2}{3} \times \frac{2}{3} =$ ___
3. $\frac{3}{4} \times \frac{1}{4} =$ ___
4. $\frac{2}{3} \times \frac{5}{7} =$ ___

5. $\frac{4}{5} \times \frac{2}{7} =$ ___
6. $\frac{1}{6} \times \frac{5}{6} =$ ___
7. $\frac{1}{3} \times \frac{2}{3} =$ ___
8. $\frac{3}{4} \times \frac{5}{6} =$ ___

9. $\frac{5}{9} \times \frac{3}{4} =$ ___
10. $\frac{7}{8} \times \frac{2}{5} =$ ___
11. $\frac{3}{5} \times \frac{3}{10} =$ ___
12. $\frac{6}{7} \times \frac{3}{4} =$ ___

Multiply. Write each product in its simplest form.
Multiplica. Simplifica todos los productos.

13. $\frac{1}{2} \times \frac{1}{6} \times \frac{2}{3} =$ ___ or ___
14. $\frac{2}{3} \times \frac{5}{6} \times \frac{1}{4} =$ ___ or ___

15. $\frac{1}{3} \times \frac{5}{7} \times \frac{3}{5} =$ ___ or ___
16. $\frac{2}{3} \times \frac{3}{4} \times \frac{1}{2} =$ ___ or ___

17. $\frac{8}{9} \times \frac{1}{3} \times \frac{3}{4} =$ ___ or ___
18. $\frac{2}{3} \times \frac{1}{2} \times \frac{3}{8} =$ ___ or ___

The Underground Railroad. Research the Underground Railroad. In each car there is a word used for a regular railroad. Underneath this word, write what each word would represent in the Underground Railroad. (Example: <u>passenger</u> would represent <u>slave</u>.) In the empty cars, come up with some of your own railroad terms. What would they represent in the Underground Railroad? (Example: <u>fuel</u> could represent <u>food</u>.)
Sigue estas instrucciones para aprender sobre el Tren Subterráneo.

Level Red

Day 14

Adverbs are words that modify or describe verbs, adjectives, and other adverbs. Adverbs tell how, when, and where. Many end with -ly. Use these adverbs to answer the questions in the chart.

Utiliza estos adverbios‡ para responder las preguntas de la tabla.

immediately	far	there	nearly	wildly
softly	lately	slowly	carefully	hard
today	often	upstairs	eagerly	
closely	soon	never	inside	

When ?					
How ?					
Where ?					

Safety.
Write down the consequence of each act and how it could have been prevented.

Escribe la consecuencia de cada acto y cómo se podría haber prevenido.

Act	Consequence	How It Could Have Been Prevented
1. Tripping on a toy		
2. Running in halls		
3. Swimming without a lifeguard		
4. Playing with matches		
5. Playing near broken glass		
6. Not wearing a seat belt		
7. Not wearing a helmet when biking		

Using a separate sheet of paper, draw a fire escape plan for your house. Make sure you have a meeting point outside for your family. Share your drawing with your family.

Dibuja un plan de escape en caso de incendio para tu hogar. Incluye un lugar de encuentro de tu familia en el exterior. Utiliza un papel aparte.

Level Red   Bridges™

Day 15

Angles. Fill in the blanks.
Completa los espacios en blanco.

When two rays share the same endpoint they form an **(1.)** _____. This endpoint is called the **(2.)** _____ of the angle. The **(3.)** _____ is the unit used for measuring angles. A **(4.)** _____ is used to measure angles. A **(5.)** _____ is marked with **(6.)** _____ degrees. You place the center of the protractor on the vertex of the angle.

The **(7.)** _____ angle looks like a square corner. It measures **(8.)** _____ degrees. An **(9.)** _____ angle is smaller than a right angle or less than 90 degrees. An **(10.)** _____ angle is larger than a right angle or greater than 90 degrees.

Label these three angles. Coloca el nombre a estos ángulos.

11. _____   **12.** _____   **13.** _____

Use a protractor to measure these angles.
Utiliza un transportador para medir estos ángulos.

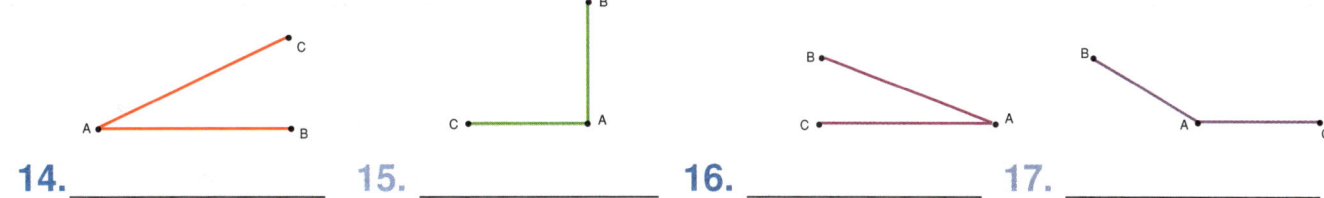

14. _____   **15.** _____   **16.** _____   **17.** _____

Use your protractor to draw an angle for these measures.
Utiliza un transportador para dibujar ángulos con estas medidas.

18. 75°   **19.** 60°   **20.** 15°

Civil War. Look at the list below. Some of the terms have to do with the Civil War. Circle in gray the terms if they refer to the Confederate side or a Confederate victory. Circle in blue the terms that refer to the Union side or a Union victory. Circle in red the terms that occurred in other periods of history.
Encierra en un círculo gris los términos que se refieran a la Confederación (incluyendo las victorias), en un círculo azul los términos que se refieran a la Unión y en un círculo rojo los términos que no se refieran a la Guerra Civil.

Abraham Lincoln	Fort Duquesne	Valley Forge
Sally Tompkins	General Thomas "Stonewall" Jackson	Frederick Douglass
Saratoga	General Ulysses S. Grant	Bill of Rights
Battle of Bull Run	Andrew Jackson	General Robert E. Lee
1776	Seven Days' Battle	Thomas Jefferson
Paul Revere	John Paul Jones	Jefferson Davis
Antietam	Eli Whitney	General William T. Sherman
Yorktown	Harriet Tubman	

© Federal Education Publishing — Level Red

Day 15

Proofread and circle the mistakes in the following paragraphs. Then rewrite the paragraphs, correcting the mistakes in spelling, punctuation, etc. Write in cursive. Try to find thirty-nine mistakes.

Revisa estos párrafos y encierra en un círculo los 39 errores. Vuelve a escribir los párrafos corrigiendo los errores.

   today the term "Native American" is used to descibe those people indigenous to america. however the firt explorers who came to America referred to them as "Indians" unknown to the exploders, most tribes had their own names. for example names used by the deleware indians of eastern north america meant "genuine men".

   the indians' languages way of life, and homes wer all very different. The aztic and maya Indians of central America built large citys The apache and Paiute used brush and mating to make simple huts the plains indians buit coneshaped tepees covered with buffalo skins Cliff dwellers and other Pueblo groups usd sun-dried bricks to make many-storyed houses

___

Use homophones or homonyms to fill in these blanks. Remember: They are words that sound or are spelled the same, but mean different things.

Usa homófonos‡ u homónimos‡ para completar estos espacios en blanco.

EXAMPLE: <u>I</u> think <u>I</u> have something in my <u>eye</u>.

1. Chris will _____ catching a bumble _____ for his insect collection.
2. My _____ Lola had an _____ bite her toe.
3. The _____ was _____ from playing at the concert.
4. _____ visit the _____ of Man in June.
5. Please _____ the door to the _____ closet.
6. Patt _____ me one _____ for good luck.
7. My _____ jeans _____ away in the wind.
8. We went _____ the mall to _____ some cards.
9. My brother _____ _____ pancakes for breakfast.
10. _____, I do not _____ how to play a musical instrument.

Level Red   96   Bridges™

High-Frequency Word List

able	class	got	making	saw	these
about	close	green	matter	sea	they're
across	comes	ground	mean	seen	thing
add	common	grow	mind	seventh	third
against	complete	hair	miss	shall	though
ago	country	half	money	ship	through
almost	course	happened	moon	short	throw
alone	dark	heart	mother	shot	times
already	deep	heavy	mouse	should	tiny
also	dinner	held	move	shown	today
although	distance	here	Mrs.	sick	too
America	doesn't	himself	music	simple	took
American	draw	hold	nothing	since	top
among	during	horse	notice	size	town
animal	early	hour	oh	sky	trouble
animals	earth	however	once	snow	true
anything	easy	hundred	open	soon	trying
area	eighth	ice	order	space	turn
ate	either	idea	outside	special	turned
ball	else	I'll	page	sport	understand
beautiful	English	inside	park	sports	united
became	enough	instead	party	stand	United States
become	ever	its	pattern	start	upon
before	everyone	it's	perhaps	state	used
begin	everything	itself	person	states	usually
behind	except	kept	pick	stay	voice
believe	eyes	killed	piece	stood	walk
best	fact	lady	plants	stopped	walked
bike	family	language	police	story	war
black	father	later	poor	strong	warm
blue	feel	lay	possible	stuff	watch
boat	felt	learned	power	sudden	weather
book	field	least	probably	suddenly	weeks
bottom	finally	leave	problem	summer	whether
box	fine	leaves	question	sun	while
bring	fire	less	quite	surface	white
brought	fix	let's	reading	surface	whole
build	floor	letter	ready	system	wide
built	follow	life	real	table	wild
cannot	foot	light	really	talk	wind
can't	free	liked	reason	talking	winter
care	friend	list	remember	tall	within
carefully	front	live	responsibilities	teach	woke
carry	full	lived	riding	ten	won't
catch	future	lives	river	Thanksgiving	would
caught	gave	living	room	that's	yard
center	glass	longer	round	their	yet
certain	gold	low	rules	themselves	young
check	gone	main	sat	there	you're

© Federal Education Publishing   Level Red

Words to Sound Out, Read, and Spell

absurdity
acceptable
accident
accidentally
accomplish
accomplished
account
accuse
accuser
ache
acquit
acquitted
actual
actually
address
addresses
adhesive
adjective
admirable
adorable
advance
adventure
adventurous
advertise
advertisement
advertiser
advice
advisable
aisle
alley
alleys
allowable
alphabetically
amazement
ambition
amuse
anchor
angel
angle
anniversary
announce
announcer
annual
annually
anxious
apologies
apologize

apology
apparently
appearance
applauded
appointment
appreciation
arches
architecture
arrange
arrival
assembly
assignment
assortment
astonished
astounded
attractive
author
autobiography
autograph
automatic
automobile
autumn
avail
available
average
aviator
avoid
avoidable
barometer
beauties
beige
bicycle
bleach
blunder
boundary
brackish
bravery
breakable
builder
buoyant
burglar
business
businesses
buyer
calculators
calendar
campus

campuses
capitalize
captivity
causes
celery
cemetery
center
chaos
chemical
chlorine
choir
chord
chorus
circular
citation
clatter
climax
climaxes
clothes
coaxed
code
collar
column
combine
command
comment
commentaries
commercial
commitment
committee
community
compare
complexion
complimentary
composition
compress
conceited
concession
condition
conduct
conductor
confiscated
confused
considerate
constitution
consult
consume

consumer
contain
contradiction
contrary
convenient
convertible
convict
convince
cost
couch
couches
counterfeit
counterfeiting
courier
criminal
criminally
cruelty
crystal
cue
cyclone
dangerous
debt
deceitful
deceive
decode
deduction
deflate
defrost
degrees
dehydrate
delay
delayed
delaying
delivery
denounce
dependable
dependent
depending
deposit
depress
depression
describe
design
desirable
destroy
destroyed
destroying

determined
determines
determining
diaries
diary
dictator
dictionary
difficult
diminutive
diploma
director
disagree
disappear
discourage
discovery
disposal
disposition
disrespectful
dissatisfied
distress
distrust
dividing
doubt
dramatize
duplex
duplexes
dynamic
earthquake
echo
ecstatic
edict
editor
either
emigrating
emission
emits
emitted
emphatically
employ
employing
enemies
enemy
engrossed
enjoy
enjoyable
enjoyed
equal

Level Red 98 Bridges™

Words to Sound Out, Read, and Spell

equally	forgivable	humiliated	journey	mentally
equator	forgiveness	humor	journeys	merchandise
equip	formation	humorous	joyous	microphone
equipped	fortune	hydrant	judge	microscope
error	forty-two	hyphen	khaki	microscopic
escort	fragile	hypnotism	knuckles	military
exaggerate	freight	ideal	labor	mirror
examine	furious	ideally	laborer	misery
examiner	further	identified	laughable	misfortune
example	fury	identifies	leashes	misplaced
exasperated	gallery	identify	legally	modern
exceed	gardener	imaginary	leisure	monarch
excellence	gauge	immediately	library	monastery
except	generally	immense	lifeguard	monotone
exception	giant	immune	loafer	monotonous
excess	gigantic	impending	locally	motto
excitable	gilded	importance	luggage	movable
excite	glamorous	impossible	lunar	muscular
exclaim	glamour	impractical	luxuries	mused
exclamation	glimpse	impression	luxurious	mystery
excuse	glorious	improvement	luxuriously	myth
exertion	glossary	incapable	luxury	mythology
exhaust	gnash	inconsiderate	lyric	national
exhibit	gnat	inconvenient	machinery	naturally
expand	gorgeous	independent	magazine	nature
expel	gossip	indignantly	magic	navigate
expelled	governor	individual	magnified	navigator
exported	gratitude	individually	mailboxes	necessary
extend	greedy	induction	manage	neither
extraordinary	grief	infernal	manager	nervous
factual	grocery	inject	manufacture	nighttime
factually	group	injection	manufacturer	nimble
famous	guard	injured	margin	normal
fashion	guesses	injuries	marvel	normally
fatal	guest	injurious	marvelous	notice
fatally	guitar	injury	mayor	nuclear
finevest	gypsy	inscribe	measurement	nursery
figure	handling	inscription	measuring	objectionable
final	hardly	inspection	mechanic	occur
flaming	haunches	intelligence	mediator	occurred
flattery	hazard	interjection	meditating	omit
flexible	hazardous	intermediate	medley	omitted
fluently	heir	introduce	megaphone	operator
forbidden	heiress	inventor	melodious	opinion
foreign	historic	invest	melodiously	opponent
foreigner	honor	invite	members	opportunity
forfeit	horror	janitor	mental	opposed

99   Level Red

Words to Sound Out, Read, and Spell

opposite	powerless	reenter	salary	submission	typhoon
opposition	practices	reexamine	salmon	submit	typical
optician	practicing	refinery	sandwiched	submitting	tyrant
optimist	precise	reformation	satisfied	subscribe	undaunted
orbit	prediction	refrigerator	satisfies	subscription	unfamiliar
orchestra	prefix	refugees	satisfy	subtract	unidentified
ordinary	prefixes	regiment	satisfying	subvert	unites
organize	preheat	register	scenery	successful	unnamed
organizer	prehistoric	regret	schedule	suffix	unnecessary
originally	prejudice	regretted	scholastic	suffixes	unretractable
outstanding	preposition	regular	search	suggestion	unsatisfactory
owing	prescribe	regulate	searches	suitable	unsuccessful
paralyze	pressure	reign	secede	supplement	unveiling
paralyzed	preview	relaxed	secretary	supplied	urgent
parents	problem	relied	seized	supposed	usable
particular	process	relies	senator	surface	use
passenger	produce	rely	separate	surgery	vanish
patrol	profitable	relying	separating	suspect	various
patrolling	propaganda	remittance	sighed	suspended	vein
peculiar	propeller	remnant	sightseers	syllable	venture
penalty	propelling	replacement	silent	sympathy	verdict
pendant	prosperous	reporter	silhouette	symphony	version
pendulum	protein	requirement	similar	symptom	victorious
penetrate	publish	requiring	simplify	system	victory
perceive	publisher	respect	sinus	talent	vigor
perception	punctual	respectable	sinuses	taxes	vigorous
performance	punctually	respectful	slavery	telegraph	villain
perishable	punishable	respond	sleigh	telepathy	vinegar
permit	purchase	resume	slogan	telephone	visitor
permitted	purchaser	retirement	solemn	temporary	visual
perpendicular	purpose	retrieve	solid	terrified	visualized
perpetually	pyramid	reverse	sorrowful	terrifies	vocabulary
personal	python	review	spaghetti	terrifying	walrus
personally	quiver	revise	speaker	territory	walruses
phonograph	raise	revolutionary	spectacle	terror	waltz
photograph	raises	rhinestone	spectacular	threat	waltzes
pillars	raising	rhinoceros	spectator	tolerance	washable
placed	reachable	rhubarb	speeches	tormentor	wearable
planet	readable	rhythm	sponsor	totally	weight
pledge	rearrange	ridicule	starved	traitor	weird
plumber	reasonable	ridiculous	statement	traitorous	weirdly
poison	receipt	robbery	stating	transfer	well-balanced
poisonous	receptacle	role	stationary	transmit	wholesale
popular	receptive	roommate	stationery	transmitting	worse
porches	recesses	routine	stomach	transportation	wrenches
position	recital	rumba	strolled	traveler	wristwatch
postpone	rectangular	rumor	studios	truthful	yacht

Level Red

Glossary

a breve (ă) — el sonido a en bat.

a larga (ā) — el sonido a en cake.

abreviatura (abbreviation) — forma corta de una palabra. Por ejemplo: dic. por diciembre, Dr. por doctor. Las abreviaturas finalizan con un punto y muchas veces comienzan con mayúscula.

adjetivo (adjective) — una palabra que califica a un sustantivo o pronombre. Los adjetivos pueden describir cuántos, de qué tipo o cuál. En la oración "El hombre delgado cepillaba tres perros con un peine azul", tres, delgado y azul son adjetivos.

adverbio (adverb) — una palabra que modifica o califica a un verbo, adjetivo u otro adverbio. Los adverbios pueden indicar cómo, cuándo y dónde. En inglés, muchos finalizan en –ly, en español, muchos finalizan en –mente.

analogía (analogy) — una comparación entre dos pares de palabras. Por ejemplo, "la manzana es al árbol como la leche a la vaca" es una analogía que compara de dónde provienen dos cosas.

antónimo (antonym) — una palabra que significa lo opuesto a otra palabra. Contento y triste son antónimos.

área (area) — la medida de la superficie de un objeto. Calculamos el área multiplicando el largo por el ancho del objeto. El área se mide en unidades cuadradas. Entonces si el área de la superficie de una mesa mide 4 pies de largo y 3 pies de ancho, tendrá 12 pies cuadrados (3 x 4 = 12).

cambio físico (physical change) — ocurre cuando una sustancia cambia pero no se forma una nueva. Por ejemplo, un cambio físico ocurre cuando el agua se convierte en hielo.

cambio químico (chemical change) — ocurre cuando dos o más sustancias se combinan y forman una nueva sustancia. Por ejemplo, hierro más oxígeno forma óxido.

categorizar (categorize/categorizing) — agrupar ítems basándose en aspectos que tienen en común. Por ejemplo, se puede incluir manzanas, peras y bananas en una categoría que se denomine "Frutas".

circunferencia (circumference) — la distancia alrededor de un círculo. Para encontrar la circunferencia de un círculo se debe multiplicar el diámetro por 3.14.

cociente (quotient) — el resultado de un problema de división.

comillas (" ") (quotation marks) — las comillas se sitúan antes y después de lo que una persona está diciendo y, además, en los títulos de historias, poemas y canciones.

contracción (contraction) — una combinación reducida de dos palabras que incluye un apóstrofe en el lugar dónde se han omitido letras. "Didn't" es una contracción de "did not".

cursiva (cursive) — una forma de escritura en la que las letras están unidas: *esto es letra cursiva*.

diferencia (difference) — la respuesta a un problema de sustracción.

doble negación (double negative) — el uso de dos palabras negativas, como "not" o "no", cuando se necesita solamente una. Por ejemplo: "He did not have no breakfast," debería escribirse "He had no breakfast" o "He did not have any breakfast."

e breve (ĕ) — el sonido e en pet.

e larga (ē) — el sonido e en sleep.

estimar (estimate) — realizar una buena aproximación.

examen de desarrollo (essay test) — un examen en el que deben contestarse las preguntas en oraciones y párrafos.

examen objetivo (objective test) — un examen en dónde se debe responder verdadero o falso, multiple choice, unir, etc., en vez de desarrollar una respuesta.

Glossary

forma estándar / notación estándar (standard form / standard notation) — la forma habitual de escribir un número. 538 ó 6,700 están escritos en notación estándar.

fracción (fraction) — un número que representa parte de un total. 1/2 2/10 y 2/3 son fracciones.

frase preposicional (prepositional phrase) — una preposición y su objeto. En la oración "El gusano está en la manzana", "en la manzana" es la frase preposicional.

grupos consonánticos (blends) — dos consonantes que se juntan para formar un cierto sonido. Pl, br, gr, cl y sp son todos grupos consonánticos.

homófonos (homophones) — ver homónimos.

homónimos (también homófonos) (homonyms or homophones) — palabras que suenan o se escriben igual pero tienen un significado distinto. Por ejemplo: see y sea en inglés, echo y hecho en español.

i breve (ĭ) — el sonido i en pit.

i larga (ī) — el sonido i en ice.

idea principal (main idea) — la idea principal indica de qué trata una historia.

lluvia de ideas (brainstorm) — lanzar ideas.

modismo (idiom) — un dicho de una lengua que significa algo diferente a lo que las palabras realmente dicen. Por ejemplo, "llueven sapos y culebras" significa que está lloviendo muy fuerte, no que están cayendo animales del cielo.

múltiplo (multiple) — un número exactamente divisible por otro número. Por ejemplo: 6, 12 , 18 , 24 ,30 son todos múltiplos de 6.

número negativo (negative number) — un número menor a 0.

número positivo (positive number) — un número mayor a cero.

o breve (ŏ) — el sonido o en pot.

o larga (ō) — el sonido o en boat.

objeto directo (direct objects) — sustantivos o pronombres que completan o reciben la acción del verbo. En la oración "Él tiró la pelota," pelota es el objeto directo.

oración (sentence) — un grupo de palabras que expresa un pensamiento completo. Una oración comienza con mayúscula y, generalmente, finaliza con un punto (.), signo de interrogación (?), o signo de exclamación (!)

oración principal (topic sentence) — una oración que indica la idea principal de un párrafo.

palabra base (o palabra raíz) (base word or root word) — una palabra a la que puede agregársele un prefijo o un sufijo. Por ejemplo, "thank" sería la palabra base en "unthankful" y "gracia" sería la palabra base en "desgraciado".

palabra compuesta (compound word) — una palabra formada por dos palabras más pequeñas como, por ejemplo, "farmhouse" o "lightbulb" en inglés, "portalámpara" o "cubrecama" en español.

palabra raíz (o palabra base) (root word or base word) — una palabra a la que puede agregársele un prefijo o un sufijo. Por ejemplo "thank" sería la palabra base en "unthankful" y "gracia" sería la palabra base en "desgraciado".

perímetro (perimeter) — la distancia alrededor de un objeto, o el largo de todos sus lados. Para obtener el perímetro, se debe sumar el largo de todos los lados.

plural (plural) — más de uno.

polígono (polygon) — una figura cerrada por cuatro líneas rectas.

porcentaje (percent) — una porción de 100. Por ejemplo, 15% significa lo mismo que 15/100 ó 15 de 100.

predicado (predicate) — indica al lector algo sobre el sujeto de una oración.

Glossary

prefijo (prefix) —una sílaba que se agrega al principio de una palabra base para formar una nueva palabra. En la palabra "untie", -un es un prefijo, en la palabra "insatisfecho", -in es un prefijo.

preposición (preposition) — palabras como en, bajo y sobre, que muestran relaciones entre otras palabras. Por ejemplo "El gusano está en la manzana."

producto (product) — el resultado de un problema de multiplicación.

pronombre (pronoun) — una palabra que reemplaza a un sustantivo. Yo, él, ellos, alguien y nosotros son todos pronombres.

pronombre posesivo (possessive pronoun) — un pronombre que muestra posesión. Suyo, nuestro y suyos son pronombres posesivos.

pronombre subjetivo (subject pronoun) — pronombres como yo, tu, él, nosotros y ellos pueden ser el sujeto de una oración.

reagrupar (regroup) — en matemática, se reagrupa cuando se "toma prestado" diez de una columna para usarlo en otra. Por ejemplo, en el problema 22-17 se mueve 1 grupo de 10 de la columna de las decenas a la columna de las unidades, para poder restar 7 a 12. Entonces queda 1 decena en la columna de las decenas y 1 menos 1 es cero.

redondear (round(ing) numbers) — una manera de estimar números para que sea más fácil utilizarlos para resolver un problema. Por ejemplo, podría redondearse el número 9 "para arriba" a 10 o el número 103 "para abajo" a 100 ó 6.72 a 7 para ayudar a realizar rápidamente un estimativo.

schwa — el sonido "uh"

sílaba (syllable) — una combinación de letras que se pronuncian como una unidad y se utilizan para dividir palabras. "Perro" tiene dos sílabas (pe-rro), "camello" tiene tres sílabas (ca-me-llo) y "elefante" tiene cuatro (e-le-fan-te).

sílaba tónica (stressed syllable) — una sílaba que se enfatiza más que las otras cuando se pronuncia una palabra. Por ejemplo, cuando se dice fútbol, se pone un poco más de énfasis en la sílaba "fút" que en "bol". Pruébalo de una manera diferente y escucha como suena.

simplificación (fracciones) (reduce (fractions)) — escribir una fracción en su forma más simple, en la que el divisor común máximo del nominador y el denominador sea 1. Por ejemplo, en la fracción 6/9, tanto 6 como 9 pueden dividirse por 3, lo que da como resultado 2/3. 2 y 3 sólo pueden dividirse por el número 1, por lo tanto 2/3 es la forma más simple de escribir 6/9.

singular — uno.

sinónimo (synonym) — una palabra que significa prácticamente lo mismo que otra. Feliz y contento son sinónimos.

sufijos (suffixes) — una sílaba que se agrega al final de una palabra base para formar una nueva palabra. En la palabra "helpless", "less" es un sufijo, en la palabra "cordialmente", "-mente" es un sufijo.

sujeto (subject) — indica sobre qué o quién es la oración.

suma (sum) — el resultado de un problema de adición.

sustantivo (noun) — una palabra que nombra a una persona, lugar, cosa o idea. Mamá, castillo, tenedor y justicia son sustantivos.

sustantivo común (common noun) — un sustantivo que no es el nombre específico de una persona, lugar o cosa. Bebé, tienda, equipo e independencia son todos sustantivos comunes. Los sustantivos comunes no se escriben con mayúscula, salvo que sean la primera palabra de una oración.

sustantivo posesivo (possessive noun) — un sustantivo que muestra posesión. Por ejemplo, en la frase "the dog's dish", "dog's" es un posesivo porque indica que el plato (dish) pertenece al perro (dog). Para formar un

Glossary

sustantivo singular posesivo se agrega 's — dog's dish. Un sustantivo plural posesivo se forma agregando s' — dogs' dish (lo que significa que el plato es usado por más de un perro).

sustantivo propio (proper noun) — el nombre específico de una persona, lugar o cosa. Por ejemplo, Rob, New York, y Oreo son todos sustantivos propios. Los sustantivos propios siempre comienzan con mayúscula.

término de la preposición (object of a preposition) — el sustantivo o pronombre que sigue a una preposición. En la oración "El gusano está en la manzana", manzana es el término de la preposición en.

transformar a número mixto (fracciones) (renaming fractions) — convertir una fracción con un numerador mayor que su denominador en un número entero y una fracción. Por ejemplo, 10/6 puede transformarse a número mixto como 1 4/6 ó 1 2/3.

transportar (suma / multiplicación) (carry [addition/multiplication]) — como reagrupar, cuando uno transporta, mueve un número de una columna a otra. Por ejemplo, en 15 + 16, se suma 5 +6, lo que da por resultado 11. Piensa en 11 como 10 + 1. Para finalizar el problema se pone el 1 en el lugar de las unidades y luego se "transporta" el 10 a la columna de las decenas, donde ahora figuran 3 decenas, o 30. Por lo tanto, el resultado es 31.

u breve (ŭ) — el sonido "u" en cup.

u larga (ū) — el sonido "u" en blue.

valor relativo (place value) — se refiere al valor de un número basado en su posición dentro de un número mayor. Por ejemplo, en el número 245, el 5 se encuentra en el lugar de las unidades y representa 5 unidades, el 4 ocupa el lugar de las decenas y representa 40 ó 4 decenas y el 2 está ubicado en el lugar de las centenas, representando 200 ó 2 centenas.

verbo (verb) — palabras que muestran una acción o un estado. Saltar, pensar, ir, es y poder son todos verbos.

verbo 'to be' ('to be" verb) — una forma del verbo que significa ser, estar o existir: is, am, are, was, were, be, being, been.

verbo activo (action verb) — una palabra para algo que se realiza. Por ejemplo: correr, gritar o dormir son verbos activos.

verbo irregular (irregular verb) — los verbos regulares muestran que la acción sucedió en el pasado agregando –ed a la palabra base. Para mostrar el tiempo pasado en los verbos irregulares, se debe cambiar la ortografía. Por ejemplo, el tiempo pasado de "run" es "ran", no "runned" y el tiempo pasado de "go" es "went".

verbos auxiliares (helping verb) — verbos que "ayudan" al verbo principal. El verbo principal muestra la acción. En la oración "El puede ir mañana", ir es el verbo principal y puede es el verbo auxiliar.

verbos copulativos (state-of-being verbs) — indican lo que algo o alguien es o hace. Son verbos copulativos: ser, parecer y semejar.

verbos en tiempo pasado (past tense verbs) — palabras que describen acciones que ya sucedieron. Escribió, caminó, olió y miró, son todos verbos en tiempo pasado.

verbos en tiempo presente (present tense verbs) —verbos que ocurren ahora. Escribe, camina y mira son todos verbos en tiempo presente.

vocal sorda (silent vowel) — una vocal como "e" al final de "cake" que no tiene sonido cuando se pronuncia la palabra.

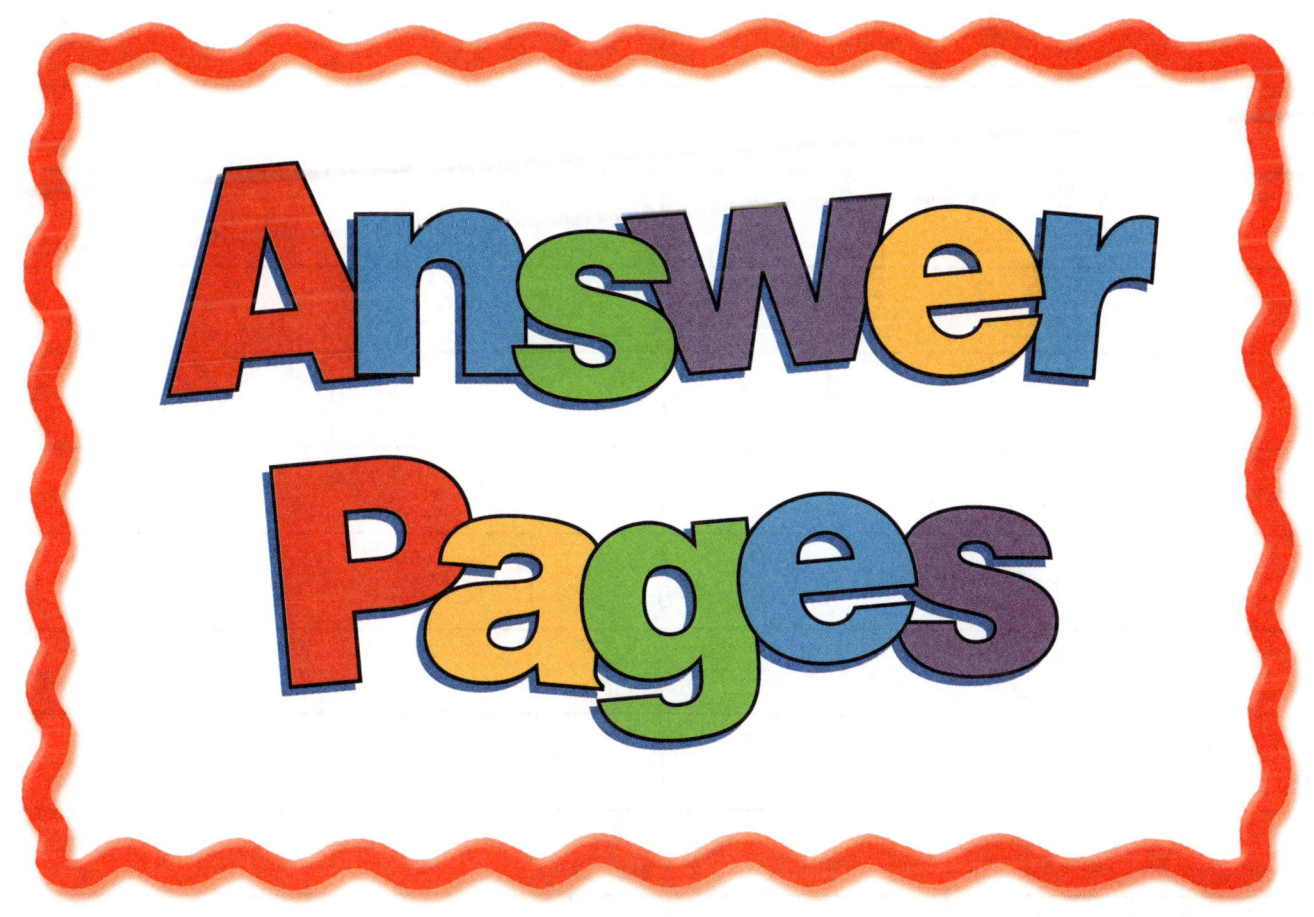

Fraction Table

1

$\frac{1}{2}$	$\frac{1}{2}$

$\frac{1}{3}$	$\frac{1}{3}$	$\frac{1}{3}$

$\frac{1}{4}$	$\frac{1}{4}$	$\frac{1}{4}$	$\frac{1}{4}$

$\frac{1}{5}$	$\frac{1}{5}$	$\frac{1}{5}$	$\frac{1}{5}$	$\frac{1}{5}$

$\frac{1}{6}$	$\frac{1}{6}$	$\frac{1}{6}$	$\frac{1}{6}$	$\frac{1}{6}$	$\frac{1}{6}$

$\frac{1}{7}$	$\frac{1}{7}$	$\frac{1}{7}$	$\frac{1}{7}$	$\frac{1}{7}$	$\frac{1}{7}$	$\frac{1}{7}$

$\frac{1}{8}$	$\frac{1}{8}$	$\frac{1}{8}$	$\frac{1}{8}$	$\frac{1}{8}$	$\frac{1}{8}$	$\frac{1}{8}$	$\frac{1}{8}$

$\frac{1}{9}$	$\frac{1}{9}$	$\frac{1}{9}$	$\frac{1}{9}$	$\frac{1}{9}$	$\frac{1}{9}$	$\frac{1}{9}$	$\frac{1}{9}$	$\frac{1}{9}$

$\frac{1}{10}$	$\frac{1}{10}$	$\frac{1}{10}$	$\frac{1}{10}$	$\frac{1}{10}$	$\frac{1}{10}$	$\frac{1}{10}$	$\frac{1}{10}$	$\frac{1}{10}$	$\frac{1}{10}$

Level Red

Bridges™

Page 3

Day 1

Use the following information to solve these place value problems.

billions			millions			thousands					
hundred-billions	ten-billions	billions	hundred-millions	ten-millions	millions	hundred-thousands	ten-thousands	thousands	hundreds	tens	ones

Remember: Commas separate millions, thousands, etc.

Write the following in expanded form.
Escribe estos números en forma expandida.

1. 72,584,361
   70,000,000 + 2,000,000 + 500,000 + 80,000 + 4,000 + 300 + 60 + 1
2. 37,126,489
   30,000,000 + 7,000,000 + 100,000 + 20,000 + 6,000 + 400 + 80 + 9
3. 56,487,320,960
   50,000,000,000 + 6,000,000,000 + 400,000,000 + 80,000,000 + 7,000,000 + 300,000 + 20,000 + 900 + 60
4. 90,675,409,783
   90,000,000,000 + 600,000,000 + 70,000,000 + 5,000,000 + 400,000 + 9,000 + 700 + 80 + 3

Write the following using the correct word form.
Escribe estos números en letras en forma correcta.

5. 826,531,947,683
   Eight hundred twenty-six billion five hundred thirty-one million nine hundred forty-seven thousand six hundred eighty-three
6. 406,723,891,534
   Four hundred six billion, seven hundred twenty-three million, eight hundred ninety-one thousand, five hundred thirty-four
7. 861,750,432,971
   Eight hundred sixty-one billion, seven hundred fifty million, four hundred thirty-two thousand, nine hundred seventy-one
8. 900,076,580,035
   Nine hundred billion, seventy-six million, five hundred eighty thousand, thirty-five

Page 4

Day 1

Write a sentence showing what the underlined words below mean. Use the underlined word in your answer.
Escribe una oración que muestre lo que significa cada palabra subrayada. Usa la palabra subrayada en tu oración.

Answers will vary.

1. Was John <u>elated</u> when he won first prize?
   No, John was not elated with a new bike. He already had one.
2. Why was there so much <u>turmoil</u> at the party?
   The turmoil was caused by a pet snake that was loose.
3. Is it <u>mandatory</u> for you to go to school until you are eighteen?
   It is mandatory to go to school until you are sixteen.
4. Why is the little boy crying so <u>dolefully</u>?
   The boy is crying so dolefully because his best friend just moved away.
5. Did the people raise enough money to <u>renovate</u> the old church?
   They were able to renovate the church and had money left over.
6. Were the Scouts <u>intrepid</u> campers?
   No, the Scouts were not very intrepid campers; three of them were afraid of the dark.
7. What was making the kitten <u>quiver</u> so hard?
   A barking dog was making the kitten quiver.
8. Do you think Mr. Brown is a <u>corpulent</u> man?
   Mr. Brown is not a corpulent man anymore. He lost 150 pounds.
9. How <u>palatable</u> are artichokes to you?
   Artichokes are very palatable to me; I love them.
10. Were the police <u>inquisitive</u> about the cause of the accident?
    The police must not have been very inquisitive because they didn't ask many questions.

Communication skills are very important. Read the sentences below. Rate yourself between 1 (lowest) and 5 (highest) on how well you communicate. Then answer the following questions.
Lee las oraciones. Califícate entre 1 (más bajo) y 5 (más alto) en lo bien que te comunicas. Responde las preguntas.

Answers will vary.   Your rating: _____

1. I speak clearly and loudly so others can hear what I am saying.   yes   no
2. I express my feelings.   yes   no
3. I try to think before I speak so I will not hurt others' feelings.   yes   no
4. I listen when others are talking.   yes   no
5. I do not share secrets that others have trusted me to keep.   yes   no

- What areas of communication are your strong points? _____
- What areas of communication do you need to improve? _____
- How might you improve in these areas? _____

Page 5

Day 2

What's in a Number?
Write a definition and some examples of the following terms.
Escribe una definición y da algunos ejemplos de estos términos.

Whole numbers
Definitions and examples will vary.
• A whole number is a number denoting one or more units or whole things.
• Cannot be a fraction. Examples: 1, 2, 3, 4, 5, 106, 110, 155, etc.

Number integers
• Number integers are any whole number. Could be a positive or negative number.
• Cannot be a fraction. Examples: 1, -1, 2, -2, 3, -3, 4, -4, 5, -5, 106, 110, 155, etc.

Prime numbers
• A prime number is a whole number that cannot be divided without a remainder by any whole number except itself and 1. Examples: 2, 3, 5, 7, 11, 13, 17, 19, 23, 29, 31, etc.

Composite numbers
• A composite number is a number divisible by a whole number other than itself or 1. Examples: 4, 6, 8, 9, 10, 12, 14, 15, 16, 18, 21, 22, 24, 25, 26, 27, 28, etc. Any whole number that is not a prime number.

Label as many states on this map as you can.
Coloca el nombre a la mayor cantidad posible de estados en este mapa.

Page 6

Day 2

Read the following paragraphs and answer the questions.
Lee estos párrafos y responde las preguntas.

Timbuktu is a small trading town in central Mali. It was established around 1100 A.D. and is located near the southern edge of the Sahara Desert. It was a trading post for products from North and West Africa. Camel caravans from the north traded salt, cloth, cowrie shells, and copper. The dealers in Timbuktu exchanged the goods for gold, kola nuts, ivory, and slaves that they got from the south.

Timbuktu's location left it open to attack, and control of the city changed many times. It has been ruled by the Mali Empire, the Songhai Empire, Morocco, nomads, and others. France controlled it from 1893 until 1960. However, as early as the 1600s it has declined in importance and population. Many of its mud and brick buildings are eroding and are half-buried in the sand.

1. What is the topic of the first paragraph?
   a small trading town called Timbuktu
2. What is the main idea of the first paragraph?
   Timbuktu was a trading city for people in Africa.
3. What is the topic of the second paragraph?
   rulers of Timbuktu
4. What is the main idea of the second paragraph?
   Because of Timbuktu's location it has been ruled by many empires.

Investigate the life of Sir Francis Drake. Compare the different ways Spain and England felt about Drake. Write these different perspectives on the T-chart below.
Investiga la vida de Sir Francis Drake. Compara qué opinaban España e Inglaterra sobre Drake. Escribe sus puntos de vista en el gráfico en forma de T.

Spain	England
The Spanish were angry at Drake and called him a pirate.	The English felt Drake was a hero.
Color may vary. Anger often portrayed as red.	Color may vary. Could be purple or blue.

Choose a color that would describe the feelings of each country towards Drake. Put the color in the appropriate box.

Page 7

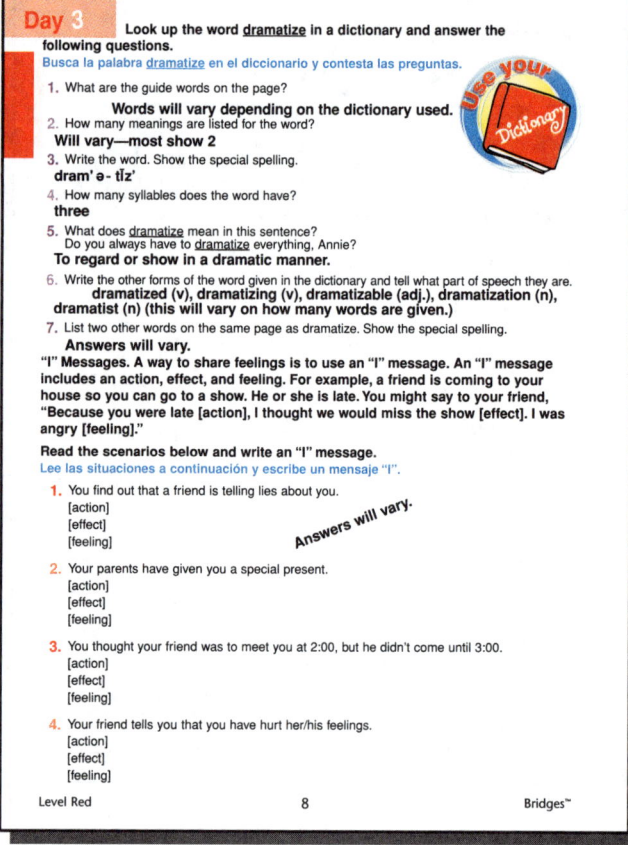

Page 8

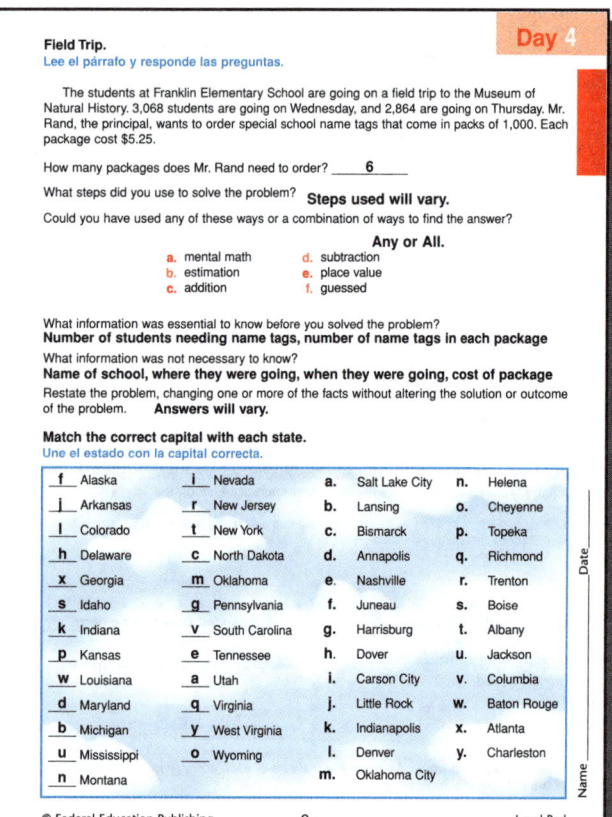

Page 9

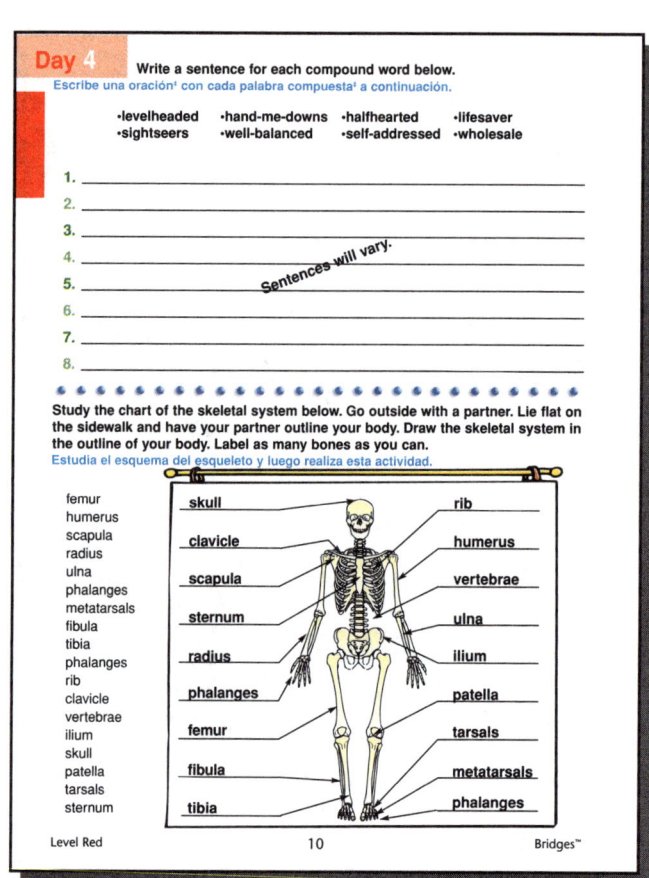

Page 10

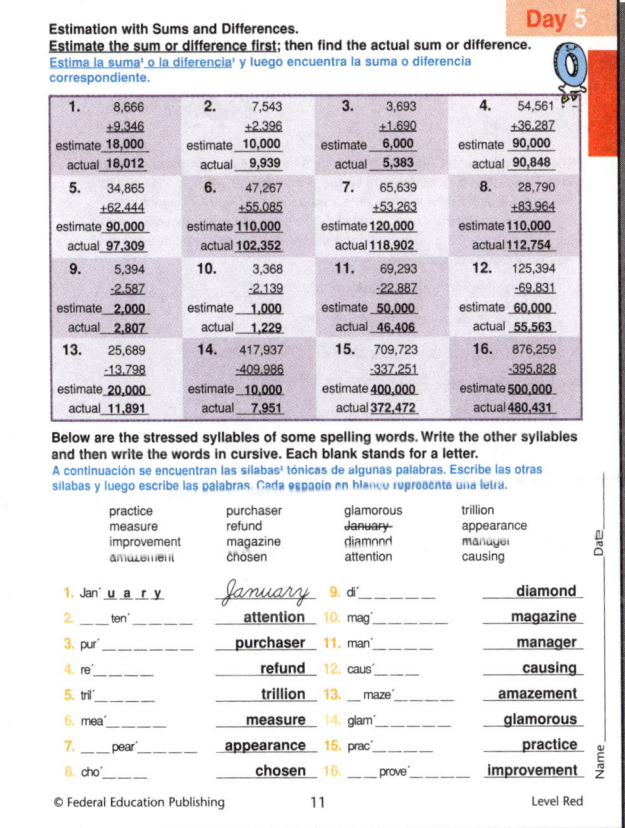

Page 11

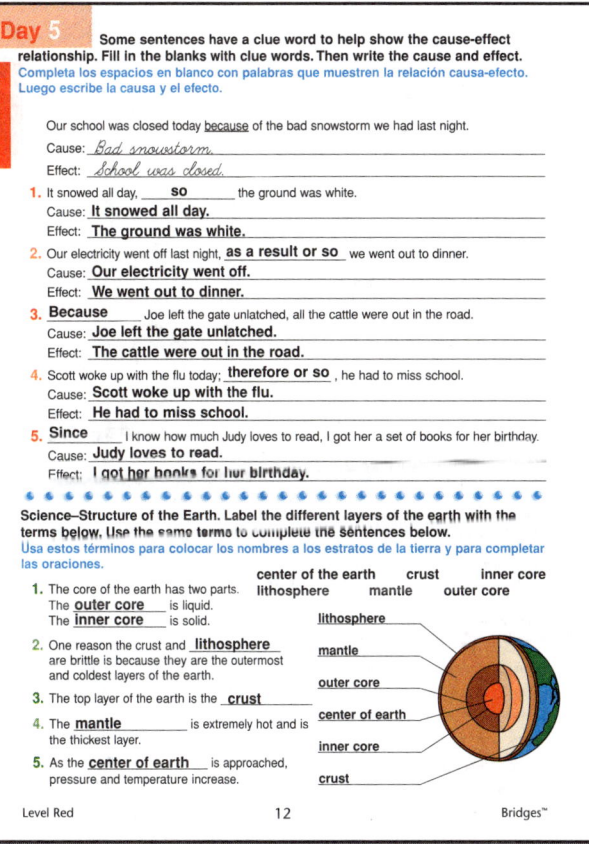

Page 12

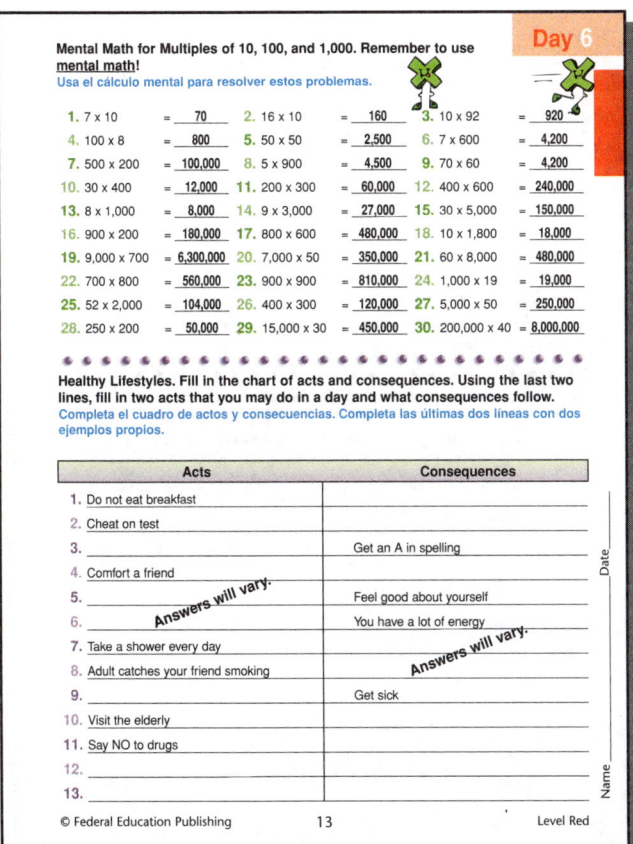

Page 13

Page 14

Page 15

Multiplying by 2- and 3-Digit Numbers.
Multiplica.

Remember:
```
    218       429       293
  x  36     x 375     x 704
   1308      2145      1172
    654      3003       000
   7848      1287      2051
          160875     206272
```

1. 826 × 47 = 38,822
2. 584 × 29 = 16,936
3. 249 × 63 = 15,687
4. 973 × 51 = 49,623
5. 670 × 94 = 62,980
6. 776 × 68 = 52,768
7. 845 × 77 = 65,065
8. 392 × 82 = 32,144
9. 628 × 274 = 172,072
10. 831 × 347 = 288,357
11. 609 × 149 = 90,741
12. 586 × 781 = 457,666
13. 196 × 175 = 34,300
14. 594 × 739 = 438,966
15. 854 × 837 = 714,798
16. 697 × 507 = 353,379

Possessive and plural forms of many nouns sound alike but are different. An 's can make the base word noun become a singular possessive. For example: All the players' (plural) coats looked the same, but one player's (singular possessive) coat was ripped in the back. In the following sentences, cross out the plurals and possessives that are incorrect. Write them correctly at the right of the sentences. If they are right, just write "correct."
Tacha los plurales¹ y posesivos incorrectos. Escríbelos correctamente en los espacios en blanco. Escribe OK si no hay errores.

1. All the news reporter's decided to stay at the Brookgreen Inn. — **reporters**
2. Ten driver's went out on the job this morning, but only nine returned on time. — **drivers**
3. One drivers truck was stuck in a huge snowdrift. — **driver's**
4. The announcer's voice sounded awful this morning. — **correct**
5. Many authors had a convention last year to come up with new ideas for books. — **correct**
6. The authors new book sold 1,000 copies in four hours. — **author's**
7. The organizer's of this party can be proud of themselves. — **organizers**

Page 16

Day 7 Sequence.
Read this paragraph; then write the main points in the correct order.
Lee y luego escribe los puntos principales en el orden correcto.

Traveling Spiders

The baby wolf spider rides on its mother's back. Jumping spiders travel by ballooning. They raise their abdomens so the wind can pull silk threads from their spinnerets. The wind then lifts the little spiders into the air like balloons on strings. Fisher spiders are very lightweight, so they can travel by walking on water. Crab spiders walk backwards and sidewards. All spiders can make and travel on a dragline (a silk thread).

1. Baby wolf spiders ride on their mother's back.
2. Jumping spiders travel by ballooning.
3. *Fisher spiders can walk on water.*
4. Crab spiders walk backwards and sidewards.
5. All spiders can travel on a dragline.

Digestive System.
Put the steps of the digestive process in the proper sequence.
Ordena las fases del proceso digestivo en la secuencia correcta.

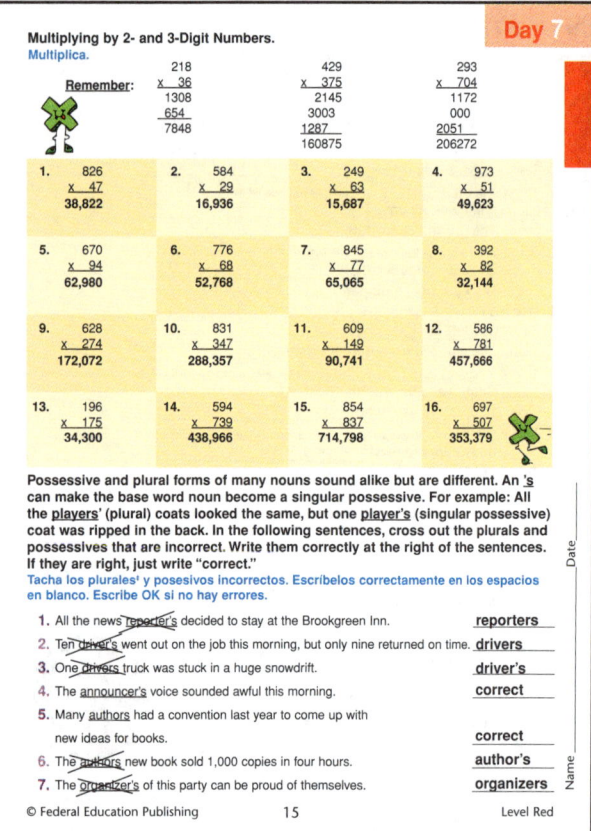

- 4 — Food moves to the small intestine.
- 2 — The tongue pushes food down the esophagus.
- 7 — Undigested food passes out of the body through the anus.
- 5 — Villi in the small intestine absorb digested food into the bloodstream.
- 1 — Teeth and saliva start to change food.
- 6 — Undigested food moves to the large intestine, or colon.
- 3 — Food goes to the stomach where it is further broken down.

Page 17

Day 8 Add, subtract, or multiply. Find the answer to each of the following story problems and tell which operation you used to solve the problem.
Suma¹, resta o multiplica para resolver los problemas. Escribe qué operación utilizaste en el espacio en blanco.

1. A person can make 36 single-dipped ice cream cones out of one gallon of ice cream. If you have 12 different flavors of one-gallon ice cream containers, how many cones do you need to use all of the ice cream? **432 cones, multiply**
2. Mrs. Stone hand-dipped 425 chocolates the first of May, 592 the middle of May, and 143 the last part of May. How many chocolates did she make in May? **1,160 chocolates, add**
3. Farmer Tim sold 4,987 pounds of potatoes last year and 12,709 pounds this year. Next year he hopes to do even better. How many more pounds of potatoes did he sell this year than last year? **7,722 pounds, subtract**
4. Denim shorts sell for $27.59 a pair at Lornet Department Store. Its regular denim jeans sell for $12.18 more than its denim shorts. How much do the store's regular denim jeans cost? **$39.77 a pair, add**
5. Mirror Park has 73 ducks on its lake. An average of 670 people visit the ducks each day. If each person fed the ducks 3 pieces of bread each day, how many pieces of bread would each duck get each day? **27.534, multiply then divide**
6. If each person in the United States drank 42 gallons of milk a year, and each gallon cost $1.98, how much would each person spend on milk a year? **$83.16 a year, multiply**
7. Vicki planted 136 red tulip bulbs, 734 white bulbs, and 400 yellow bulbs. How many flowers will she have if each bulb blooms? **1,270 tulips, add**
8. Gloria bought 25 pairs of socks at $5.80 a pair. If her mother gave her $500, would she have enough money left to buy 6 pairs of shoes at $30.00 each? **Yes, multiply, subtract**
9. Griffin came home with 12 popsicles that cost him $3.00 a dozen. He sold 2 popsicles to his sister, Brynn, at 50¢ each and 4 popsicles to his brother, Tyler, at 50¢ each. How much profit will Griffin make after he sells the rest to his Grandma Dorene at 50¢ each? **$3.00, multiply, add, subtract, or multiply, subtract**

Look in an atlas. Which states contain the following latitude and longitude?
Busca en un atlas. ¿Qué estados contienen estas latitudes y longitudes?

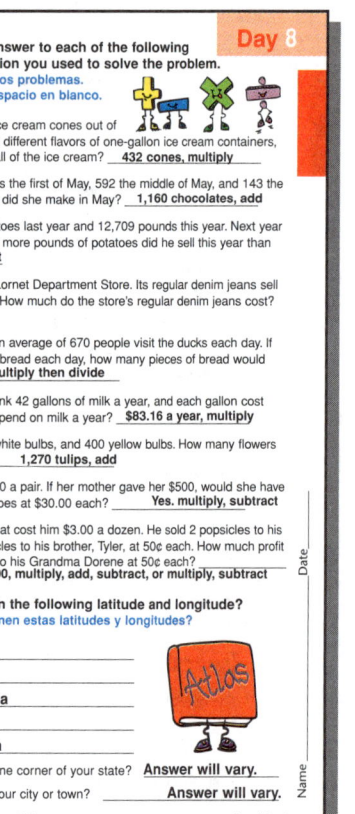

1. 40° N, 110° W — **Utah**
2. 35° N, 110° W — **Arizona**
3. 35° N, 120° W — **California**
4. 40° N, 83° W — **Ohio**
5. 33° N, 87° W — **Alabama**
6. What is the latitude and longitude of one corner of your state? **Answer will vary.**
7. What is the latitude and longitude of your city or town? **Answer will vary.**

Page 18

Day 8 Context clues help you learn new words and their meanings. Use the context clues in the following sentences to tell what the underlined words mean.
Utiliza las pistas del contexto de la oración¹ para determinar qué significan las palabras subrayadas. Escribe el significado.

1. Mary feigned surprise when her friends had a birthday party for her.
   feigned – **pretended**
2. My colleagues and I work together on many new projects.
   colleagues – **people who work together**
3. Maurice looks at his watch often to make sure he is always punctual.
   punctual – **on time**
4. Joseph, a philatelist, has a large collection of stamps.
   philatelist – **a stamp collector**
5. The pig napping in the mud was hardly able to bestir itself for its dinner.
   bestir – **awaken**

Read the following passage and answer the questions below.
Lee los párrafos y responde las preguntas.

Englishman Sir Walter Raleigh wanted to start a colony in the New World (North America). In 1585, Raleigh sent colonists to what is now North Carolina. The colonists did not want to work and almost starved to death. They were taken back to England. Two years later a second group of colonists sailed over to the same place as the previous colonists. They worked very hard to survive.

Because of a war involving England, Raleigh lost track of the colonists. In 1591, a ship from England finally arrived to check on the colonists, but the colonists had disappeared. There was no sign of life. All the sailors found were some empty trunks, rotted maps, and the word CROATOAN carved on the doorpost of the fort. Croatoan was an island 100 miles south of The Lost Colony. No one knows if the colonists were attacked by the Croatoan Indians or if the settlers went to live on Croatoan Island. The Lost Colony has been a great mystery in American history.

1. How many years has it been since the first colony settled in North Carolina?
   Subtract 1585 from present year.
2. What year did Raleigh send the second set of colonists to North Carolina?
   1587
3. How many years did it take Raleigh to send a ship to check on the second set of colonists?
   4 years
4. Why was this colony called The Lost Colony?
   No one knows what happened to the settlers. They disappeared.
5. State what you think might have happened to The Lost Colony.
   Answer will vary.
6. Think of a title that would be appropriate for this passage.
   Answer will vary.

Page 19

Day 9 — Find the quotient when dividing whole numbers.
Encuentra el cociente y el resto.

EXAMPLE: $829 ÷ 9 = 92$ with the remainder of 1

Use mental math or scratch paper if needed.

1. 8)231 — 28 R7
2. 4)394 — 98 R2
3. 9)894 — 99 R3
4. 5)3,305 — 661
5. 6)56,707 — 9,451 R1
6. 7)6,845 — 977 R6
7. 90)270 — 3
8. 60)480 — 8
9. 20)1,900 — 95
10. 42)336 — 8
11. 75)675 — 9
12. 63)315 — 5
13. 52)4,173 — 80 R13
14. 70)5,844 — 83 R34
15. 84)4,978 — 59 R81
16. 59)4,538 — 76 R54
17. 94)2,980 — 31 R66
18. 41)3,613 — 88 R5
19. 27)6,641 — 245 R26
20. 52)9,385 — 180 R25
21. 44)9,599 — 218 R7
22. 57)92,831 — 1,628 R35
23. 40)73,847 — 1,846 R7
24. 62)79,365 — 1,280 R5
25. 31)62,620 — 2,020

Spelling. Find the word that is misspelled in each row and spell it correctly.
Encuentra la palabra escrita incorrectamente en cada línea y escríbela de manera correcta.

1.	refund	remodel	decode	previw	**preview**
2.	deposet	pretend	deflate	pace	**deposit**
3.	mold	respond	brutel	revise	**brutal**
4.	fiction	grieff	unsafe	equip	**grief**
5.	transfer	defend	truthful	penlty	**penalty**
6.	prdict	decide	gossip	fragile	**predict**
7.	beware	precice	porches	capital	**precise**
8.	leashes	cipher	volt	climack	**climax**
9.	month	friendly	wrench	businiss	**business**
10.	jiant	angle	guest	greet	**giant**
11.	surgery	magnit	usually	bearish	**magnet**
12.	slogan	gigantck	beast	galley	**gigantic**

Page 20

Day 9 — Prefixes are added to the beginning of base words. Add prefixes to these base words. Use as many prefixes as you can with the base words and see how many you can make. Use prefixes mis-, re-, un-, non-, and pre-.

EXAMPLE: view – preview   review

Base words:
- join — rejoin
- name — misname, rename
- spell — misspell, respell
- treat — retreat, mistreat
- stop — nonstop, unstop
- sure — unsure
- call — recall, miscall
- trace — retrace
- heat — preheat, reheat
- cut — precut, uncut, recut, miscut
- turn — return
- read — misread, reread
- fit — unfit, misfit
- place — misplace, replace

Choose one word for each of the prefixes and write a sentence with it.

mis 1. I misread the directions.
re 2. Denise had to retrace her steps to find the key.
un 3. He was very unsure of the answers.
non 4. We rode nonstop for three hours.
pre 5. Will you please preheat the oven before baking?

Answers may vary.

Circulatory System. Label the different parts of the heart with the terms listed. Color the side of the heart that has oxygen-rich blood red. Color the side of the heart where the blood is lacking oxygen blue.

- aorta
- left ventricle
- tricuspid valve
- cardiac septum
- left atrium
- aortic valve
- pulmonary valve
- right ventricle
- right atrium
- bicuspid valve
- pulmonary artery
- pulmonary vein

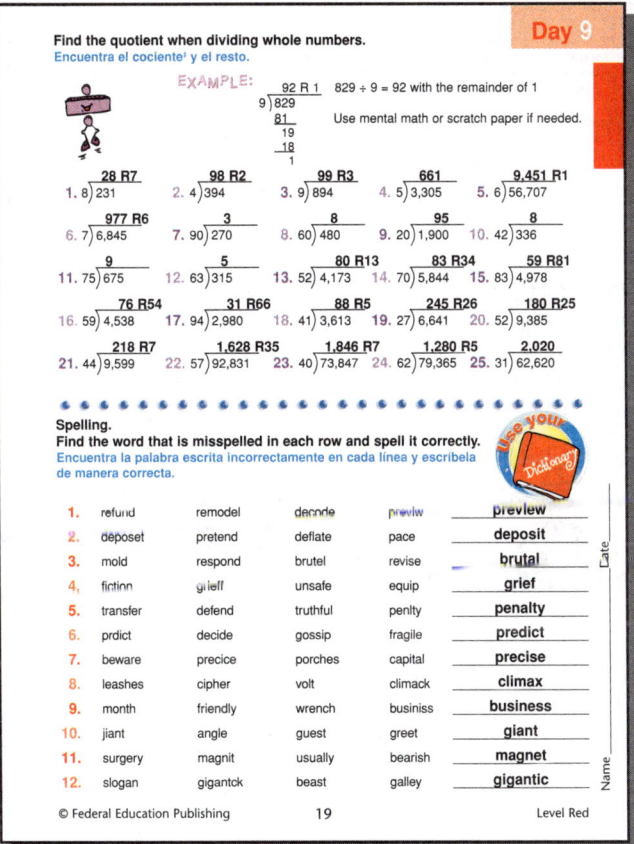

Page 21

Day 10 — Mixed Practice. Be sure to watch the signs. You can use mental math or a piece of scratch paper if needed.
Práctica matemática.

1. 684 ÷ 9 = **76**
2. 356 ÷ 8 = **44 R4**
3. 793 × 27 = **21,411**
4. 469 ÷ 7 = **67**
5. 7,133 ÷ 8 = **891 R5**
6. 4,036 × 9 = **36,324**
7. 143 + 973 = **1,116**
8. 72,483 + 56,774 = **129,257**
9. 8)9,696 = **1,212**
10. 63,459 − 21,365 = **42,094**
11. 90)48,713 = **541 R23**
12. 569,040 ÷ 8 = **71,130**
13. 53,907 × 6 = **323,442**
14. 483 × 175 = **84,525**
15. 763,947 − 244,398 = **519,549**
16. 45)29,705 = **660 R5**
17. 14,008 ÷ 60 = **233 R28**
18. $678.14 + $990.27 = **$1,668.41**
19. 297 × 47 = **13,959**
20. 3,046 × 70 = **213,220**
21. 34,148 + 95,228 = **129,376**
22. 49,375 ÷ 71 = **695 R30**
23. 573 + 4,935 + 7,340 = **12,848**
24. 75)566,212 = **7,549 R37**
25. 456,350 ÷ 32 = **14,260 R30**
26. 3,804 × 43 = **163,572**

Matter. Matter exists in three states: solid, liquid, and gas. Put the following words in the appropriate categories.
La materia existe en estado sólido, líquido o gaseoso. Coloca estas palabras en la categoría correcta.

butter, lava, oxygen, water, box, dust, ice, radon, milk, juice, nitrogen, vapor

Solid	Liquid	Gas
butter	milk	oxygen
box	lava	nitrogen
dust	juice	radon
ice	water	vapor

Water can be in three different states: liquid-water, solid-ice, gas-vapor. See if you can come up with some items in your home that can be in more than one state.
Piensa en items de tu hogar que puedan presentarse en más de un estado.

Solid	Liquid	Gas
	Answers will vary.	

Page 22

Day 10 — You have taken two kinds of tests in the past year: essay and objective tests. When you take an essay test you write out the answers. When you take an objective test you have multiple-choice, true-false, matching, and completion questions. When you take a test, read the directions carefully before you begin. Think about how much time you should take for each question and then begin. Answer the following questions and tell what kind of test they would be on. Also, if the question is from an objective test, write the type of question.

1. Match the words below to their meaning.

   - equip — to furnish
   - clatter — confused noise
   - penalty — punishment
   - bleach — to make whiter
   - consult — to ask for advice

   Kind of test **Objective test**   Kind of question **Matching**

2. Write a paragraph about the produce grown in the state where you live.

   Answers will vary.

   Kind of test **Essay test**   Kind of question **none**

3. Fill in the blanks.
   a. Most cars run on a fuel called **gasoline**.
   b. **Fudge** is candy made with milk, sugar, chocolate, and butter.
   c. **Walt Disney** is famous for his animated movies.
   d. This state does not border any other state or nation. It is **Hawaii**.
   e. A sombrero is a kind of **hat**.

   Kind of test **Objective test**   Kind of question **Completion**

4. Write F for false, T for true.
   a. All mammals live on land. **F**
   b. After the Industrial Revolution, many people moved to the cities. **T**
   c. Eli Whitney invented the cotton gin. **T**
   d. A census worker helps find out how many people live in the United States. **T**

   Kind of test **Objective test**   Kind of question **True or False**

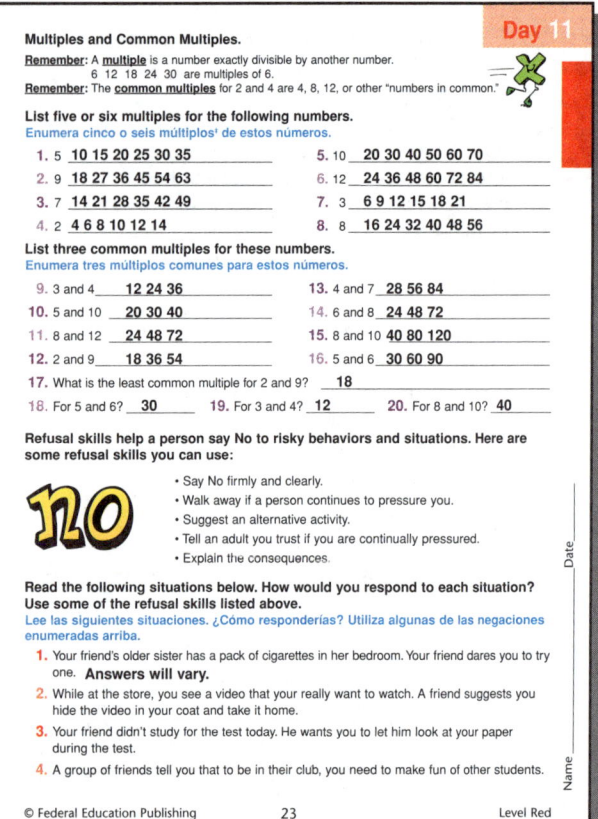

Page 23

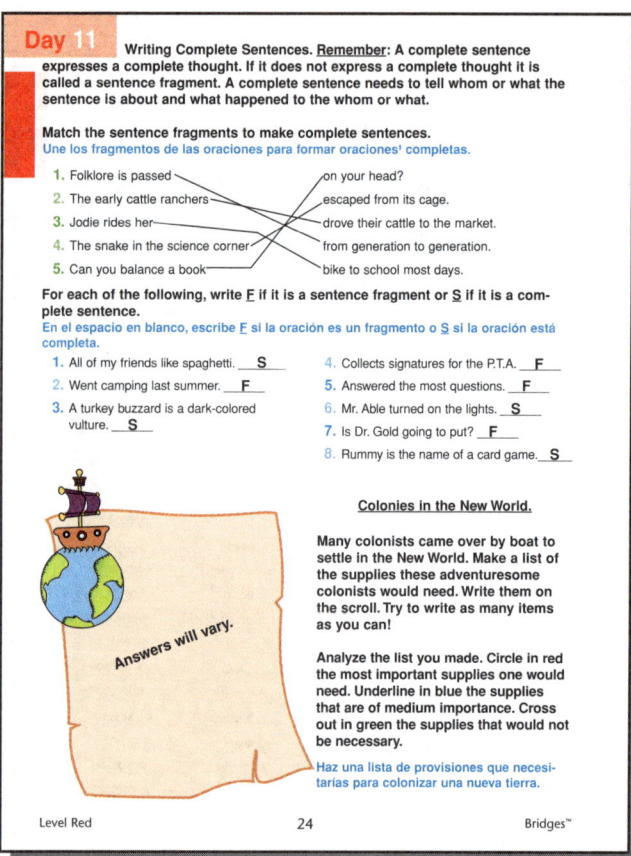

Page 24

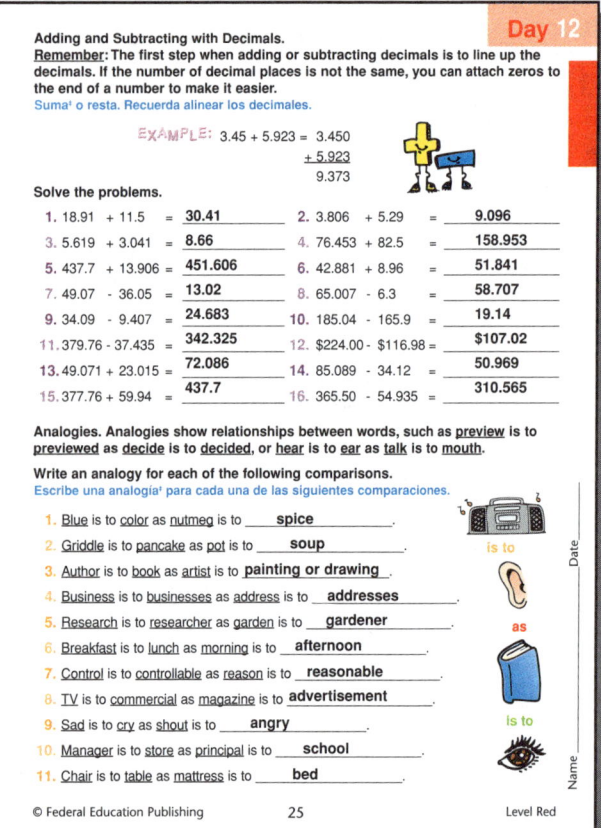

Page 25

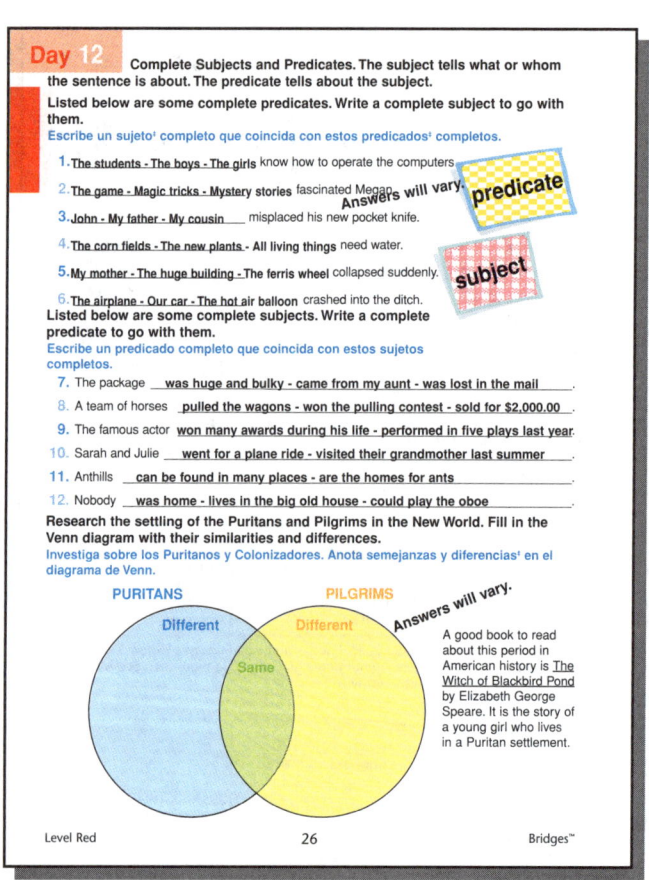

Page 26

Page 27

Day 13

Multiplying Whole Numbers and Decimals.
Remember to put the decimal point in the correct place in the product.
Multiplica. Recuerda ubicar el decimal en el lugar correcto del producto¹.

1.	0.12	2.	0.08	3.	4.6	4.	5.05	5.	2.9	6.	2.71
	x 6		x 7		x 3		x 8		x 5		x 4
	.72		.56		13.8		40.40		14.5		10.84
7.	6.5	8.	1.906	9.	7.0216	10.	6.65	11.	5.364	12.	0.0352
	x 13		x 28		x 52		x 77		x 93		x 49
	84.5		53.368		365.1232		512.05		498.852		1.7248
13.	3.613	14.	40.35	15.	7.735	16.	9.546	17.	7.263	18.	9.634
	x 84		x 38		x 47		x 68		x 87		x 54
	303.492		1,533.30		363.545		649.128		631.881		520.236
19.	359.073	20.	5.9081	21.	12.504	22.	8.709	23.	27.035	24.	7.893
	x 24		x 71		x 99		x 56		x 93		x 32
	8,617.752		419.4751		1,237.896		487.704		2,514.255		252.576

25. Jan works delivering pizza and gets paid $37.40 a night. She works 23 nights each month. How much does Jan earn each month? __$860.20__

26. Jake works at a grocery store. He gets paid $8.65 an hour for each hour he works. He usually works 37 hours a week. How much does he earn in a week? How much would he earn in a 4 weeks? __$320.05__ __$1,280.20__

Chemical Change. With chemical change, two or more substances are combined to form a completely new substance. For example, iron plus oxygen makes rust. Physical change occurs when a substance changes but no new substance is formed (e.g., water to ice).

Read the list below. Determine if a physical change and/or chemical change has occurred. Then come up with some of your own ideas!
Lee la lista a continuación. Determina si ocurre un cambio físico y/o un cambio químico¹. ¡Luego da tus propias ideas!

Activity	Physical Change	Chemical Change	Own Ideas
Chopping wood	X		Answers will vary.
Baking cookies	X	X	
Burning wood		X	
Painting a door	X		
Making ice cubes	X		
Cutting tomatoes	X		
Making ice cream	X	X	

Page 28

Day 13

Two Kinds of Verbs: Action Verbs and State-of-Being Verbs.

Action verbs tell about an action you can see (ran) or an action you cannot see (hear).
State-of-being verbs tell what something or someone is (is, are, am, appear, look, etc.).

Make a design by coloring the action verbs orange and the state-of-being verbs green. Color the empty spaces any color you like, except orange or green.
Colorea los verbos¹ activos de naranja y los verbos copulativos¹ de verde. Colorea los espacios vacíos de cualquier otro color.

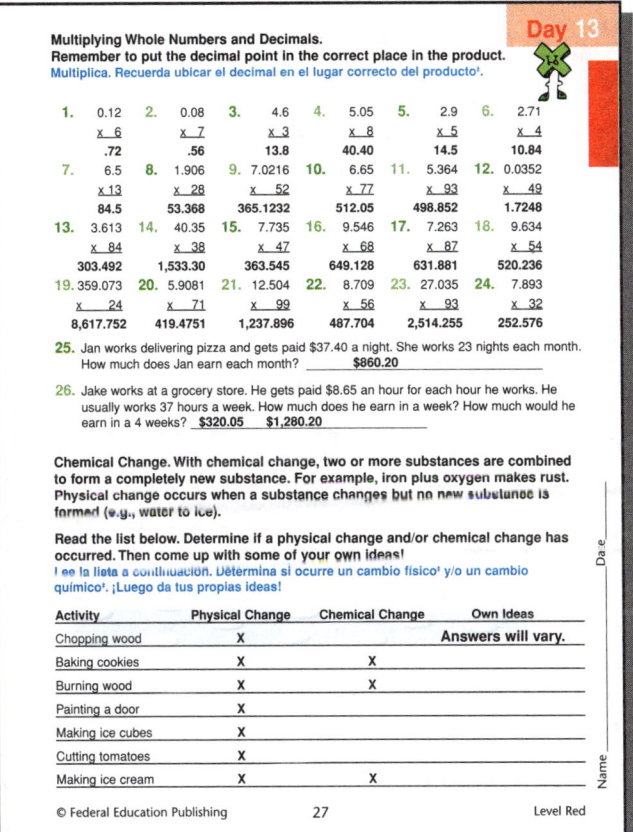

Page 29

Day 14

Measuring with Metrics.

1 centimeter = 10 millimeters
1 decimeter = 10 centimeters
1 decimeter = 100 millimeters
1 meter = 10 decimeters
1 meter = 100 centimeters
1 meter = 1,000 millimeters
1 kilometer = 1,000 meters

Estimate and then measure the following using the metric system.
Estima y luego mide las siguientes cosas utilizando el sistema métrico.

	Estimation	Measurement (Use more than one term of measurement.)
a book		
a toaster		
width of a drawer		Measurements will vary.
your little finger		
a can of soup		
a necklace		
a spatula		
an eraser		
the bathroom floor		
a garbage can		
a flashlight		

Choose things that you would like to measure.

Answers will vary.

Page 30

Day 14

Pronunciation and Spelling.
Do you remember that **g** and **c** both have a hard and soft sound? **G** as in sugar (hard) and **g** as in giant (soft), **c** as in camel (hard) and **c** as in city (soft). In the first column of blanks, put **S** or **H** after each word to tell if the **c** or **g** is soft or hard. In the second column, match the hard or soft **c** and **g** words to another word or words that mean about the same.
En la primera columna de espacios en blanco, coloca S o H luego de cada palabra para indicar si el sonido de c o g es suave (S) o fuerte (H). En la segunda columna, une las palabras que sean sinónimos¹.

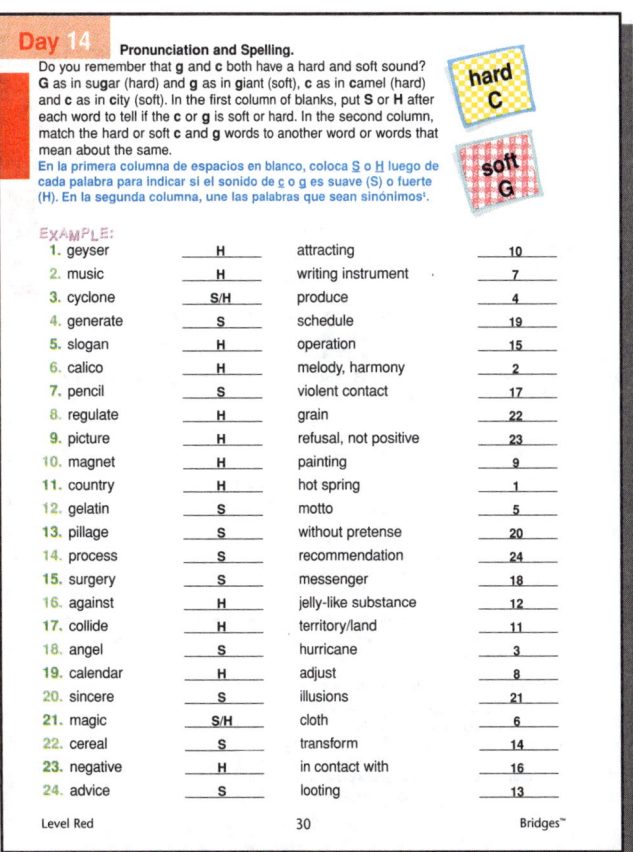

EXAMPLE:
1. geyser — H — attracting — 10
2. music — H — writing instrument — 7
3. cyclone — S/H — produce — 4
4. generate — S — schedule — 19
5. slogan — H — operation — 15
6. calico — H — melody, harmony — 2
7. pencil — S — violent contact — 17
8. regulate — H — grain — 22
9. picture — H — refusal, not positive — 23
10. magnet — H — painting — 9
11. country — H — hot spring — 1
12. gelatin — S — motto — 5
13. pillage — S — without pretense — 20
14. process — S — recommendation — 24
15. surgery — S — messenger — 18
16. against — H — jelly-like substance — 12
17. collide — H — territory/land — 11
18. angel — S — hurricane — 3
19. calendar — H — adjust — 8
20. sincere — S — illusions — 21
21. magic — S/H — cloth — 6
22. cereal — S — transform — 14
23. negative — H — in contact with — 16
24. advice — S — looting — 13

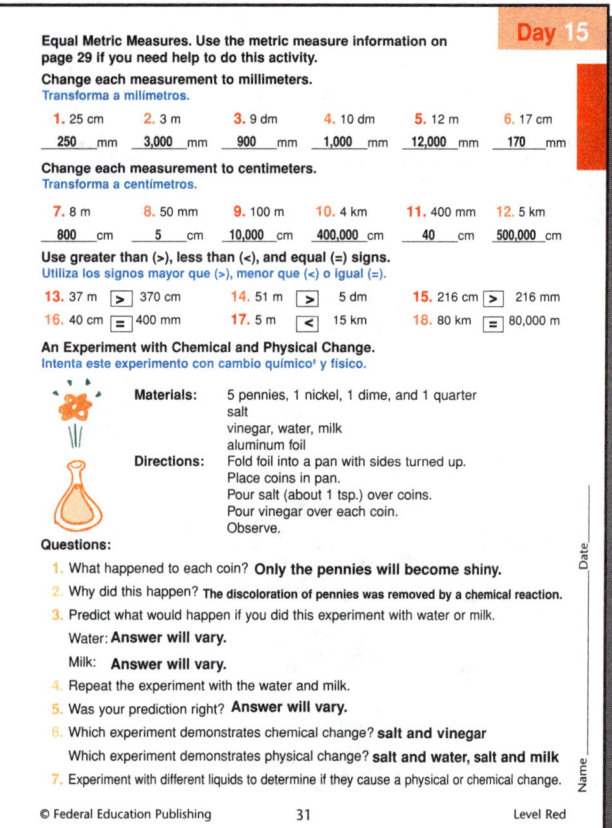

Page 37

Deposits and Deductions. **Day 2**

Amanda opened a checking account on May 15th with $500.25. On May 31st she deposited another $496.80. On June 4th she withdrew $145.00 to buy a bicycle. On June 15th she deposited $435.20. On June 30th she deposited $600.00. On July 1st she withdrew $400.00 to go to Camp Rockland, plus she also needed $63.00 for a sleeping bag. On July 15th she deposited $110.00. On July 24th she withdrew $900.00 to buy a compact TV with a built-in VCR.

Use the chart below to record Amanda's checking account record.
Utiliza la información del párrafo para completar los cuadros.

DATE	DEPOSITED	WITHDREW	TOTAL $
May 15	$500.25		$500.25
May 31	$496.80		$997.05
June 4		$145.00	$852.05
June 15	$435.20		$1,287.25
June 30	$600.00		$1,887.25
July 1		$463.00	$1,424.25
July 15	$110.00		$1,534.25
July 24		$900.00	$634.25

Remember, when you deposit money you add, and when you withdraw money you subtract.

Use Amanda's checking account record to graph the total dollar amounts.

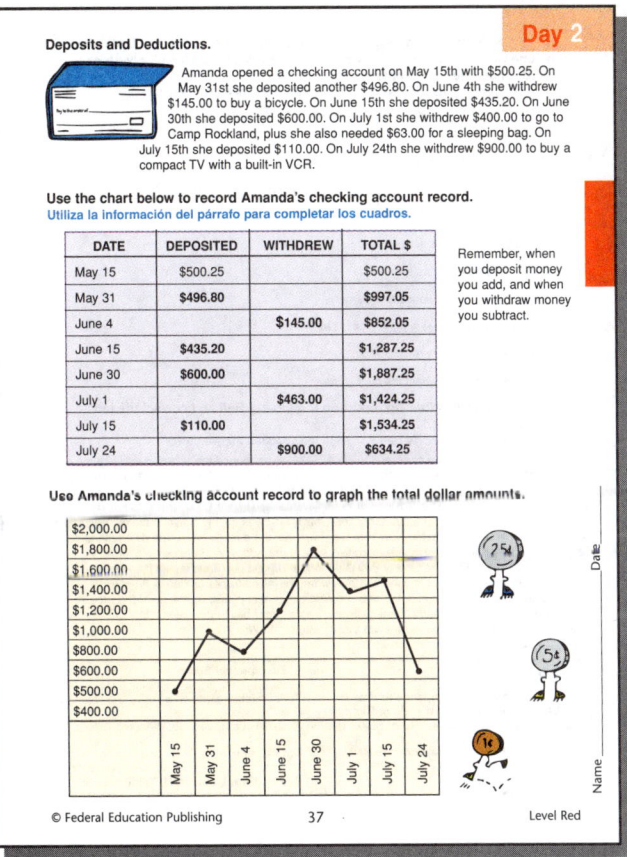

Page 38

Day 2 **Topic Sentences.**
Remember: The topic sentence expresses the main idea of the paragraph.
Underline the topic sentences of these paragraphs.
Subraya las oraciones principales de estos párrafos.

1. **The beginning of his life was very unusual.** He was born in Texas into a large family. He fell out of a covered wagon and was not missed for many days because he had so many brothers and sisters. His parents couldn't find him, so he was raised by coyotes. He thought he was a coyote until he discovered he didn't have four feet and a tail.

2. **Nuclear energy is the most awesome power that exists.** It produces tremendous heat and light. It has been used to produce hydrogen and atomic bombs. It results from changes in the core of atoms. One important use of nuclear energy is in producing electricity. Scientists believe that if it were fully developed, nuclear energy could produce all the world's electricity for millions of years.

Now it's your turn! Write a topic sentence for these two paragraphs. Try to make it interesting so others will want to read the paragraph.
Escribe una oración principal para estos dos párrafos.

3. _Sentences will vary._
They are among the world's oldest and largest living things. Some are thousands of years old and over 200 feet tall. Some of them are about 100 feet around at the base. You can see them in California and Oregon. They are the giant sequoia and redwood trees.

4. _Sentences will vary._
It ranges from great works like Michelangelo's carvings to African masks. A piece of sculpture can be very large, like the Statue of Liberty, or small enough to sit on a table or hold in your hand. It has always played an important part in the history of man. Sculpture is an excellent way to express your own ideas and feelings.

Fill in the vowels for these words. Write each word three times in cursive.
Completa estas palabras con las vocales. Escribe cada palabra en cursiva tres veces.

1. rh_n_c_r_s *rhinoceros rhinoceros rhinoceros*
2. ch_m_c_l *chemical chemical chemical*
3. st_m_ch *stomach stomach stomach*
4. rh_b_rb *rhubarb rhubarb rhubarb*
5. sch_l_st_c *scholastic scholastic scholastic*
6. rh_thm *rhythm rhythm rhythm*
7. l_gg_g_ *luggage luggage luggage*
8. r_m__nd_r *remainder remainder remainder*
9. _m_tt_d *omitted omitted omitted*
10. m_l_t_r_ *military military military*

Page 39

Fractions. Remember: When talking about fractions, the denominator names the number of equal parts of a whole amount, and the numerator names the number of parts being taken from the whole. **Day 3**

Write the fraction that tells what part is shaded.
Escribe la fracción que indica cuánto está sombreado.

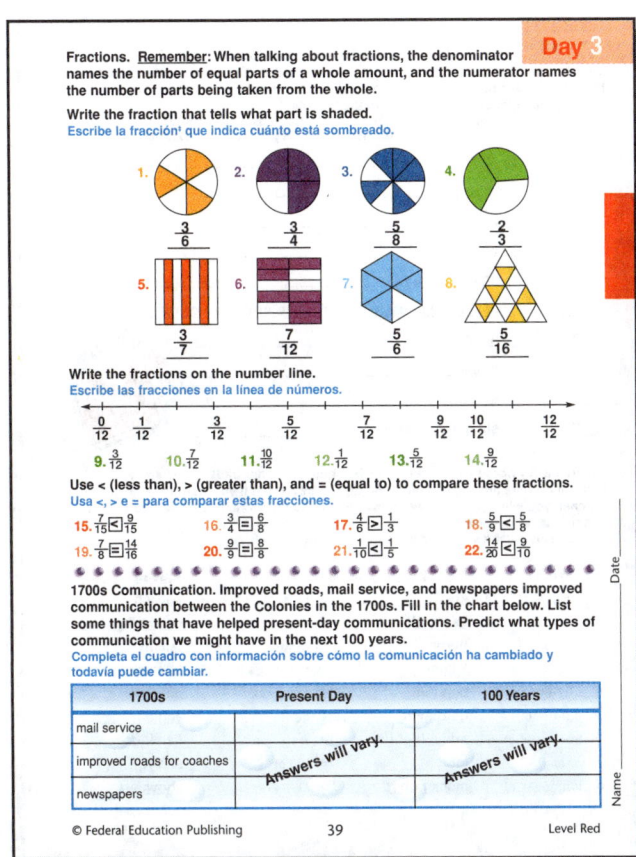

1. $\frac{3}{6}$ 2. $\frac{3}{4}$ 3. $\frac{5}{8}$ 4. $\frac{2}{3}$
5. $\frac{3}{7}$ 6. $\frac{7}{12}$ 7. $\frac{5}{6}$ 8. $\frac{5}{16}$

Write the fractions on the number line.
Escribe las fracciones en la línea de números.

9. $\frac{3}{12}$ 10. $\frac{7}{12}$ 11. $\frac{10}{12}$ 12. $\frac{1}{12}$ 13. $\frac{5}{12}$ 14. $\frac{4}{12}$

Use < (less than), > (greater than), and = (equal to) to compare these fractions.
Usa <, > e = para comparar estas fracciones.

15. $\frac{7}{15} < \frac{9}{15}$ 16. $\frac{4}{8} = \frac{3}{8}$ 17. $\frac{4}{6} > \frac{1}{3}$ 18. $\frac{9}{5} < \frac{5}{5}$
19. $\frac{2}{6} = \frac{3}{6}$ 20. $\frac{9}{8} = \frac{8}{8}$ 21. $\frac{7}{10} < \frac{9}{10}$ 22. $\frac{14}{20} < \frac{9}{10}$

1700s Communication. Improved roads, mail service, and newspapers improved communication between the Colonies in the 1700s. Fill in the chart below. List some things that have helped present-day communications. Predict what types of communication we might have in the next 100 years.
Completa el cuadro con información sobre cómo la comunicación ha cambiado y todavía puede cambiar.

1700s	Present Day	100 Years
mail service		
improved roads for coaches	*Answers will vary.*	*Answers will vary.*
newspapers		

Page 40

Day 3 Read a book or story of your choice and do the following.
Elige un libro o una historia para leer y luego haz lo siguiente.

1. Write the names of four characters and tell why they were important to the story.
   a. _____
   b. _____   *Answers will vary.*
   c. _____
   d. _____

2. What are some important details or events of the story you read? List at least three.
   a. _____
   b. _____   *Answers will vary.*
   c. _____
   d. _____

3. How did the story end?   *Answers will vary.*

4. Would you like it to end differently? If so, how would you have it end?   *Answers will vary.*

Plate Tectonics. Circle the seven major plates of the earth's surface. On the world map below, divide the earth into the seven plates. See if you can label them correctly. Check the answers in the back to see how close you came!
Encierra en un círculo los nombre de las siete placas tectónicas más importantes de la superficie de la tierra. Marca y coloca el nombre a las placas en el mapa.

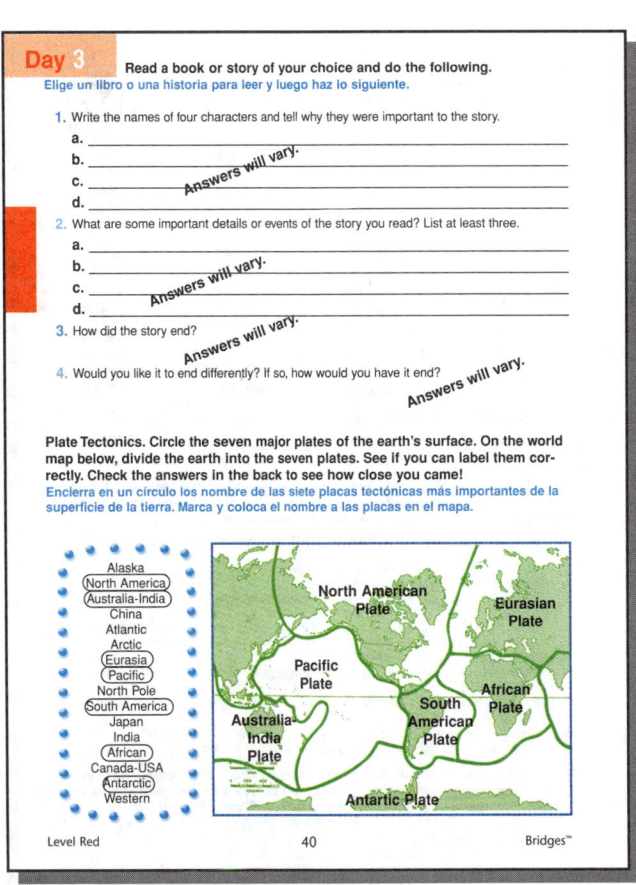

Page 41

Divide to find the fraction of a number. *Divide para encontrar la fracción.*

1. $\frac{1}{2}$ of 10 = __5__
2. $\frac{1}{8}$ of 24 = __3__
3. $\frac{1}{6}$ of 48 = __8__
4. $\frac{1}{5}$ of 45 = __9__
5. $\frac{1}{4}$ of 32 = __8__
6. $\frac{1}{3}$ of 60 = __20__
7. $\frac{1}{7}$ of 56 = __8__
8. $\frac{1}{12}$ of 36 = __3__

Divide to find the equivalent fractions. *Divide para encontrar las fracciones equivalentes.*

9. $\frac{3}{4} = \frac{6}{8}$
10. $\frac{5}{8} = \frac{10}{16}$
11. $\frac{10}{25} = \frac{2}{5}$
12. $\frac{4}{9} = \frac{16}{36}$
13. $\frac{7}{12} = \frac{28}{48}$
14. $\frac{6}{6} = \frac{12}{12}$
15. $\frac{3}{4} = \frac{15}{20}$
16. $\frac{7}{15} = \frac{21}{45}$

Multiply to find the equivalent fractions. *Multiplica para encontrar las fracciones equivalentes.*

17. $\frac{9}{12} = \frac{36}{48}$
18. $\frac{2}{3} = \frac{10}{15}$
19. $\frac{3}{10} = \frac{18}{60}$
20. $\frac{1}{3} = \frac{3}{9}$
21. $\frac{5}{8} = \frac{45}{72}$
22. $\frac{2}{5} = \frac{8}{20}$
23. $\frac{3}{12} = \frac{15}{36}$
24. $\frac{11}{24} = \frac{44}{96}$

Reduce the fractions to the lowest terms that make whole or mixed numbers. *Simplifica las fracciones.*

25. $\frac{56}{6} = 9\frac{1}{3}$
26. $\frac{14}{4} = 3\frac{1}{2}$
27. $\frac{38}{8} = 4\frac{3}{4}$
28. $\frac{51}{8} = 6\frac{3}{8}$
29. $\frac{17}{2} = 8\frac{1}{2}$
30. $\frac{35}{5} = 7$
31. $\frac{14}{6} = 2\frac{1}{3}$
32. $\frac{10}{8} = 1\frac{1}{4}$

Health—Communicable Diseases. Answer T for true or F for false to the following statements. If false, correct the sentence so it is true.
Contesta T para verdadero o F para falso. Si es falso corrige las oraciones para convertirlas en verdaderas.

__F__ 1. Pathogens are people who build roads. **They are germs that cause disease.**
__T__ 2. Communicable diseases are spread by contact with an infected person.
__T__ 3. The common cold, flu, and sore throat are considered communicable diseases.
__F__ 4. Pathogens cannot spread by touch or through the air. **Pathogens can be spread...**
__F__ 5. Washing hands does not reduce the risk of pathogens entering the body. **Washing hands does reduce...**
__T__ 6. Medicines that kill some pathogens are called antibiotics.

Imagine you are principal of your school. As principal, you must write some rules that would help the school be free from the spread of pathogens that can cause communicable diseases. Write five rules you would enforce.
Imagina que eres el director de una escuela. Escribe cinco reglas para evitar la diseminación de agentes patógenos que puedan causar enfermedades contagiosas.

1. Answers will vary. Suggestions:
2. Wash hands.
3. Avoid harmful drugs & smoking.
4. Be vaccinated.
5. Avoid others if they have a communicable disease.

Page 42

Main Verbs and Helping Verbs. Remember: The verb in a sentence may be one word or a few words. Some words can be either a helping verb or a main verb. Underline the complete verb in these sentences.
Subraya los verbos completos en estas oraciones. Incluye los verbos auxiliares.

EXAMPLE: Jack <u>was</u> in town. Or, Jack <u>was working</u> in town.

1. Joseph <u>is walking</u> to the park with his friends.
2. My mother <u>has been working</u> at Sears for many years.
3. I <u>might have called</u> if I <u>had known</u> you <u>were</u> home.
4. The snowstorm yesterday <u>buried</u> all the beautiful flowers.
5. Jim <u>does enjoy</u> sports.
6. Mark <u>is playing</u> outdoors with Sam.
7. David <u>does</u> his homework every day.
8. Misty and Courtney <u>are watching</u> television.
9. The hikers <u>were</u> thirsty and hungry.
10. I <u>have been thinking</u> about the play all day.

Liberty Bell. Read the following report on the Liberty Bell and correct the ten facts that are inaccurate.
Lee este informe sobre Liberty Bell y corrige diez hechos incorrectos.

The Liberty Bell was rung at noon on July 4, 1776, to announce the adoption and signing of the Bill of Rights. Its inscription, "Proclaim Liberty throughout all the land unto all the inhabitants thereof," is from Shakespeare (1564–1616). The bell originally had a different name. It was first called Independence Bell. The province of Pennsylvania paid about $300 for it in 1752. The Liberty Bell weighs more than 2,080 tons. The Liberty Bell was cast in Spain. It broke in ringing after its arrival and was recast in New York City from the same metal but with a different inscription in 1753. It rang at each successive anniversary of the Adoption of the Declaration of Independence until 1935. The Liberty Bell is no longer rung, since it broke, but it has been struck on special occasions. On June 6, 1944, when the Allied forces landed in France, Philadelphia officials struck the bell. Special sound equipment picked up the tone and broadcast it to all parts of the United States. Officials rang a larger bell in the steeple of Independence Hall to announce America's entry into World War III.

Corrections:

1. July 8, not July 4
2. Declaration of Independence four days before, not signing of the Bill of Rights
3. The Bible, Leviticus instead of Shakespeare
4. Province Bell, not Independence Bell
5. pounds, not tons
6. England, not Spain
7. Philadelphia, not New York
8. same inscription, not different
9. 1835, not 1935
10. World War I, not World War III

Page 43

Mixed Practice.
Estimate first, then solve the problem to see how close you got.
Haz primero una estimación y luego resuelve el problema.

EXAMPLE:
1. 6,525 / 3,910 / +2,335 ; actual __12,770__ ; estimate __13,000__ (Est. 7,000 / 4,000 / 2,000 = 13,000)
2. 1,236 / 4,253 / +7,237 ; actual __12,726__ ; estimate __12,000__
3. 74,652 / 75,843 / +18,284 ; actual __168,779__ ; estimate __170,000__
4. 28,746 / 93,009 / +88,537 ; actual __210,292__ ; estimate __210,000__
5. 365,244 − 79,087 ; actual __286,157__ ; estimate __300,000__
6. 866,533 − 278,184 ; actual __588,349__ ; estimate __600,000__
7. 904,568 − 578,179 ; actual __326,389__ ; estimate __300,000__
8. 350,859 − 126,388 ; actual __224,471__ ; estimate __300,000__
9. 533 × 24 ; actual __12,792__ ; estimate __10,000__
10. 975 × 53 ; actual __51,675__ ; estimate __50,000__
11. 4,675 × 85 ; actual __397,375__ ; estimate __450,000__
12. 342,250 × 27 ; actual __9,240,750__ ; estimate __9,000,000__
13. 164 ÷ 24 ; actual __6 R20__ ; estimate __6__
14. 286 ÷ 80 ; actual __3 R46__ ; estimate __3__
15. 190 ÷ 62 ; actual __3 R4__ ; estimate __3__
16. 1,494 ÷ 73 ; actual __20 R34__ ; estimate __20__

George Washington. Below are some sentences about our first president, George Washington. Read the sentences and put them in the correct chronological order.
Lee las oraciones y colócalas en el orden cronológico correcto.

__3__ When his father died in 1743, Washington went to live on a plantation known as Mount Vernon.
__1__ George Washington was born in 1732 in Virginia.
__6__ Washington married Martha Dandridge Custis in 1759.
__9__ After the Revolutionary War, Washington was elected first president of the United States in 1789.
__2__ During his childhood years, Washington enjoyed reading about battles and war heroes.
__5__ In 1758 Washington became a member of the Virginia House of Burgesses.
__10__ George Washington died in 1799.
__4__ Beginning his military career at age 21, Washington served in the French and Indian War from 1754–1758.
__7__ During the Revolutionary War, Washington won victories at Trenton in 1776 and Yorktown in 1778.
__8__ Washington believed America needed independence from England. In 1778, he was chosen to lead the Continental Army against the British soldiers.

"Washington" is the name of our nation's capital, a state, 31 counties and at least 16 cities. Why do you think so many places are named after George Washington?
¿Por qué crees que tantos lugares llevan el nombre de George Washington?
Answers will vary.

Page 44

Syllables. Write your telephone number down the side of the paper. Include your area code. For each digit, write a word that has that number of syllables. If you have numerals over 5 you can use two words to total the number. If your phone number has a zero, leave the line blank.
Utiliza tu número telefónico para practicar escribir palabras multi-silábicas.

Answers will vary. Here is an example.

1	carp
0	
1	please
5	en thu si as tic
4	liq ue fac tion
7	et y mo log i cal ly (or) fu gi tive AND gig a cy cle
2	nib ble
1	prank
2	wa ter
3	sta di um

The following words are names of birds. Some are water birds, some are land birds, and some are tropical birds. Some can't even fly! If you want to be a bird-watcher, you will need to know the names of birds. Unscramble these bird names. The first letter is underlined.
Ordena estos nombres de pájaros. La primera letra está subrayada.

1. <u>a</u>ayrcn — **canary**
2. <u>w</u>iik — **kiwi**
3. <u>d</u>irnaalc — **cardinal**
4. <u>h</u>eonr — **heron**
5. <u>r</u>lekelid — **killdeer**
6. <u>u</u>npiegn — **penguin**
7. <u>h</u>gldinocf — **goldfinch**
8. <u>h</u>bdrmuimgni — **hummingbird**
9. <u>o</u>nol — **loon**
10. <u>i</u>dnmcgkriob — **mockingbird**
11. <u>n</u>acuot — **toucan**
12. <u>i</u>cosrht — **ostrich**
13. <u>d</u>kheaciec — **chickadee**
14. <u>n</u>foacl — **falcon**
15. <u>t</u>snahape — **pheasant**
16. <u>p</u>eatreak — **parakeet**
17. <u>g</u>eela — **eagle**
18. <u>m</u>aiofgln — **flamingo**
19. <u>p</u>rworas — **sparrow**
20. <u>e</u>lehovsr — **shoveler**

Page 45

Day 6

Grocery Store Estimation in Weight and Cost.
Before you go to the grocery store, estimate at home how much you think certain produce will weigh. Make a chart showing your results; then go to the grocery store and actually weigh the produce. Chart these results. Remember: Most scales in the United States will be in pounds and ounces, whereas other countries use grams and kilograms.
Haz una estimación de lo que crees que un producto¹ puede pesar. Ve al negocio y averigua el peso verdadero. Haz una tabla con tus resultados.

EXAMPLE:

produce	estimated weight	actual weight	estimated cost	actual cost
6 apples	3 pounds	2 pounds 3 oz	$3.00	$3.15

Answers Will Vary.

Precursors to the Revolutionary War.
Answer the following questions. Use the time line.
Usa la línea del tiempo para responder las siguientes preguntas.

1754 French and Indian War | 1763 King George III gives proclamation to limit western settlement | 1765 Stamp Act | 1770 Boston Massacre | 1773 Boston Tea Party | 1774 Intolerable Acts | 1775 Battles fought at Lexington and Concord

1. How many years after the French and Indian War did the Boston Massacre occur? **16 years**
2. Which events occurred in Boston? **Boston Massacre**, **Boston Tea Party**
3. Which occurred first—the Stamp Act or the Intolerable Acts? How many years are there between these events? **Stamp Act**, **9 years**
4. Choose four events on the time line. Draw and color four pictures in the rectangles below that show the sequence of those events. **Pictures will vary.**

Page 46

Day 6

Verbs. Circle the correct form of the be verb.
Encierra en un círculo la forma correcta del verbo¹ to be.

1. I (be, **am**) guessing the number of pennies in the jar.
2. What (**is**, be) your favorite month of the year?
3. The workmen (been, **were**) repairing the road in front of our house.
4. Carla (**was**, were) laughing very loud.
5. (Is, **Are**) you the team leader?
6. My Uncle Clint (been, **has been**, have been) an astronaut, an explorer, and is now a teacher.
7. The haunted house (**is being**, are being) torn down.
8. We (be, **will be**) playing in the orchestra on Saturday night.

Now write a sentence for each of these words. Make sure your sentences are different from the ones above.
Escribe una oración¹ con cada una de estas palabras.

9. were — Answers will vary.
10. has been —
11. was being —
12. are —

Plate Movement. Match the type of plate boundary with the correct synonyms and definitions.
Une el tipo de límite de placas tectónicas con el sinónimo¹ y la definición correctos.

Synonyms | Definitions
1. sliding | a. plates push against each other
2. spreading | b. plates move away from each other
3. colliding | c. plates slide by each other

Synonyms	Definitions	Type of Plate Boundary
2	b	divergent boundary
3	a	convergent boundary
1	c	transform boundary

Look at the pictures below. Determine which picture represents each type of plate boundary listed above.
¿Qué dibujo representa cada tipo de límite de placas tectónicas?

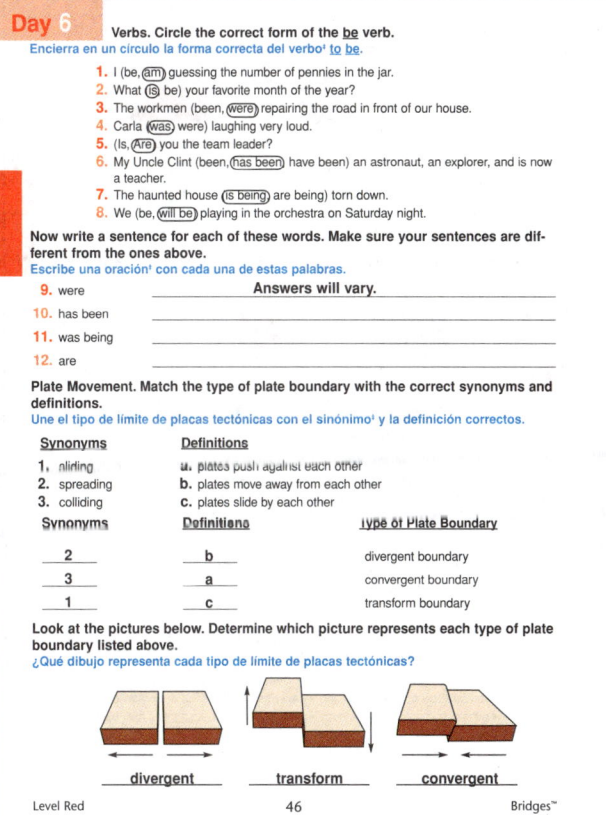

divergent | transform | convergent

Page 47

Day 7

Geometric Lines. Match the terms with their definitions.
Une los términos con sus definiciones.

- **d** segment
- **c** ray
- **f** angles
- **e** perpendicular lines
- **b** parallel lines
- **h** congruent
- **a** symmetric
- **l** congruent segments
- **k** circumference
- **j** radius
- **i** diameter
- **g** AB or BA

a. A figure that can be folded and both parts fit perfectly.
b. Lines that never meet.
c. Has an end point or a starting point and can go from there in one direction.
d. A part of a line that can be named by its endpoints.
e. Lines that intersect to form right angles of 90 degrees.
f. Rays with the same endpoint.
g. Ways of labeling endpoints on a segment.
h. Figures having the same shape and size.
i. Segment that passes through the center of a circle and has both endpoints on the circle.
j. A line connecting the center of a circle to a point on the outside of a circle.
k. The distance around a circle.
l. Have equal lengths.

Illustrate each of these geometric terms.
Ilustra estos términos geométricos.

1. segment
2. ray
3. angle
4. perpendicular lines
5. parallel lines
6. congruent
7. symmetric
8. congruent segments
9. circumference
10. radius
11. diameter
12. AB or BA

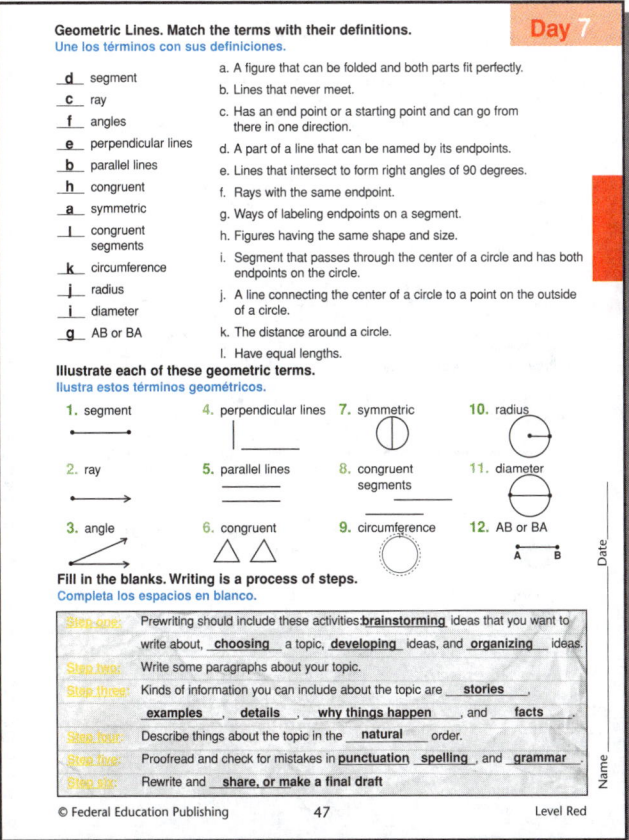

Fill in the blanks. Writing is a process of steps.
Completa los espacios en blanco.

Step one:	Prewriting should include these activities: **brainstorming** ideas that you want to write about, **choosing** a topic, **developing** ideas, and **organizing** ideas.
Step two:	Write some paragraphs about your topic.
Step three:	Kinds of information you can include about the topic are **stories**, **examples**, **details**, **why things happen**, and **facts**.
Step four:	Describe things about the topic in the **natural** order.
Step five:	Proofread and check for mistakes in **punctuation**, **spelling**, and **grammar**.
Step six:	Rewrite and **share, or make a final draft**.

Page 48

Day 7

Read this part of the Declaration of Independence and answer the questions.
Lee esta parte de la Declaración de la Independencia y responde las preguntas.

> We hold these truths to be self-evident, that all men are created equal, that they are endowed by their Creator with certain unalienable Rights, that among these are Life, Liberty and the pursuit of Happiness.
> That to secure these rights, Governments are instituted among Men, deriving their just powers from the consent of the governed.
> That whenever any Form of Government becomes destructive of these ends, it is the Right of the People to alter or to abolish it, and to institute new Government, laying its foundation on such principles and organizing its powers in such form, as to them shall seem most likely to effect their Safety and Happiness.

1. What are the basic rights of all people in accordance to the Declaration of Independence?
   Life, liberty, and the pursuit of happiness.
2. Why are governments "instituted," or created?
   To secure the rights of the people.
3. If people feel the government is not acting in their best interest, what should they do?
   People need to change or abolish the old government and create a new one.
4. On what principles will the new American government be founded?
   Founded on principles that will effect the safety and happiness of people.
5. Draw and color a flag below that expresses the feelings and beliefs of the Declaration of Independence.
   Pictures will vary.

Earth's Magnetic Field. Read the following passage and answer the questions below.
Lee el párrafo y responde las preguntas.

The earth is like a huge magnet. It has a magnetic field. Its magnetism is the strongest at the North and South Poles. When rock forms, any magnetic particles will align themselves with the earth's magnetic field. They will point towards either the North or South Poles. There are some rocks that do not point to the current North and South Poles. Scientists conclude that either the North and South Poles have moved, or the rocks themselves have moved since they were formed. Most feel the rocks and continents have moved. Geologists use this information to determine how the continents have moved over time.

1. Why is the earth compared to a magnet?
   It has a magnetic field.
2. Where are the earth's strongest points of magnetism?
   North and South poles
3. How can geologists study the movements of the continents?
   The geologists study rocks that have been formed. They note where the rocks have moved from the current North and South poles.
4. How might the magnetism of the earth affect a compass?
   A compass is made so it will turn toward the North Pole and away from the South Pole.
5. What would happen to a ship and its compass if the earth's magnetic strong area became the western part of the earth and NOT the North Pole?
   The compass would point to the new point of magnetism.

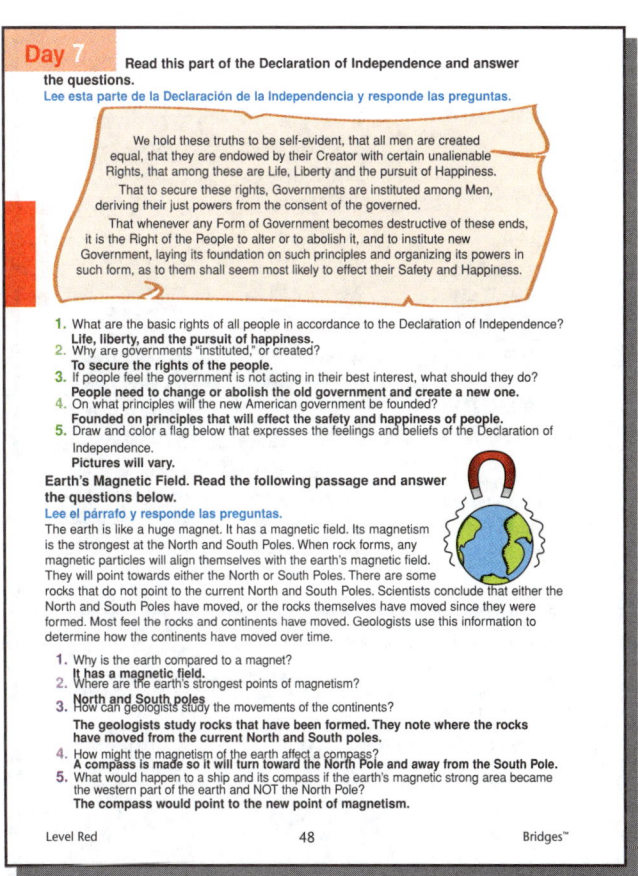

Page 49

Find the Perimeter.
Remember: To find the perimeter, you have to add the lengths of each side.
Encuentra el perímetro.

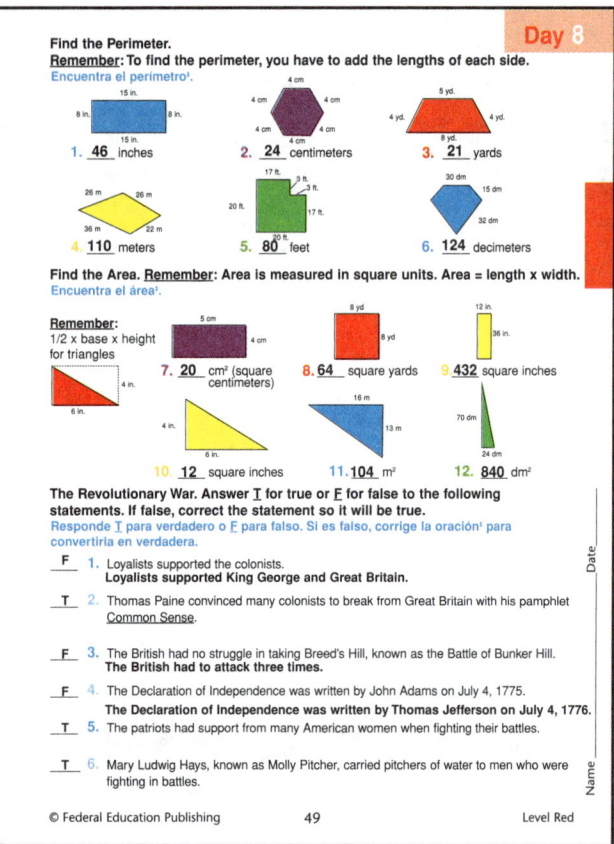

1. **46** inches
2. **24** centimeters
3. **21** yards
4. **110** meters
5. **80** feet
6. **124** decimeters

Find the Area. Remember: Area is measured in square units. Area = length x width.
Encuentra el área.

Remember: 1/2 x base x height for triangles

7. **20** cm² (square centimeters)
8. **64** square yards
9. **432** square inches
10. **12** square inches
11. **104** m²
12. **840** dm²

The Revolutionary War. Answer T for true or F for false to the following statements. If false, correct the statement so it will be true.
Responde T para verdadero o F para falso. Si es falso, corrige la oración para convertirla en verdadera.

- **F** 1. Loyalists supported the colonists.
  Loyalists supported King George and Great Britain.
- **T** 2. Thomas Paine convinced many colonists to break from Great Britain with his pamphlet Common Sense.
- **F** 3. The British had no struggle in taking Breed's Hill, known as the Battle of Bunker Hill.
  The British had to attack three times.
- **F** 4. The Declaration of Independence was written by John Adams on July 4, 1775.
  The Declaration of Independence was written by Thomas Jefferson on July 4, 1776.
- **T** 5. The patriots had support from many American women when fighting their battles.
- **T** 6. Mary Ludwig Hays, known as Molly Pitcher, carried pitchers of water to men who were fighting in battles.

Page 50

Earthquakes. Many earthquakes occur at the plate boundaries. Study the map of earthquake epicenters and answer the questions below.
Estudia el mapa de los epicentros de terremotos y responde las preguntas.

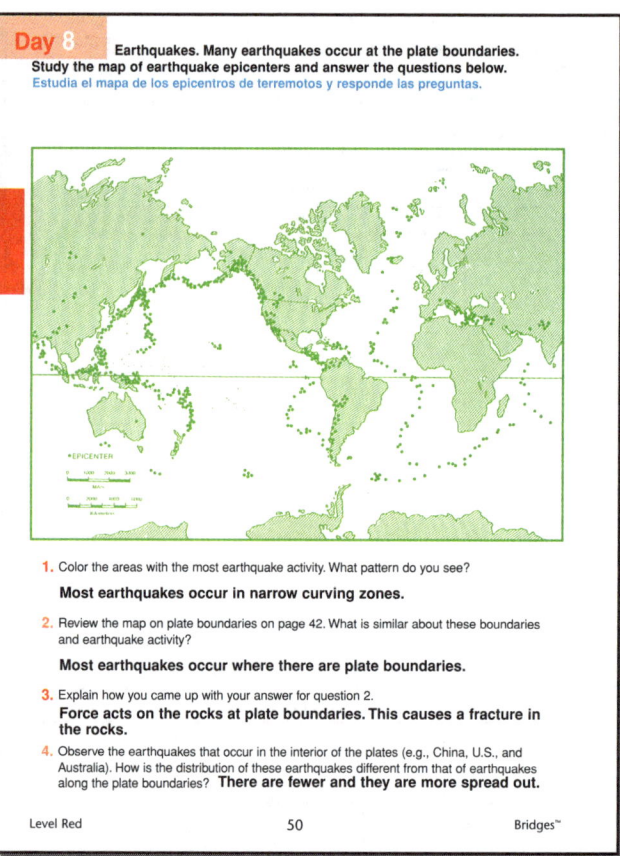

1. Color the areas with the most earthquake activity. What pattern do you see?
   Most earthquakes occur in narrow curving zones.
2. Review the map on plate boundaries on page 42. What is similar about these boundaries and earthquake activity?
   Most earthquakes occur where there are plate boundaries.
3. Explain how you came up with your answer for question 2.
   Force acts on the rocks at plate boundaries. This causes a fracture in the rocks.
4. Observe the earthquakes that occur in the interior of the plates (e.g., China, U.S., and Australia). How is the distribution of these earthquakes different from that of earthquakes along the plate boundaries? **There are fewer and they are more spread out.**

Page 51

Write the rest of the number families.
Escribe el resto de las familias de números.

1. 78 x 42 = 3,276
   42 x 78 = 3,276
   3,276 ÷ 42 = 78
   3,276 ÷ 78 = 42

2. 39 x 56 = 2,184
   56 x 39 = 2,184
   2,184 ÷ 56 = 39
   2,184 ÷ 39 = 56

3. 95 x 37 = 3,515
   37 x 95 = 3,515
   3,515 ÷ 37 = 95
   3,515 ÷ 95 = 37

4. 49 x 76 = **3,724**
   76 x 49 = 3,724
   3,724 ÷ 76 = 49
   3,724 ÷ 49 = 76

5. 141 x 27 = **3,807**
   27 x 141 = 3,807
   3,807 ÷ 27 = 141
   3,807 ÷ 141 = 27

6. 3,762 ÷ 38 = **99**
   3,762 ÷ 99 = 38
   99 x 38 = 3,762
   38 x 99 = 3,762

7. 26,320 ÷ 47 = **560**
   26,320 ÷ 560 = 47
   560 x 47 = 26,320
   47 x 560 = 26,320

8. 48,306 ÷ 83 = **582**
   48,306 ÷ 582 = 83
   582 x 83 = 48,306
   83 x 582 = 48,306

9. 194 x 92 = **17,848**
   92 x 194 = 17,848
   17,848 ÷ 92 = 194
   17,848 ÷ 194 = 92

10. 16,019 ÷ 83 = **193**
    16,019 ÷ 193 = 83
    193 x 83 = 16,019
    83 x 193 = 16,019

11. 2,650 x 54 = **143,100**
    54 x 2,650 = 143,100
    143,100 ÷ 54 = 2,650
    143,100 ÷ 2,650 = 54

12. 876,600 ÷ 360 = **2,435**
    876,600 ÷ 2,435 = 360
    2,435 x 360 = 876,600
    360 x 2,435 = 876,600

Respiratory System. There are a lot of ways you can take care of your respiratory system. Some ways are exercising regularly, not smoking, and not inhaling chemicals produced by products such as paint or glue.

Look at some old magazines and ask your parents if you can cut out pictures of people caring for their respiratory system. If you don't have any old magazines, draw and color pictures.
Recorta de revistas viejas fotos de personas que se preocupan por su sistema respiratorio o haz y colorea dibujos.

Answers will vary.

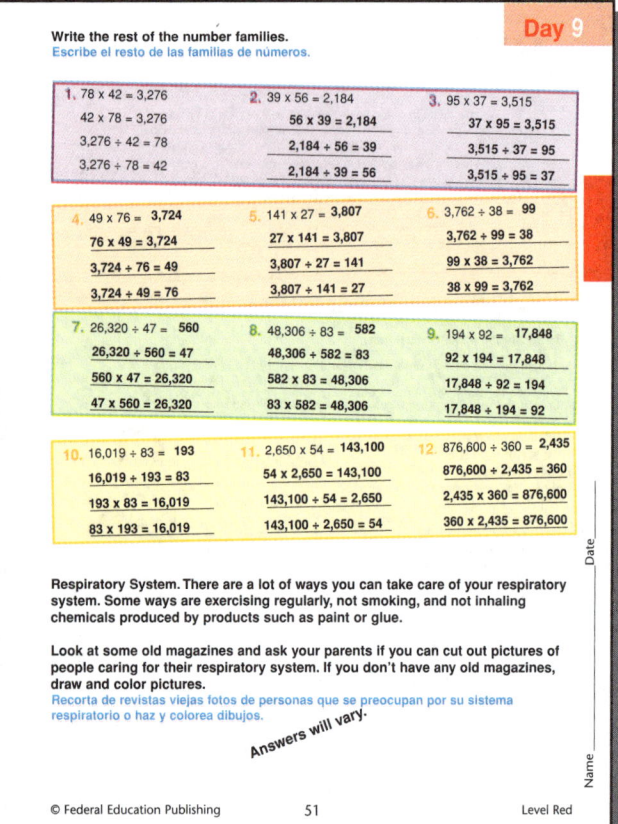

Page 52

Read these paragraphs. Remember to ask yourself:
1. Does the paragraph have one main idea?
2. Do all the sentences in the paragraph tell about the main idea?
3. Is every sentence in the paragraph a complete sentence?

Cross out any sentences that do not belong in the paragraph. Tell why.
Tacha las oraciones que no pertenezcan al párrafo. Explica por qué no pertenecen.

1. Water in the ocean never stops moving. The most well-known movements are waves. Waves are set in motion by earthquakes, winds, and the gravitational pull of the sun and moon. ~~The ocean water is also very salty.~~ On shore, we see waves caused by the wind. Their size depends on whether they come from far across the ocean or are caused by winds from nearby storms.
   It does not tell about the main idea.

2. The beaver is a furry animal with a flat, wide tail that looks like a paddle. There are more beavers in the U.S. and Canada than anywhere else. The beaver's strong front teeth are used for cutting down trees. They use the branches to build dams and homes, but they eat the bark from them first. ~~Beavers almost always seem.~~ We often call people who work hard "eager beavers."
   It is not a complete sentence.

3. Write a paragraph. Try to remember the three rules as you write.
   Answers will vary.

Earthquakes. Read the paragraph and fill in the blanks with the words listed.
Lee el párrafo. Completa los espacios en blanco con las palabras de la lista.

seismologists	earthquake	seismic waves	energy
epicenter	fault	above	fracture
focus			beneath

An **earthquake** is sudden shaking of the ground that happens when **energy** stored in rock is released. A **fault** is a break, or **fracture**, in the Earth's crust. As rock breaks, stored energy moves along the fault. The hypocenter, or **focus**, is where an earthquake begins. This occurs **beneath** the Earth's surface. The point on the Earth's crust which is directly **above** the focus is called the **epicenter**. **Seismic waves**, or shock waves, move out from the focus and cause the ground to shake. **Seismologists** study and record these shock waves and determine the size of the earthquake.

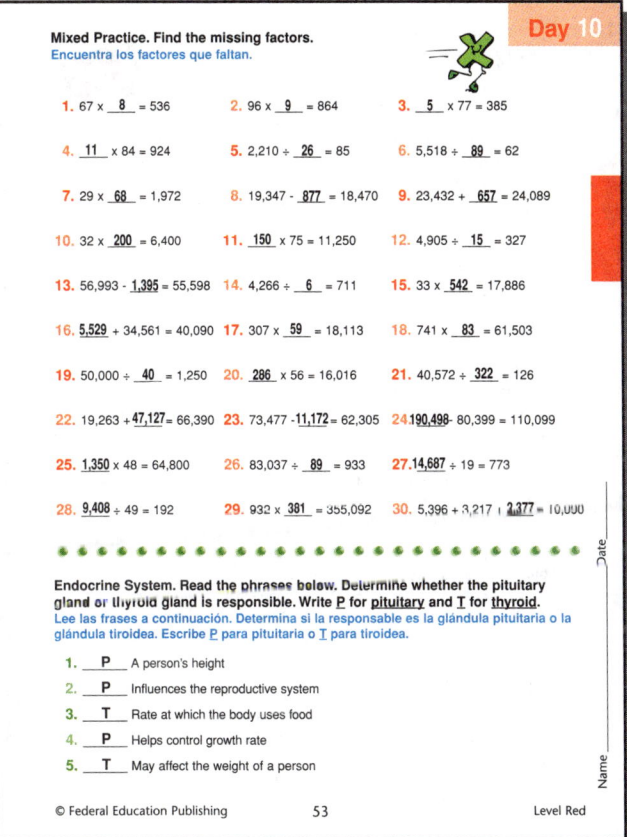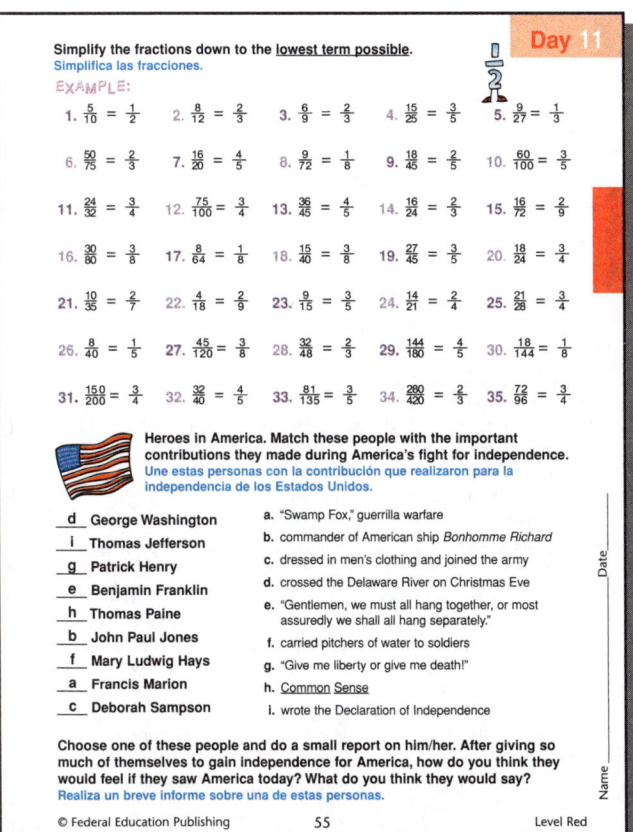

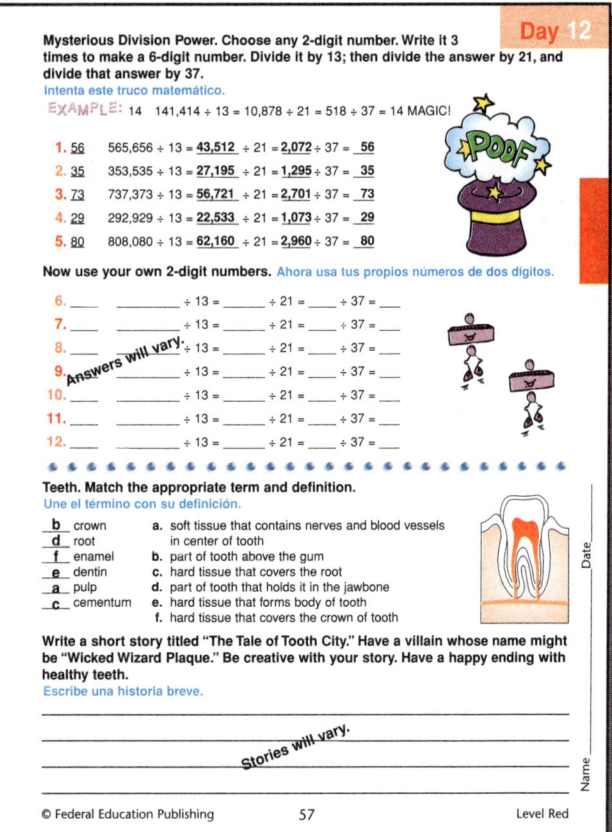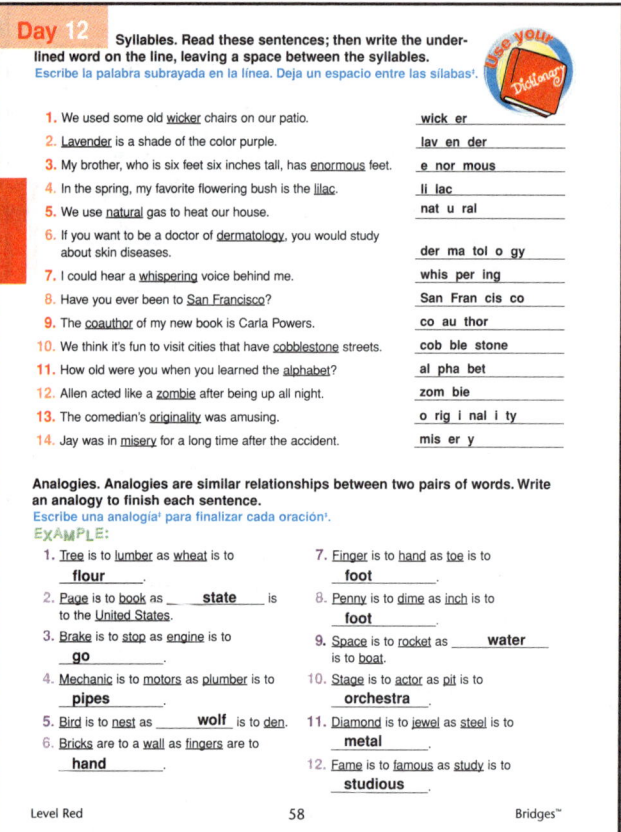

Page 61

Day 14 — Exchange and Share $906.00. You have $906.00 to share among 7 family members. Find out if you can share it equally. To begin with, you have nine $100 bills, no $10 bills, and six $1 bills. Share and exchange down.
Intenta repartir $906.00 en partes iguales entre siete miembros de una familia.

1. You have nine $100 bills. How many $100 bills does each family member get? __1__
   How many are left? __2__
2. Exchange the $100 bills you have left for __20__ $10 bills.
3. Each family member gets __2__ $10 bills. How many are left? __6__
4. Exchange your $10 bills for __60__ $1 bills. How many $1 bills do you have altogether? __66__
5. Each family member gets __9__ $1 bills. How many are left? __3__
6. Each family member gets __1__ $100 bills, __2__ $10 bills, and __9__ $1 bills.
7. How much money does each family member get? __$129__
8. What could you do with the amount left over? __Answers will vary.__
9. Is there another way to share the money equally? Show us! __Answers will vary.__

Make up your own "Exchange and Share" situation or use the following: $504 among 21 people. Use the above method.

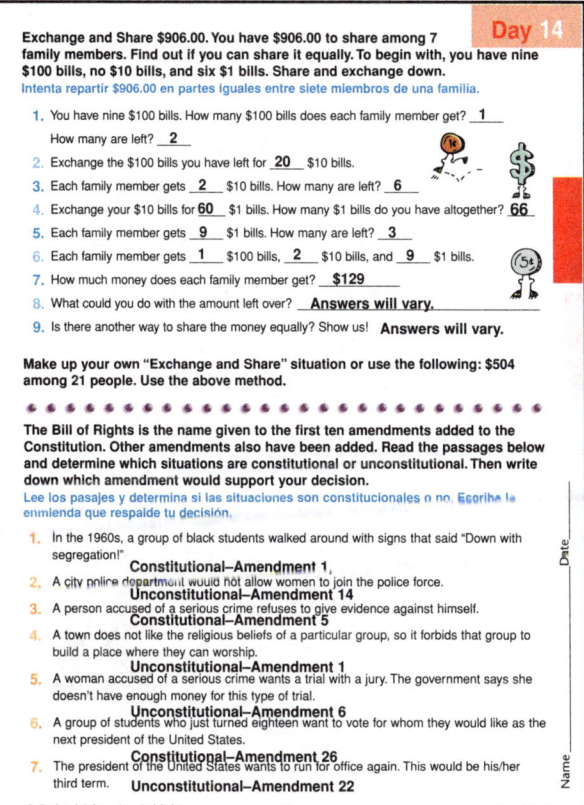

The Bill of Rights is the name given to the first ten amendments added to the Constitution. Other amendments have also been added. Read the passages below and determine which situations are constitutional or unconstitutional. Then write down which amendment would support your decision.
Lee los pasajes y determina si las situaciones son constitucionales o no. Escribe la enmienda que respalde tu decisión.

1. In the 1960s, a group of black students walked around with signs that said "Down with segregation!"
   __Constitutional–Amendment 1__
2. A city police department would not allow women to join the police force.
   __Unconstitutional–Amendment 14__
3. A person accused of a serious crime refuses to give evidence against himself.
   __Constitutional–Amendment 5__
4. A town does not like the religious beliefs of a particular group, so it forbids that group to build a place where they can worship.
   __Unconstitutional–Amendment 1__
5. A woman accused of a serious crime wants a trial with a jury. The government says she doesn't have enough money for this type of trial.
   __Unconstitutional–Amendment 6__
6. A group of students who just turned eighteen want to vote for whom they would like as the next president of the United States.
   __Constitutional–Amendment 26__
7. The president of the United States wants to run for office again. This would be his/her third term. __Unconstitutional–Amendment 22__

Page 62

Day 14 — Contractions. Words like *let's* (let us), *you'll* (you will), etc., are contractions. Contractions that have the word *not* in them are called negatives. The rule is NEVER use double negatives when you write or speak. Other words like *nothing*, *never*, and *nobody* are also negatives. In these sentences, find the double negatives and rewrite the sentence in cursive, using the correct word.
Vuelve a escribir estas oraciones para eliminar la doble negación.

EXAMPLE: The fight didn't solve nothing. *The fight didn't solve anything.*

1. The team didn't want no trouble.
   The team didn't want any trouble.
2. Haven't you never seen Yellowstone Park?   *Answers may vary.*
   Haven't you ever seen Yellowstone Park?
3. There weren't no eggs left in the carton.
   There were no eggs left in the carton. Or: There weren't any eggs left in the carton.
4. I haven't never been happier to finish a school year.
   I have never been happier to finish a school year. Or: I haven't ever been happier...
5. This path doesn't lead nowhere.
   This path doesn't lead anywhere.
6. Can't no one in this class solve the puzzle?
   Can't anyone in this class solve the puzzle?
7. Richard didn't have nothing to read.
   Richard didn't have anything to read.
8. Nanette said that she hadn't never thought of that idea.
   Nanette said that she had never thought of that idea.
9. Don't spill none of the juice on the carpet.
   Don't spill any of the juice on the carpet.
10. There isn't nothing you can do about the weather.
    There isn't anything you can do about the weather.
11. Thad doesn't know nobody in his algebra class.
    Thad doesn't know anybody in his algebra class.
12. The bus didn't have no empty seats when we got on.
    The bus didn't have any empty seats when we got on.

Page 63

Day 15 — Eggs? What eggs? Chicken eggs! Down through the ages, eggs have been eaten around the world. In America, the most popular eggs to eat are chicken eggs. Chicken eggs are classified primarily by their weight. Small eggs weigh approximately 18 ounces a dozen. Medium eggs weigh 21 ounces a dozen. Large eggs weigh 24 ounces a dozen. Extra large eggs weigh a hefty 27 ounces a dozen. Jumbo eggs, which are classified as the largest sellable eggs, weigh 30 ounces a dozen.
Lee el párrafo y responde las preguntas sobre huevos.

1. 6 dozen __jumbo__ eggs weigh a total of 180 ounces.
2. How many eggs are in 6 dozen? __72__
3. How many eggs are in 12 dozen? __144__ What are two different ways you can use to find the answer to this question? __12 x 12 = 144__, __72 x 2 = 144__
4. Which weighs more—3 dozen jumbo eggs or 5 dozen small eggs?
   __They both total 90 ounces.__
5. If 5 dozen eggs weigh a total of 150 ounces, which eggs would they be? __jumbo__
6. If you wanted to boil a total of 120 eggs for an Easter egg hunt and you wanted an equal number of each size of egg, how many of each size would you boil? __2 dozen__
7. What is the minimum weight you can have if you have 4 dozen eggs? __72__ ounces of __small__ eggs.
8. If you bought a dozen of each size of egg, what should be the total weight in ounces? __120 ounces__
9. Jan gathered 4 dozen medium-sized eggs, 3 dozen small eggs, 1 dozen large eggs, 2 dozen extra-large eggs, and 1/2 dozen jumbo eggs. How many eggs did she gather? __126__ How many ounces did she have altogether? __231 ounces__
10. Mother bought 3 dozen eggs, but some broke on the way home. When she got home, she tried to divide them evenly between 2 bowls, but she had 1 left over. With 3 and 4 bowls she again had 1 left over. When she divided them into 5 bowls, they came out exactly even! How many eggs did she have? __25 eggs__

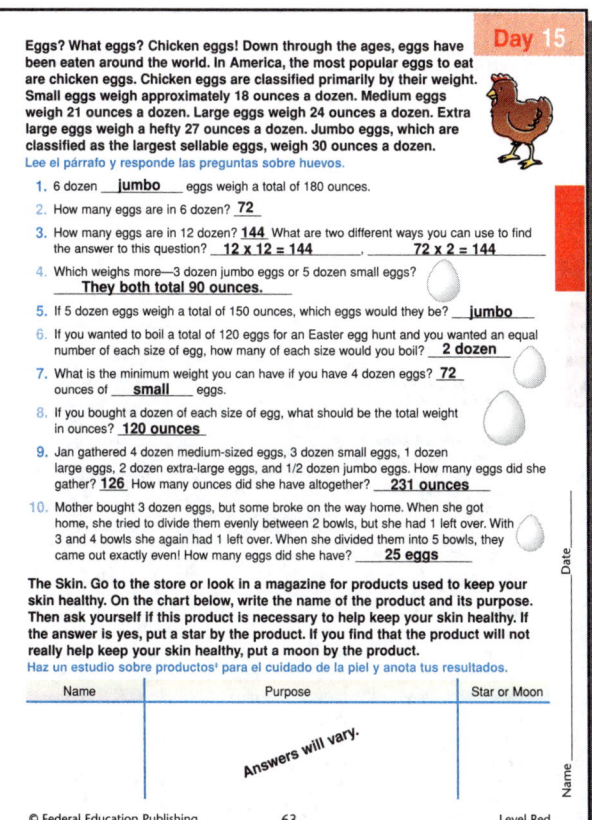

The Skin. Go to the store or look in a magazine for products used to keep your skin healthy. On the chart below, write the name of the product and its purpose. Then ask yourself if this product is necessary to help keep your skin healthy. If the answer is yes, put a star by the product. If you find that the product will not really help keep your skin healthy, put a moon by the product.
Haz un estudio sobre productos para el cuidado de la piel y anota tus resultados.

Name	Purpose	Star or Moon
	Answers will vary.	

Page 64

Day 15 — Pronouns. Fill in the blanks with pronouns.
Completa los espacios en blanco con pronombres.

EXAMPLE: Maggie collects books. **She** likes old books best.   **Some answers will vary.**

1. Nancy's parents collect books also; __they__ are professors.
2. Mark had a pet wolf. __His__ wolf was named Silver.
3. Andrew handed Mary the rock. Mary showed __us or him__ the fossils in __it__.
4. Emily washed __her__ hair.
5. I asked __my__ sister to give __me__ a ride home.
6. The cat washed __its__ baby kittens.
7. The girls made lunch for __their__ family.
8. "Craig, will __you__ give __them__ __your__ phone number?"

The pronouns *we* and *us* are sometimes used with nouns. Fill in the blanks with *we* or *us*. Use *we* when the noun is the subject; use *us* when it is not.
Completa los espacios en blanco con we o us.

9. __We__ Americans have a lot of pride in our country.
10. At the dinner party, __we__ guests made sandwiches.
11. The stranger made a map for __us__ travelers.
12. Will the teacher give __us__ students good grades?

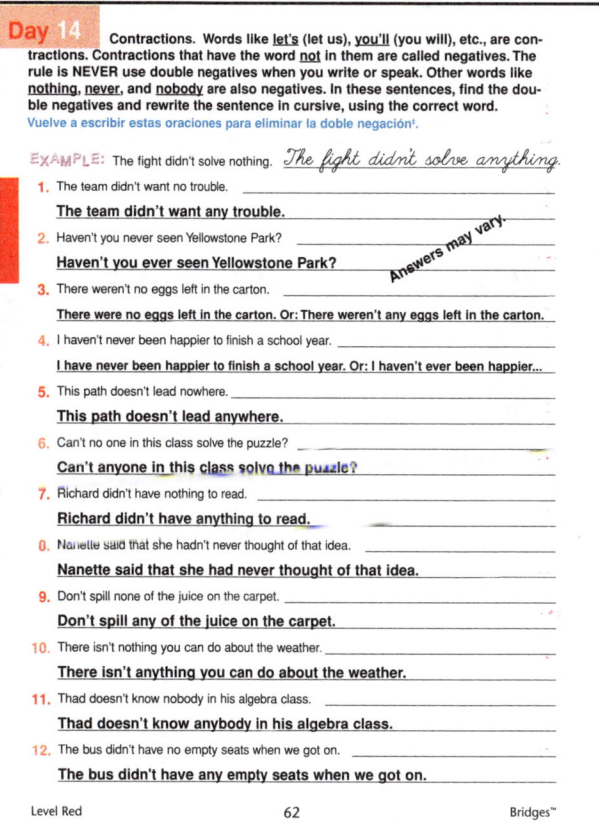

Use the letters from these spelling words to make three or four new words. Try to make four- and five-letter words also. Use a letter only once in each word.
Utiliza las letras de estas palabras para formar nuevas palabras.

EXAMPLE: journeys *our* *runs* *yes* *nose*

1. enemies	men	is	mine	seem
2. intermediate	ate	term	men	time
3. vocabulary	cab	lay	buy	vocal
4. inscription	ton	script	point	rip
5. purpose	so	purse	rose	us
6. suspended	pen	us	depend	end
7. examiner	exam	near	examine	mine
8. pendulum	pen	mud	plume	plum
9. luxurious	ours	sir	sour	soil
10. monotonous	not	ton	noun	mount

Page 67

Day 1

Let's Go with Division.
Choose a place you would like to go that you can drive to in a few days. Find a map and chart your course. Estimate, then check how many miles it is from your house. Decide how fast you can drive and how many hours you are going to travel each day. Using division, figure out how many days it will take. Make a chart using the information you have. Decide how long you can stay. Remember, you have to save some time to drive home. Try a one-week trip, then a three-week trip. Remember, you have to travel by car. Could you chart your results? Can you estimate the cost of your trip? Involve your parents to help you in this plan!
Lee el párrafo y utiliza la división como ayuda para planear un viaje.

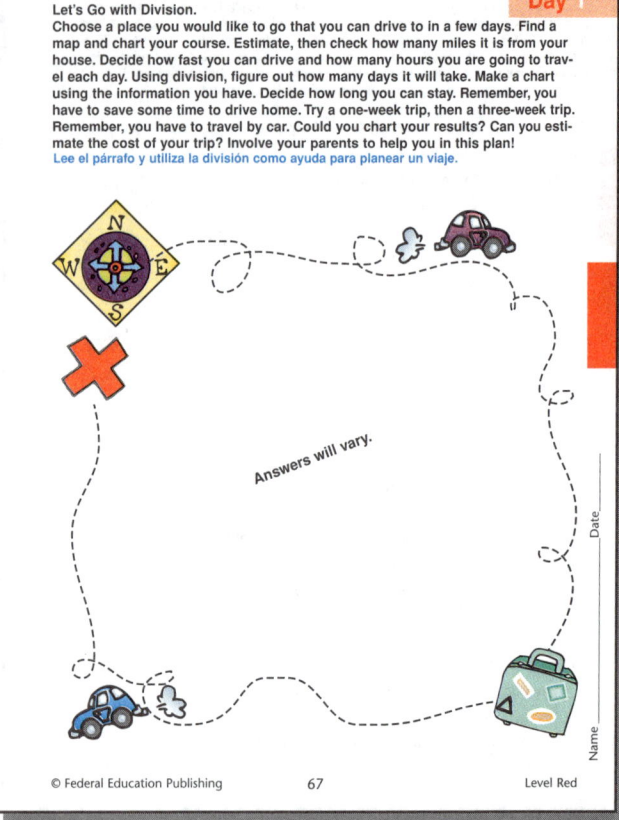

Answers will vary.

Page 68

Day 1 — **More Pronouns.**
Use **I** or **me** in these sentences. When **I** is part of a compound subject, use it last.
Utiliza I o me en estas oraciones.
EXAMPLE: She and **I** made a cake.

1. Mom and __I__ went to the store.
2. When will you come to see Kent and __me__?
3. Karen asked __me__ to answer the door.
4. Ann Marie and __I__ ate our lunch outside.
5. Snakes scare __me__ to death.
6. The gift was sent by Aunt Jean and __me__.
7. Carla and __I__ were both born in May.

Possessive pronouns show ownership. Use possessive pronouns in these sentences.
Utiliza pronombres posesivos en estas oraciones.

8. Did you see __their__ faces when they saw Santa?
9. __Your__ handwriting is very neat.
10. The prize is __ours__ for the asking.
11. The book you gave to Leza was __mine__.
12. __My__ uncle, Clint, is coming for a visit.
13. The prints on the mirror are __his or hers__ or mine.
14. The elephant stood on __its__ drum.

Volcanoes. Answer **T** for true or **F** for false to the following statements. If false, correct the sentence so it will be true.
Responde T para verdadero o F para falso. Si es falso, corrige la oración para convertirla en verdadera.

__T__ 1. A volcano is an opening in the crust of the Earth through which lava, gases, ash, and rocks erupt.
__F__ 2. In a short time, volcanic material can build up to form mountains. **It takes a long time.**
__F__ 3. These mountains can form only on land. **They also form on the ocean floor.**
__F__ 4. All magma comes from the Earth's core. **Magma comes from the upper mantle.**
__T__ 5. Most volcanoes happen underwater.
__T__ 6. Mid-ocean ridges are formed from underwater volcanoes.
__T__ 7. Mid-ocean ridges happen when lava builds up under water and creates underwater mountain chains.
__F__ 8. Most volcanoes on land occur at diverging plate boundaries. **They occur at converging plate boundaries.**
__F__ 9. Mid-ocean ridges form at convergent boundaries. **They occur at divergent boundaries.**
__T__ 10. Volcanoes on land occur on the edge of a continent or on islands.
__T__ 11. When two plates converge, compression forces some rocks upward to make mountains.

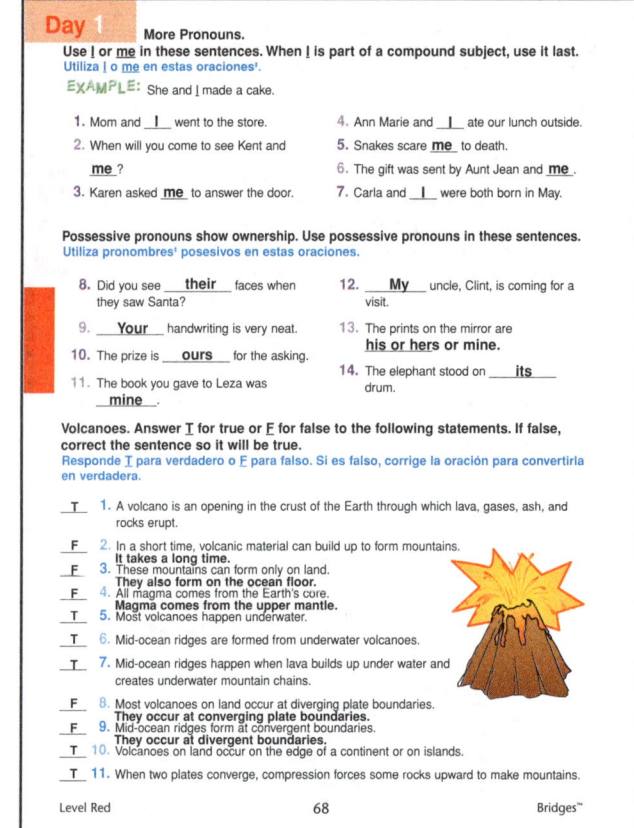

Page 69

Day 2

Sharpen your skills with this timed multiplication test! Estimate how much time you think it will take you to do these problems. _____ Now do the actual test. How long did it take you to do it? _____ What's the difference between the two times? _____
Agudiza tus habilidades haciendo este examen de multiplicación en tiempo limitado.

1. 6 x 7 = __42__
2. 12 x 2 = __24__
3. 5 x 10 = __50__
4. 9 x 6 = __54__
5. 7 x 8 = __56__
6. 11 x 12 = __132__
7. 7 x 5 = __35__
8. 11 x 2 = __22__
9. 10 x 3 = __30__
10. 5 x 6 = __30__
11. 9 x 5 = __45__
12. 8 x 4 = __32__
13. 8 x 0 = __0__
14. 6 x 12 = __72__
15. 8 x 2 = __16__
16. 10 x 2 = __20__
17. 6 x 6 = __36__
18. 8 x 9 = __72__
19. 7 x 2 = __14__
20. 8 x 7 = __56__
21. 11 x 7 = __77__
22. 5 x 2 = __10__
23. 10 x 6 = __60__
24. 9 x 4 = __36__
25. 6 x 3 = __18__
26. 8 x 9 = __72__
27. 6 x 9 = __54__
28. 11 x 10 = __110__
29. 10 x 9 = __90__
30. 9 x 11 = __99__
31. 7 x 3 = __21__
32. 12 x 10 = __120__
33. 9 x 9 = __81__
34. 8 x 8 = __64__
35. 7 x 7 = __49__
36. 10 x 10 = __100__
37. 11 x 3 = __33__
38. 6 x 5 = __30__
39. 5 x 3 = __15__
40. 5 x 2 = __10__
41. 12 x 5 = __60__
42. 10 x 0 = __0__
43. 9 x 10 = __90__
44. 8 x 2 = __16__
45. 11 x 5 = __55__
46. 8 x 8 = __64__
47. 6 x 7 = __42__
48. 7 x 7 = __49__
49. 11 x 9 = __99__
50. 5 x 12 = __60__
51. 5 x 5 = __25__
52. 9 x 0 = __0__
53. 9 x 3 = __27__
54. 7 x 4 = __28__
55. 12 x 4 = __48__
56. 9 x 9 = __81__
57. 7 x 9 = __63__
58. 7 x 8 = __56__
59. 10 x 4 = __40__
60. 9 x 8 = __72__
61. 7 x 6 = __42__
62. 10 x 5 = __50__
63. 11 x 4 = __44__
64. 7 x 5 = __35__
65. 12 x 12 = __144__
66. 9 x 7 = __63__
67. 7 x 11 = __77__
68. 5 x 4 = __20__
69. 9 x 7 = __63__
70. 10 x 8 = __80__
71. 9 x 11 = __99__
72. 8 x 12 = __96__
73. 8 x 6 = __48__
74. 12 x 3 = __36__
75. 5 x 7 = __35__
76. 11 x 5 = __55__
77. 9 x 6 = __54__
78. 9 x 12 = __108__
79. 6 x 8 = __48__
80. 7 x 10 = __70__
81. 5 x 11 = __55__
82. 10 x 10 = __100__
83. 6 x 11 = __66__
84. 12 x 11 = __132__
85. 12 x 9 = __108__
86. 8 x 7 = __56__
87. 5 x 8 = __40__
88. 0 x 8 = __0__
89. 6 x 8 = __48__
90. 11 x 8 = __88__
91. 11 x 12 = __132__
92. 10 x 7 = __70__
93. 8 x 11 = __88__
94. 11 x 6 = __66__
95. 6 x 10 = __60__
96. 4 x 6 = __24__
97. 11 x 8 = __88__
98. 12 x 6 = __72__
99. 8 x 10 = __80__
100. 12 x 12 = __144__
101. 8 x 10 = __80__
102. 10 x 0 = __0__
103. 7 x 9 = __63__
104. 10 x 11 = __110__
105. 7 x 12 = __84__
106. 12 x 12 = __144__
107. 11 x 9 = __99__
108. 12 x 7 = __84__
109. 11 x 6 = __66__
110. 9 x 5 = __45__
111. 9 x 3 = __27__
112. 12 x 9 = __108__
113. 11 x 7 = __77__
114. 5 x 9 = __45__
115. 9 x 10 = __90__
116. 9 x 8 = __72__
117. 9 x 4 = __36__
118. 10 x 12 = __120__
119. 8 x 12 = __96__
120. 11 x 11 = __121__
121. 7 x 12 = __84__
122. 8 x 11 = __88__
123. 11 x 11 = __121__
124. 0 x 9 = __0__
125. 12 x 8 = __96__

Cover up the answers with another sheet of paper and try it again!

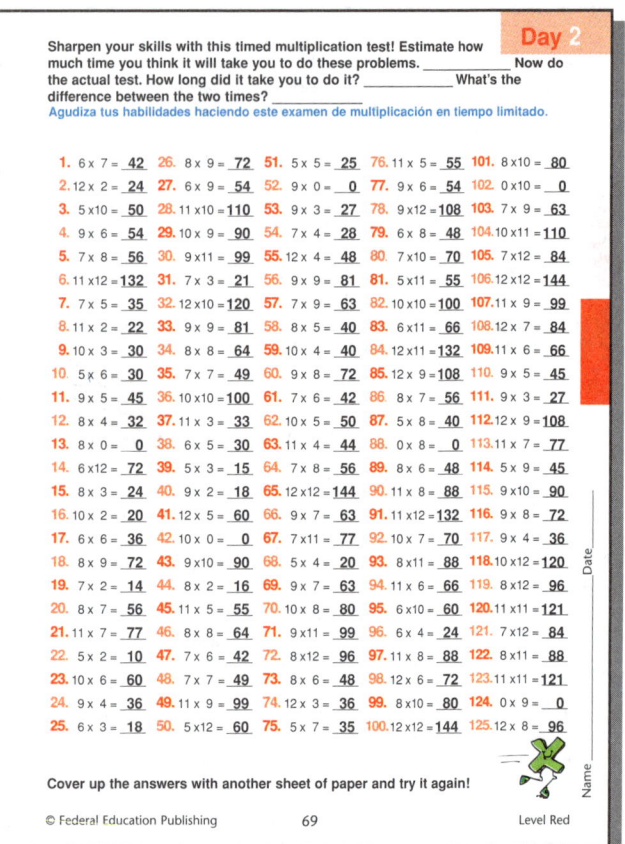

Page 70

Day 2 — **Subject Pronouns and Object Pronouns.** If the pronoun is not part of the subject it is an object pronoun. Write **SP** if the pronoun is a subject pronoun. Write **OP** if it is an object pronoun.
Si el pronombre no es parte del sujeto es un pronombre objetivo. Escribe SP si el pronombre forma parte del sujeto y OP si el pronombre es objetivo.

__OP__ 1. The funny story made **us** laugh.
__OP__ 2. McCall held the dance trophy in front of **her** and Ted.
__SP__ 3. Will **we** see any sharks at Sea Life Park?
__SP-OP__ 4. Kathy and **I** went ice skating with **her** family.
__OP__ 5. Don't give **her** the present until noon.
__SP__ 6. Did **they** fly or take the train home?
__SP__ 7. **We** are going to Washington D.C. this summer.
__SP__ 8. Are **you** a cousin to Hal Tomlyn?
__SP-OP__ 9. **I** bought blue gym shoes this year because I like **them**.
__OP__ 10. The dog got **its** paw caught in the bear trap.

Verbs. Regular verbs show action that happened in the past by adding **-ed** to the base word. But to show past tense for irregular verbs, you have to change the spelling.
EXAMPLE: sit - sat
In the square there are some irregular verbs. Write them under the correct heading below.
En el cuadrado aparecen algunos verbos irregulares. Escríbelos bajo el encabezado correcto.
Remember: The past participle is used with a helping word when in a sentence.

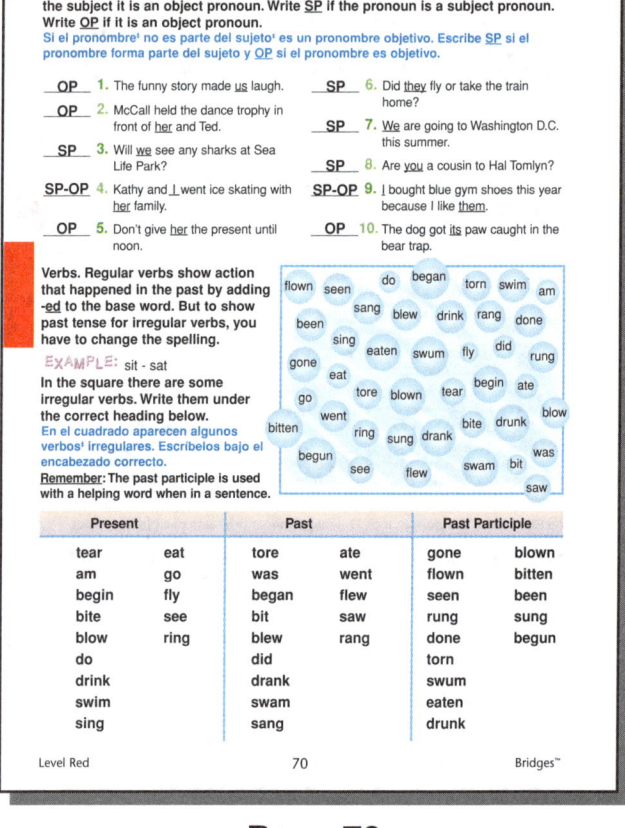

Present	Past	Past Participle
tear	tore	torn
am	was	been
begin	began	begun
bite	bit	bitten
blow	blew	blown
do	did	done
drink	drank	drunk
swim	swam	swum
sing	sang	sung
eat	ate	eaten
go	went	gone
fly	flew	flown
see	saw	seen
ring	rang	rung

Page 71

Choices. Clayton's mother bought him some new clothes to go to camp. She bought him 4 pairs of shorts—red, blue, green, and white. She also bought him 8 t-shirts—2 red, 2 blue, 2 green, and 2 white. She bought him 4 long-sleeved sweatshirts—2 white and 2 blue.

Use a tree diagram to organize the data to find out how many different choices of shorts and shirts Clayton can wear. __24__ total choices

Lee el párrafo. Usa el diagrama en forma de árbol para determinar cuántas combinaciones de pantalones y camisetas Clayton puede usar.

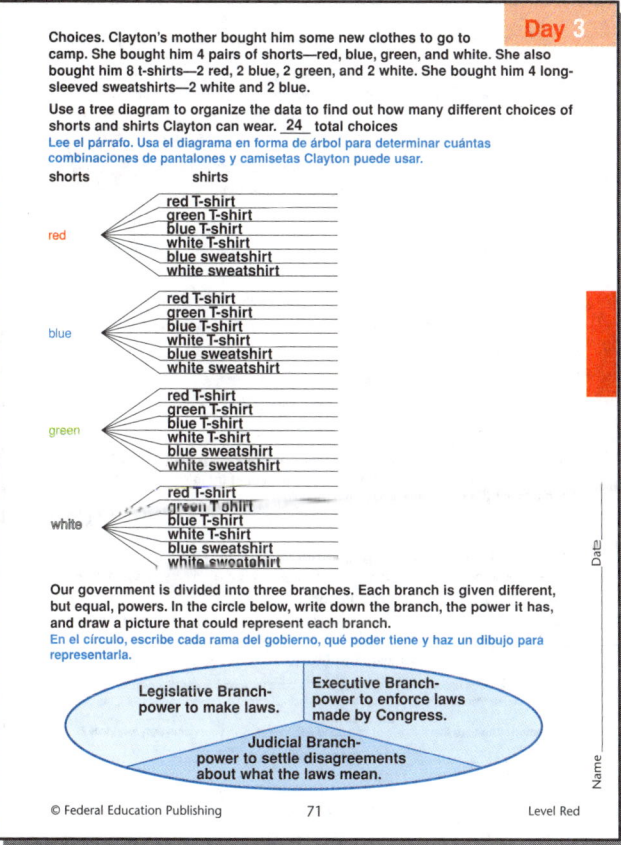

Our government is divided into three branches. Each branch is given different, but equal, powers. In the circle below, write down the branch, the power it has, and draw a picture that could represent each branch.

En el círculo, escribe cada rama del gobierno, qué poder tiene y haz un dibujo para representarla.

- Legislative Branch- power to make laws.
- Executive Branch- power to enforce laws made by Congress.
- Judicial Branch- power to settle disagreements about what the laws mean.

Page 72

Day 3 Below are some parts of sentences that give the cause. Finish the sentence by writing what the effect might be. Look for clue words.
Estas partes de oraciones establecen una causa. Completa la oración escribiendo cuál puede ser el efecto. **Answers will vary.**

EXAMPLE: (cause) The old house had not been painted for years, (effect) so the first thing we did was paint it. (The clue word is "so.")

1. Our Thanksgiving turkey was burned because __the oven was not working right__
2. __My feet hurt at the end of the day__ because my new shoes were too tight.
3. The wind was blowing hard, so __we decided not to go gliding that day__.
4. Because I didn't get up early enough this morning, __I was late for school__
5. Some children were playing with matches; as a result, __the house burned down__.

Now it's your turn to write the cause to the effects.

6. The plane crashed due to __the thick fog__
7. __Because I had eaten so much__, my stomach hurt.
8. __Our class won the prize__, so we decided to celebrate.
9. The drinks were very sweet because __Ronda spilled sugar in the punch bowl__
10. __Since we had such a cold spell in April__, there was no fruit on the trees this summer.

Electricity. In the table below, make a list of things you enjoy that use electricity. Now ask a parent, adult, or grandparent to list things that use electricity that we have now, but they did not have when they were your age.

Haz una lista de cosas que disfrutas y que usen electricidad, cosas que tus padres y abuelos no tenían, y cosas que vayan a existir en el futuro.

Compare the differences and similarities on your table. Next, create a list of things children in 30 years may have that use electricity that we do not have today. Be creative!

You	Parent/Adult
Answers will vary.	
Grandparent/Elderly Person	Future

Page 73

Broken Line Graphs, "Using Leisure Time."

Keep track of how much television you watch daily in a two-week period, then graph the results. Do the same with how much time you play computer games or TV games, then graph the results. Now do the same with how much time you spend with your friends, then graph the results. You can use the same graph for all three if you use different colored pens or pencils.

Realiza un gráfico para hacer el seguimiento de tu tiempo libre.

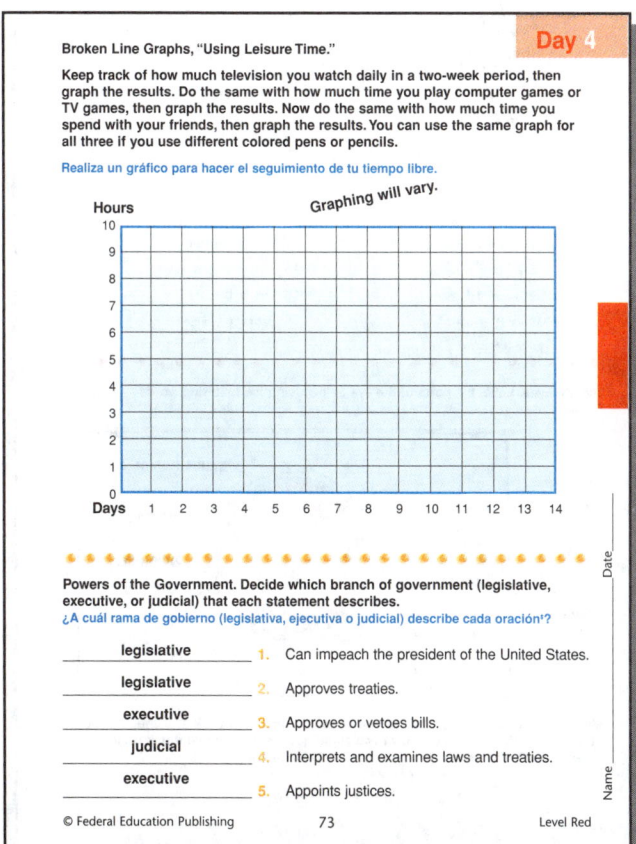

Graphing will vary.

Powers of the Government. Decide which branch of government (legislative, executive, or judicial) that each statement describes.

¿A cuál rama de gobierno (legislativa, ejecutiva o judicial) describe cada oración?

1. __legislative__ Can impeach the president of the United States.
2. __legislative__ Approves treaties.
3. __executive__ Approves or vetoes bills.
4. __judicial__ Interprets and examines laws and treaties.
5. __executive__ Appoints justices.

Page 74

Day 4 Adjectives make reading more interesting. Adjectives modify or describe nouns and pronouns. Read the clues and do the crossword puzzle. The answers are adjectives listed below.

Lee las pistas y completa el crucigrama. Las respuestas son adjetivos del Recuadro de Palabras.

Across
1. satisfied
4. dignified, lofty, noble
8. filled with fear
11. critical, immediate
12. rough voice
13. courageous, valiant, gallant
14. headstrong, inflexible

Down
1. skilled, competent
2. commanding
3. unbelievable, amazing
5. unable to put up with others' beliefs
6. lively, playful
7. childish, foolish
9. ill-disposed, hateful
10. made of wood

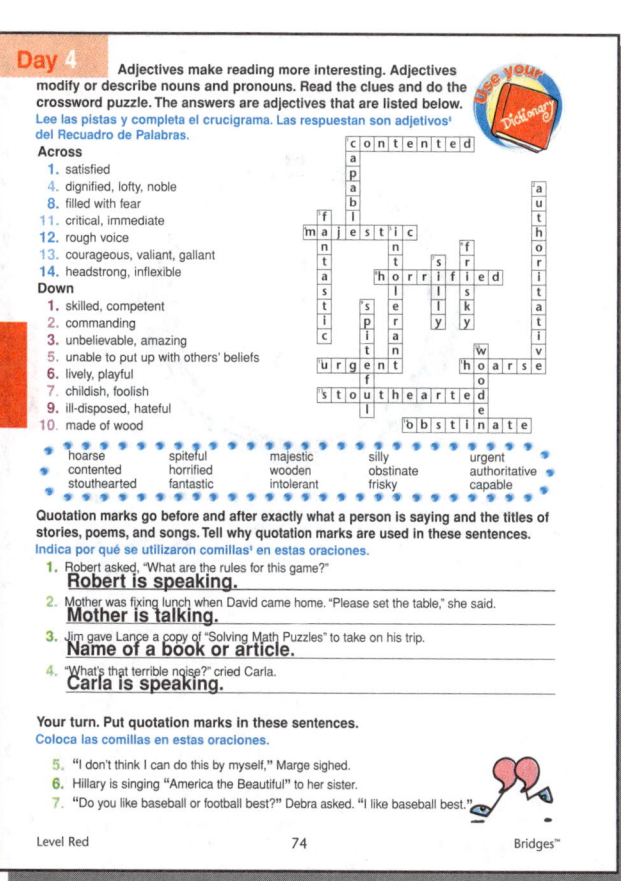

hoarse, spiteful, majestic, silly, urgent, contented, horrified, wooden, obstinate, authoritative, stouthearted, fantastic, intolerant, frisky, capable

Quotation marks go before and after exactly what a person is saying and the titles of stories, poems, and songs. Tell why quotation marks are used in these sentences.
Indica por qué se utilizaron comillas en estas oraciones.

1. Robert asked, "What are the rules for this game?"
   __Robert is speaking.__
2. Mother was fixing lunch when David came home. "Please set the table," she said.
   __Mother is talking.__
3. Jim gave Lance a copy of "Solving Math Puzzles" to take on his trip.
   __Name of a book or article.__
4. "What's that terrible noise?" cried Carla.
   __Carla is speaking.__

Your turn. Put quotation marks in these sentences.
Coloca las comillas en estas oraciones.

5. "I don't think I can do this by myself," Marge sighed.
6. Hillary is singing "America the Beautiful" to her sister.
7. "Do you like baseball or football best?" Debra asked. "I like baseball best."

Page 75

Day 5

Complete this table to see which of these numbers can be divided by 2, 3, 5, 9, and 10 without remainders. After you have finished the chart, see if you can come up with some hypotheses to form some divisibility rules.
¿Qué números de la tabla pueden dividirse por 2,3,5,9 y 10 sin resto? ¿Puedes determinar alguna hipótesis para reglas de división?

y = yes and n = no

Hypotheses of 2, 3, 5, 9, and 10

2 Hypothesis: The number can be divided equally by 2 if a 0, 2, 4, 6, or 8 is found in the one's place.

3 Hypothesis: The number can be divided equally by 3 if the sum of the numbers when added together can be divided by 3.

5 Hypothesis: The number can be divided equally by 5 if 0 or 5 is found in the one's place.

9 Hypothesis: The number can be divided equally by 9 if the sum of the numbers when added together can be divided by 9.

10 Hypothesis: The number can be divided equally by 10 if a 0 is found in the one's place.

Divisible by	2	3	5	9	10
3,825	n	y	y	y	n
930	y	y	y	n	y
792	y	y	n	y	n
856	y	n	n	n	n
1,440	y	y	y	y	y
6,825	n	y	y	n	n
1,854	y	y	n	y	n
41,004	y	y	n	n	n
85,010	y	n	y	n	y
314,402	y	n	n	n	n
4,277,133	n	y	n	n	n
10,009,407	n	y	n	n	n
9,617,590	y	n	y	n	y
9,591,314	y	n	n	n	n

Try out your hypotheses on number combinations of your own to see if they really work.

The Expansion West. Write a dialogue that might have happened between the following people during the expansion west: an Indian, a settler, and a soldier. Remember to keep an open mind about their different points of view. Have your parents, brothers, sisters, or friends read the parts in costume!
Escribe un diálogo que pueda haber sucedido entre las siguientes personas durante la expansión hacia el oeste: un Indio, un colono y un soldado.

Answers will vary.

Page 76

Day 5

Fill in the blank in each sentence with a synonym of the boxed word.
Completa el espacio en blanco con un sinónimo¹ de la palabra en el recuadro.

EXAMPLE: I had to [finish] *complete* my work before I could go with my friends.

Answers will vary.

1. Sarah and Angie go for a [walk] __stroll__ every day except Sunday.
2. It's fun to watch the little colts [play] __frolic or romp__ in the green pastures.
3. The electricians have done [enough] __sufficient__ work for this week.
4. I cannot [find] __locate__ the information I [need] __require__ for my report.
5. You will have to [write] __record__ all the important events of your [trip] __journey__.
6. The lost couple had not had any [food] __nourishment__ for six days.
7. Will you please [show] __demonstrate__ how your new invention works?
8. They will [try] __attempt/ endeavor__ to climb Mount Everest again next summer.
9. Tourists [might] __may__ be able to travel to the moon by the year 2010.
10. The value of this coin will [grow] __increase__ over the years.
11. The applicant must [reply] __respond__ within three weeks.
12. I think your [story] __tale__ was a little farfetched!

Electric Current. Read each passage on electricity. One sentence in each passage is false. Cross out the false sentence and try to correct it. Then answer the questions after each passage.
Cruza la oración¹ falsa de cada párrafo e intenta corregirla. Luego responde las preguntas.

1. An electrical current is moving energy. You can see electricity at work in lights, motors, computers, and some toys. Any material that allows an electric current to pass through is called a ~~battery.~~ **a conductor**

   Question: How many things can you think of in 1–2 minutes that need electricity? Have a race with someone to see who can think of the most ideas.
   Answers will vary.

2. Material that does not allow an electric current to pass through it is called a ~~circuit.~~ This material covers conducting materials. It stops electricity from escaping and causing harm. **an insulator**

   Question: What are five things you can do to ensure safety in your home with electricity?
   1. ____ 2. **Answers will vary.** 3. ____
   4. ____ 5. ____

Page 77

Day 6

Choose numbers between 10 and 100 and put them in the outer circle. Next, put numbers between 1 and 12 in the following circle. Then multiply the outer circle's number by the second circle's number.
Escribe números entre 10 y 100 en el círculo exterior. Coloca números entre 1 y 12 en el círculo siguiente y luego multiplica ambos números.

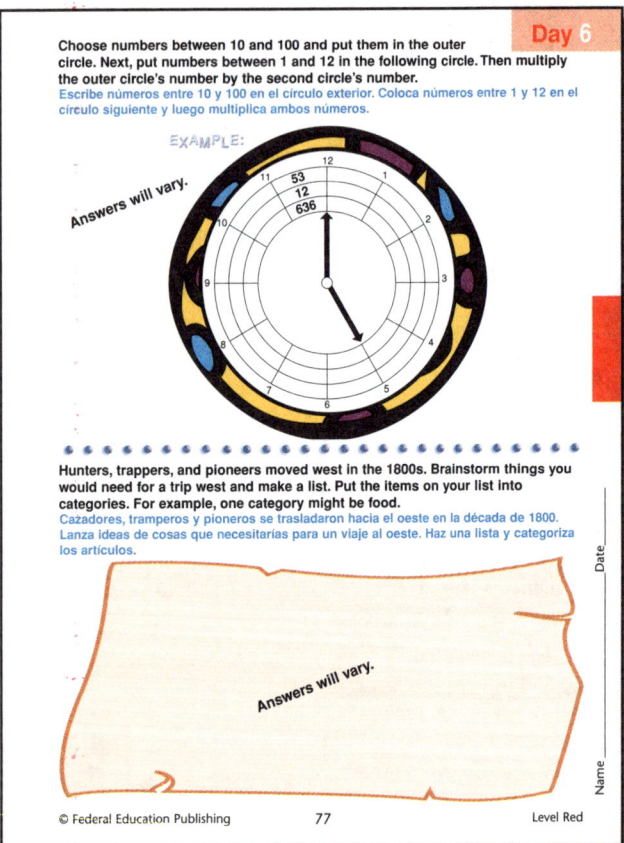

EXAMPLE: 53 × 12 = 636
Answers will vary.

Hunters, trappers, and pioneers moved west in the 1800s. Brainstorm things you would need for a trip west and make a list. Put the items on your list into categories. For example, one category might be food.
Cazadores, tramperos y pioneros se trasladaron hacia el oeste en la década de 1800. Lanza ideas de cosas que necesitarás para un viaje al oeste. Haz una lista y categoriza los artículos.

Answers will vary.

Page 78

Day 6

Spelling. What double consonants go in these spelling words?
¿Qué consonantes dobles van en estas palabras?

1. i__m__ediately
2. su__p p__ort
3. i__r r__egular
4. a__t t__ribute
5. di__f f__erence
6. a__s s__e__s s__ment
7. i__r r__emovable
8. a__b b__reviation
9. exce__l l__ence
10. a__n n__ual
11. su__p p__osed
12. po__s s__ible
13. inte__l l__igence
14. a__l l__egiance
15. bu__t t__ernut
16. i__n n__ocent
17. di__s s__atisfied
18. a__c c__e__s s__ible
19. scri__b b__le
20. permi__t t__ing

Health—Eyes. Label the parts of the eye below using the following words:
Coloca los nombres de las partes del ojo utilizando las palabras a continuación.

retina, cornea, lens, iris, pupil, vitreous humor, optic nerve

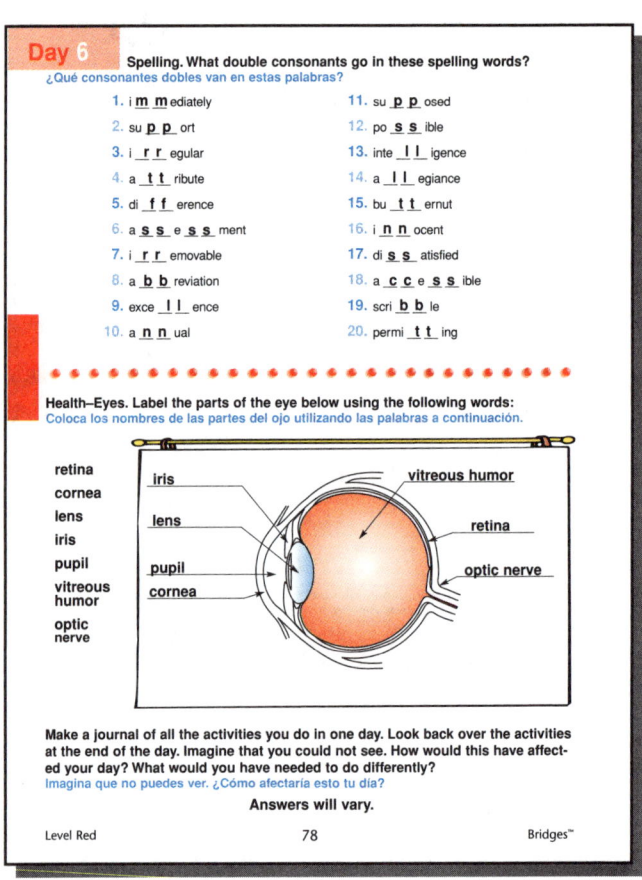

Make a journal of all the activities you do in one day. Look back over the activities at the end of the day. Imagine that you could not see. How would this have affected your day? What would you have needed to do differently?
Imagina que no puedes ver. ¿Cómo afectaría esto a tu día?

Answers will vary.

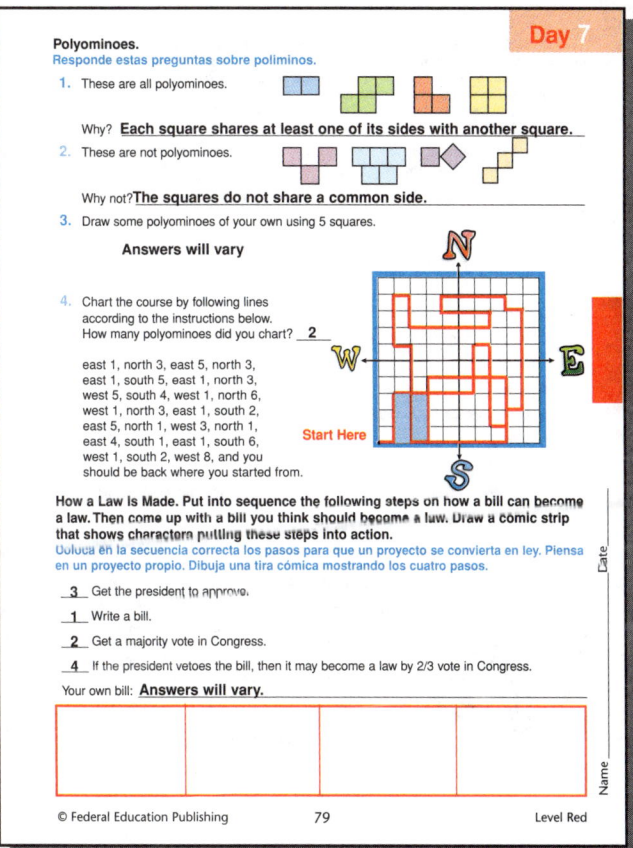

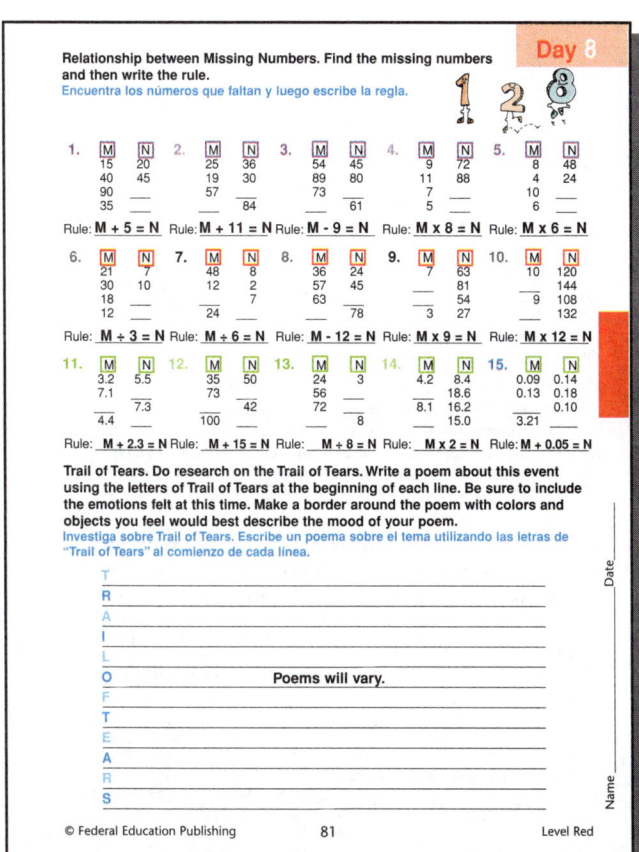

Page 83

Day 9

Match the term to the mathematical definition dealing with fractions.
Une el término con la definición correcta.

1. fraction — a. It's the answer you get by dividing one number by another number.
2. improper fraction — b. It's the number found below the line in a fraction.
3. quotient — c. It's a number that names a part of a set or part of a whole.
4. mixed number — d. It's the number found above the line in a fraction.
5. denominator — e. It's a number that has a whole number and a fraction number.
6. numerator — f. It's a fraction whose numerator is greater than its denominator or can be equal to its denominator.

Show your understanding. *Sigue las instrucciones.*

7. Show 15 ÷ 7 as an improper fraction. $\frac{15}{7}$
8. Show 2 ÷ 9 as a fraction. $\frac{2}{9}$
9. Show 11 ÷ 7 as an improper fraction. $\frac{11}{7}$
10. 82 ÷ 7 can be written $\frac{82}{7}$ or $7\overline{)82}$
    What is the divisor? 7
    What is the remainder? 5
    Write it as a mixed number. $11\frac{5}{7}$
11. What kind of fractions are these: $\frac{28}{5}\ \frac{17}{12}\ \frac{59}{7}$? improper fraction
    Write a mixed fraction for each. $5\frac{3}{5}\ \ 1\frac{5}{12}\ \ 8\frac{3}{7}$
12. Write a mixed fraction for the following:
    $7\overline{)29}\ \ 8\overline{)143}\ \ 25\overline{)90}\ \ 10\overline{)433}$
    $4\frac{1}{7}\ \ 17\frac{7}{8}\ \ 3\frac{3}{5}\ \ 43\frac{3}{10}$

A Trailblazer. On his expeditions, Meriwether Lewis kept an illustrated journal on things he discovered. Imagine that you are also an explorer. Go outside and study natural objects or look at photographs of plants, animals, and physical features in your area. Write a journal entry on one of the objects you have found. Look at it as though you have never seen it before. Describe the structure of the object and hypothesize its function. After writing the description, draw and label the object.
Imagina que eres explorador. Estudia o mira fotografías de plantas, animales y características físicas de tu área¹. Describe una de las cosas como si fuera la primera vez que la vieras. Luego haz un dibujo y colócale el nombre a las partes.

Date: _____
Location: _____
Observations: _____

Answers will vary.

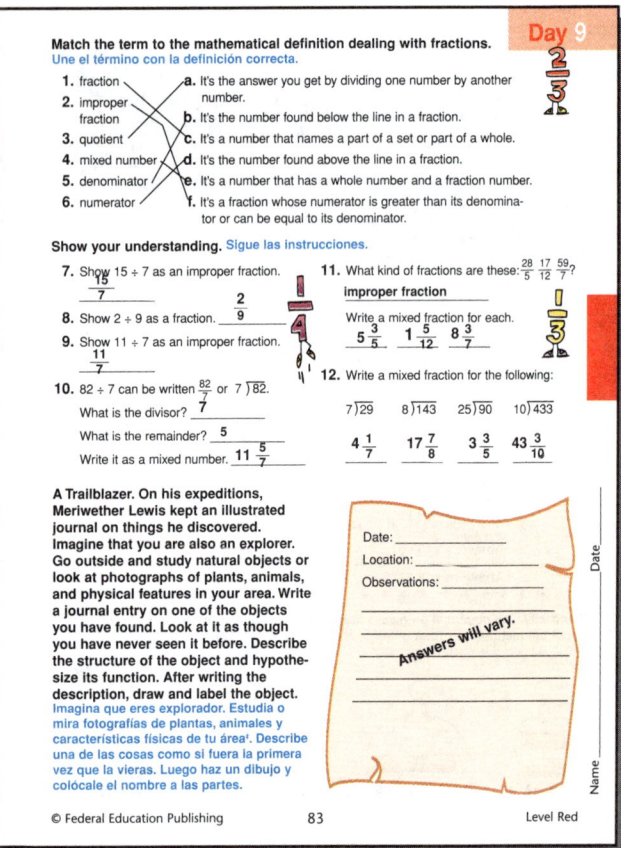

Page 84

Day 9

Conclusions Versus Facts. People, young and old, often jump to conclusions. They frequently make up their mind without looking for facts or reasons behind a situation. Write a conclusion for each situation given and then think of facts you need to verify your conclusion.
Escribe una conclusión para cada situación dada. Luego piensa hechos necesarios para verificar tu conclusión.

1. There is a large package with your name on it at your doorstep without a note saying who it's from. It's not your birthday.
   Conclusion:
   Facts needed:

2. Your teacher sends a note home with you addressed directly to your parents. He/she tells you to make sure your parents get it.
   Conclusion:
   Facts needed:

3. When you go to the game, no one will speak to you or play with you.
   Conclusion:
   Facts needed:

4. The house is dark and the doors are locked when you get home.
   Conclusion:
   Facts needed:

5. You have looked all through the house and all over the yard, and you cannot find your pet turtle.
   Conclusion:
   Facts needed:

Answers will vary.

Natural Resources. Create a poster that reminds us of the importance of the 3 Rs: Reduce, Reuse, and Recycle!
¡Crea un poster que les recuerde a las personas reducir, reusar y reciclar!

Posters will vary.

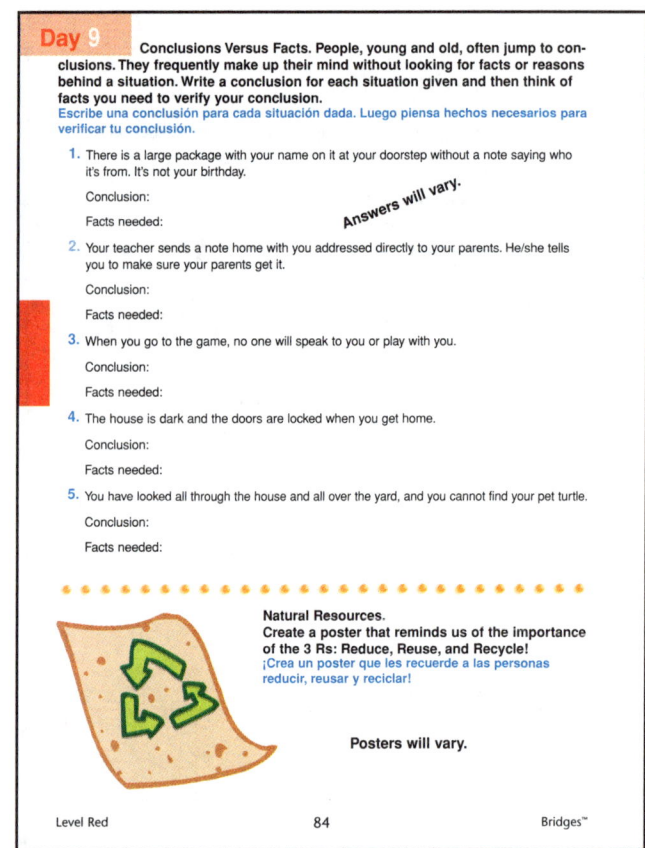

Page 85

Day 10

Add to find the fraction. The sum of each is found in the center.
Suma¹ para encontrar la fracción¹. La suma se encuentra en el centro.

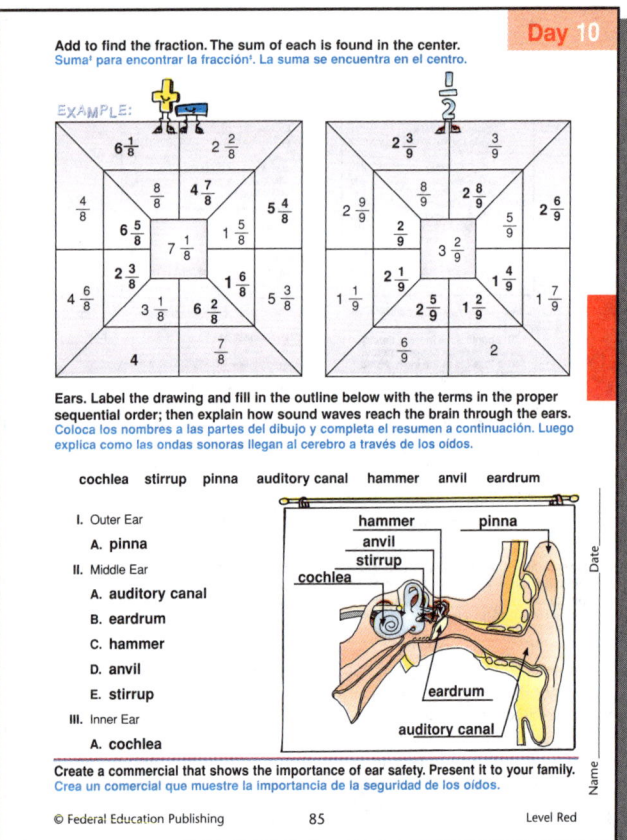

Ears. Label the drawing and fill in the outline below with the terms in the proper sequential order; then explain how sound waves reach the brain through the ears.
Coloca los nombres a las partes del dibujo y completa el resumen a continuación. Luego explica como las ondas sonoras llegan al cerebro a través de los oídos.

cochlea   stirrup   pinna   auditory canal   hammer   anvil   eardrum

I. Outer Ear
   A. pinna
II. Middle Ear
   A. auditory canal
   B. eardrum
   C. hammer
   D. anvil
   E. stirrup
III. Inner Ear
   A. cochlea

Create a commercial that shows the importance of ear safety. Present it to your family.
Crea un comercial que muestre la importancia de la seguridad de los oídos.

Page 86

Day 10

Adverbs. Underline the adverb in each sentence. At the end of the sentence, write the word it modifies.
Subraya el adverbio¹ de cada oración¹. Luego escribe la palabra a la que modifica.

1. Brent's broken arm hurts <u>badly</u>. **hurts**
2. The train moved <u>rapidly</u> down the tracks. **moved**
3. That chorus sang <u>well</u>. **sang**
4. Our three bulldogs waited <u>eagerly</u> for their walk. **waited**
5. The monkeys chattered <u>noisily</u> in the trees. **chattered**
6. <u>Yesterday</u> Todd and Travis flew to London. **flew**

Fill in the blanks with adverbs.
Completa los espacios en blanco con adverbios.
Answers will vary.

7. The children ran **excitedly** down the stairs.
8. Delicate white snowflakes were falling **gently** to the ground.
9. Kirk spoke **quietly** to his father on the phone.
10. April drove her new car **proudly** through the middle of town.
11. The old windmill worked **perfectly** after he oiled it.
12. Seven baby possums clung **tightly** to their mother's back.

Categories. Find the word that does not belong in the category. Draw a line through it and write a sentence using the word you drew a line through to tell why it doesn't belong.
Tacha la palabra que no pertenezca a la categoría. Escribe una oración usando esa palabra para indicar por qué no pertenece a la categoría.

EXAMPLE: street - road - ~~turnpike~~ - railroad - freeway - highway Cars do not travel on a railroad.

1. software - mouse - ~~depth~~ - program - disk Depth has nothing to do with computers.
2. dawn - daytime - twilight - sunrise - ~~hyphen~~ A hyphen is a punctuation mark.
3. spaghetti - meatballs - ~~menu~~ - rhubarb - lasagna I do not want to eat the menu.
4. cyclone - ~~generator~~ - tornado - hurricane - monsoon A generator is not related to the weather.
5. ~~mythology~~ - petrology - geology - biology - zoology Mythology is the study of myths.
6. ~~almond~~ - chocolate - caramel - butterscotch Almonds are nuts.
7. exception - export - ~~impolite~~ - examiner - excavate Impolite does not have an ex- prefix.
8. ~~proverb~~ - pronoun - adjective - noun - preposition - verb A proverb is not one of the eight parts of speech.
9. period - comma - apostrophe - colon - ~~clause~~ A clause is part of a sentence, not punctuation.
10. export - portable - support - importance - ~~medieval~~ Medieval does not have the letters p o r t in it.

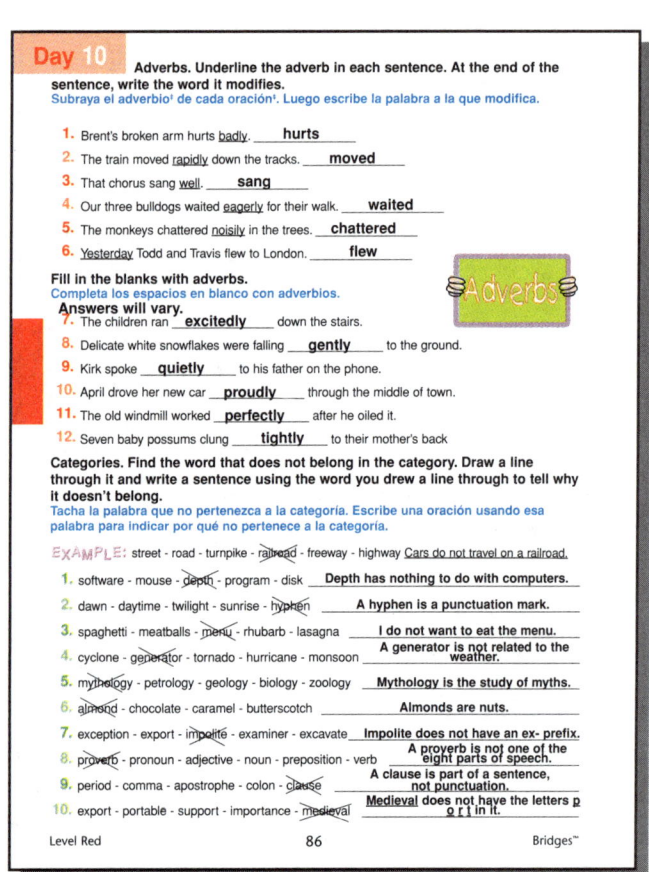

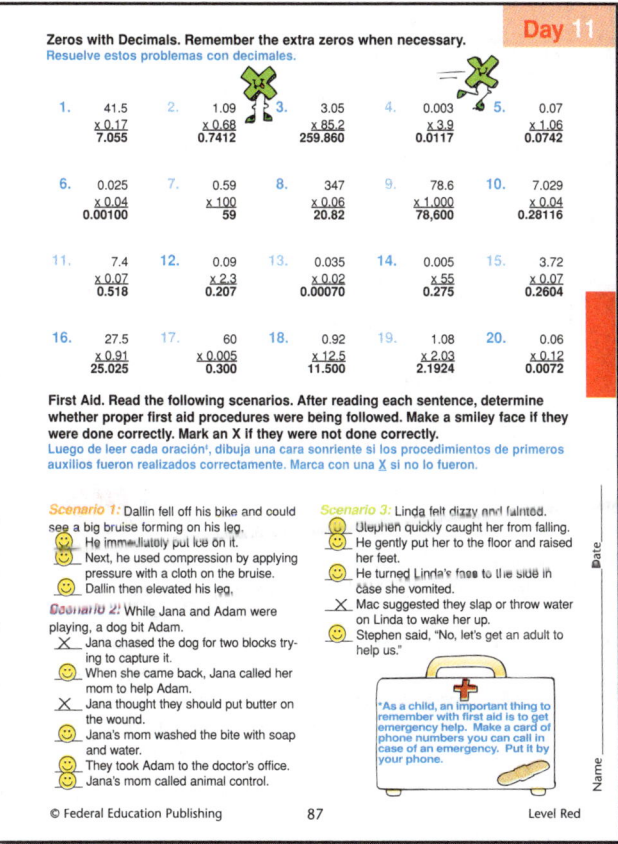

Page 87

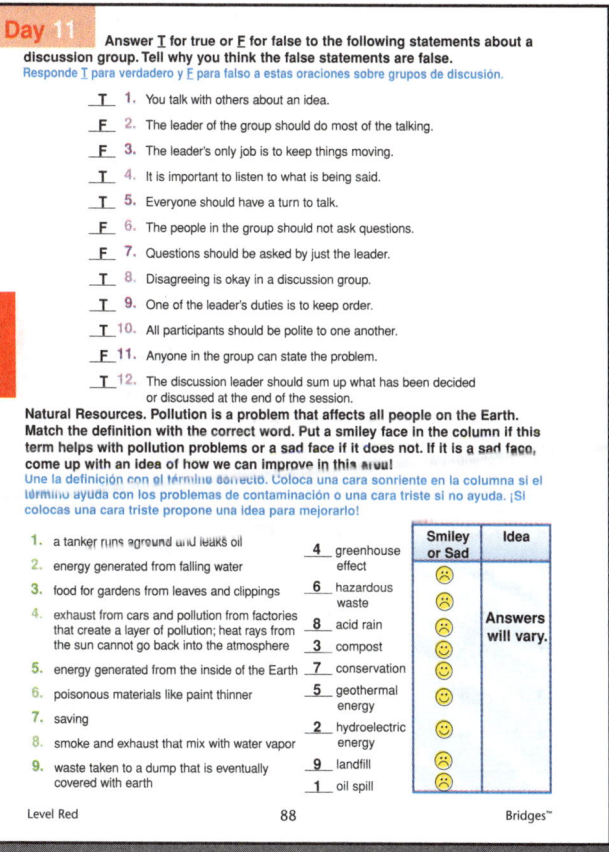

Page 88

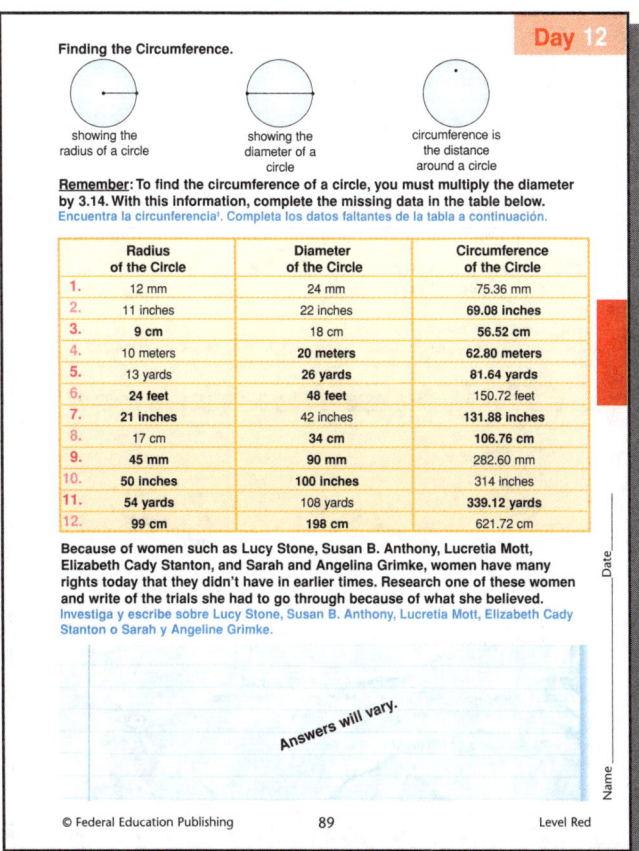

Page 89

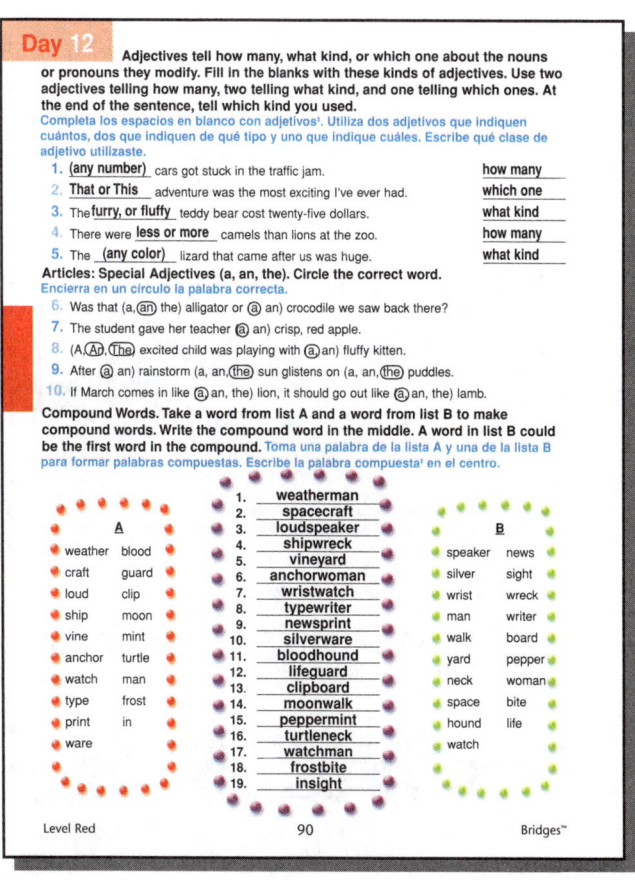

Page 90

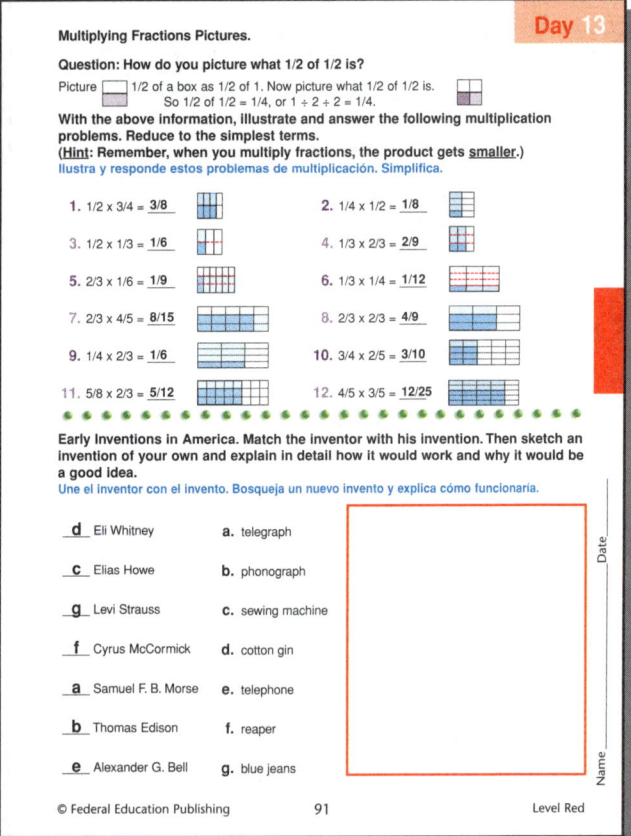

Page 91

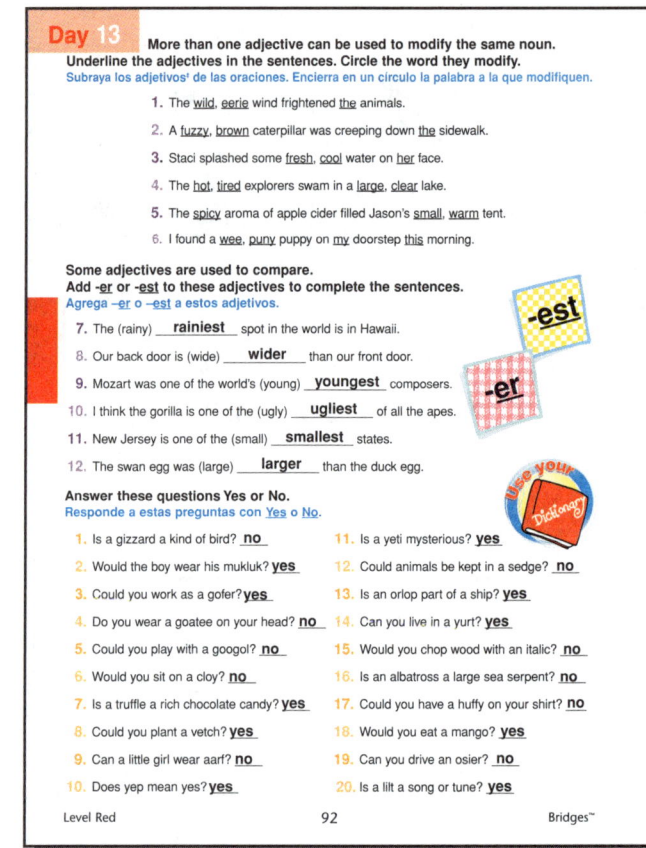

Page 92

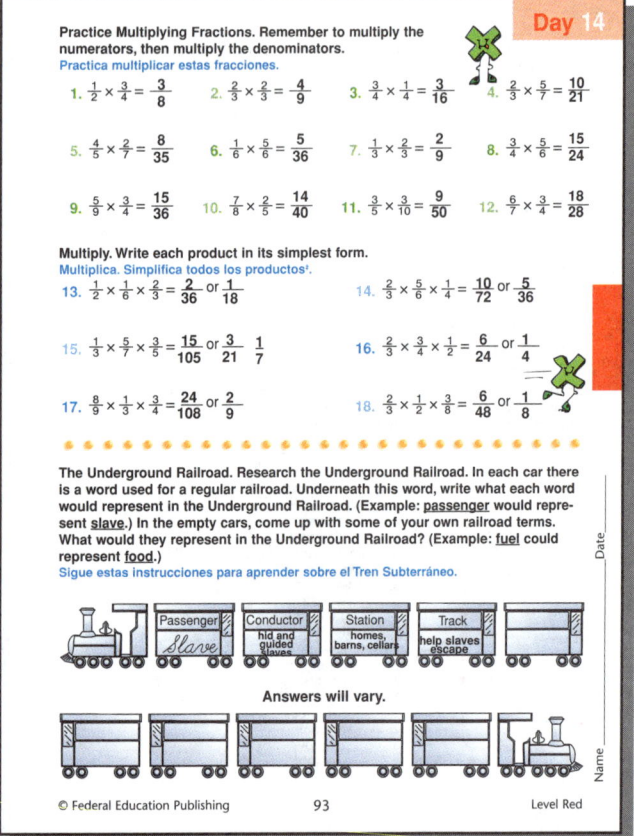

Page 93

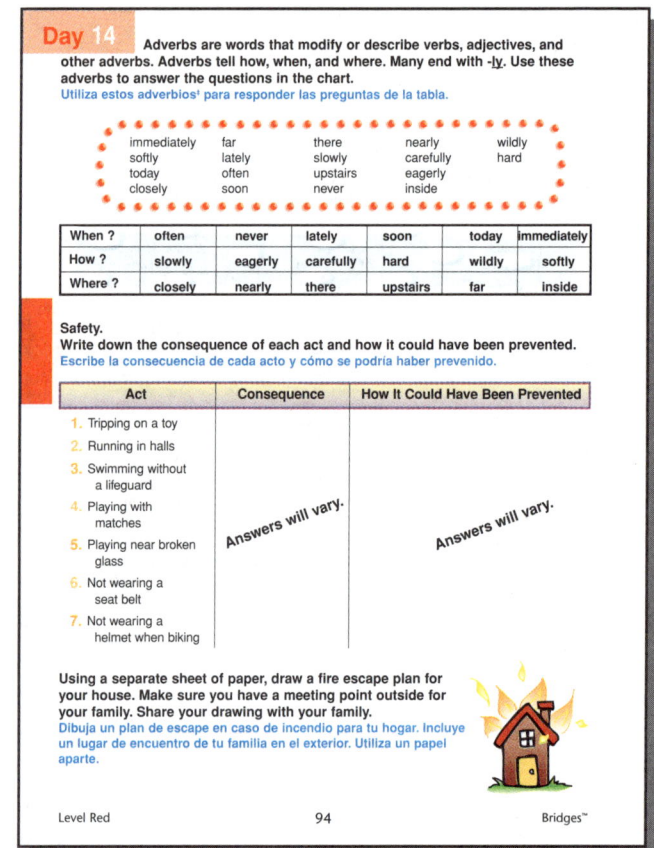

Page 94

Day 15

Angles. Fill in the blanks.
Completa los espacios en blanco.
When two rays share the same endpoint they form an (1.) __angle__. This endpoint is called the (2.) __vertex__ of the angle. The (3.) __degree__ is the unit used for measuring angles. A (4.) __protractor__ is used to measure angles. A (5.) __protractor__ is marked with (6.) __180__ degrees. You place the center of the protractor on the vertex of the angle.

The (7.) __right__ angle looks like a square corner. It measures (8.) __90__ degrees. An (9.) __acute__ angle is smaller than a right angle or less than 90 degrees. An (10.) __obtuse__ angle is larger than a right angle or greater than 90 degrees.

Label these three angles. Coloca el nombre a estos ángulos.

11. __acute angle__ 12. __right angle__ 13. __obtuse angle__

Use a protractor to measure these angles.
Utiliza un transportador para medir estos ángulos.

14. __25 degrees__ 15. __90 degrees__ 16. __20 degrees__ 17. __150 degrees__

Use your protractor to draw an angle for these measures.
Utiliza un transportador para dibujar ángulos con estas medidas.

18. 75° 19. 60° 20. 15°

Civil War. Look at the list below. Some of the terms have to do with the Civil War. Circle in gray the terms if they refer to the Confederate side or a Confederate victory. Circle in blue the terms that refer to the Union side or a Union victory. Circle in red the terms that occurred in other periods of history.
Encierra en un círculo gris los términos que se refieran a la Confederación (incluyendo las victorias), en un círculo azul los términos que se refieran a la Unión y en un círculo rojo los términos que no se refieran a la Guerra Civil.

Abraham Lincoln	Fort Duquesne	Valley Forge
Sally Tompkins	General Thomas "Stonewall" Jackson	Frederick Douglass
Saratoga	General Ulysses S. Grant	Bill of Rights
Battle of Bull Run	Andrew Jackson	General Robert E. Lee
1776	Seven Days' Battle	Thomas Jefferson
Paul Revere	John Paul Jones	Jefferson Davis
Antietam	Eli Whitney	General William T. Sherman
Yorktown	Harriet Tubman	

Day 15

Proofread and circle the mistakes in the following paragraphs. Then rewrite the paragraphs, correcting the mistakes in spelling, punctuation, etc. Write in cursive. Try to find thirty-nine mistakes.
Revisa estos párrafos y encierra en un círculo los 39 errores. Vuelve a escribir los párrafos corrigiendo los errores.

today the term "Native American" is used to descibe those people indigenous to america, however the firt explorers who came to America referred to them as "Indians" Unknown to the exploders, most tribes had their own names. for example, names used by the deleware indians of eastern north america meant "genuine men".

the Indians' languages way of life, and homes wer all very different. The aztic and maya Indians of central America built large citys. The apache and Paiute used brush and mating to make simple huts the plains indians built coneshaped tepees covered with buffalo skins Cliff dwellers and other Pueblo groups usd sun-dried bricks to make many storyed houses.

Today the term "Native American" is used to describe those people indigenous to America. However, the first explorers who came to America referred to them as "Indians". Unknown to the explorers, most tribes had their own names. For example, names used by the Delaware Indians of eastern North America meant "genuine men".

The Indians' languages, way of life, and homes were all very different. The Aztec and Maya Indians of Central America built large cities. The Apache and Paiute used brush and matting to make simple huts. The Plains Indians built cone-shaped tepees covered with buffalo skins. Cliff Dwellers and other Pueblo groups used sun-dried bricks to make many-storied houses.

Use homophones or homonyms to fill in these blanks. Remember: They are words that sound or are spelled the same, but mean different things.
Usa homófonos u homónimos para completar estos espacios en blanco.

EXAMPLE: I think I have something in my _eye_.

1. Chris will __be__ catching a bumble __bee__ for his insect collection.
2. My __aunt__ Lola had an __ant__ bite her toe.
3. The __band__ was __banned__ from playing at the concert.
4. __I'll__ visit the __Isle__ of Man in June.
5. Please __close__ the door to the __clothes__ closet.
6. Patt __sent__ me one __cent__ for good luck.
7. My __blue__ jeans __blew__ away in the wind.
8. We went __by__ the mall to __buy__ some cards.
9. My brother __ate__ __eight__ pancakes for breakfast.
10. __No__, I do not __know__ how to play a musical instrument.

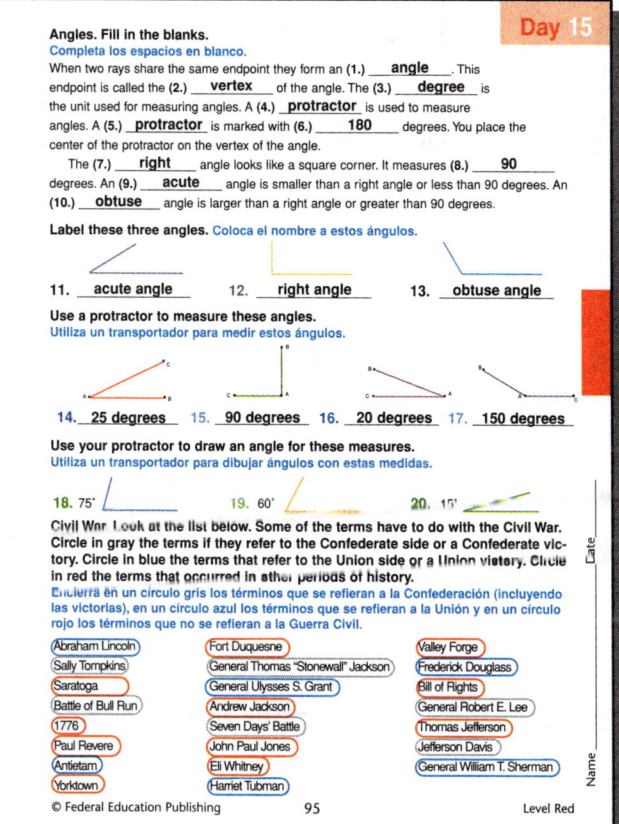

Multiplication and Division

Developing multiplication and division math skills can be a challenging experience for both parent and child.

- Have a positive attitude.
- Relax and enjoy the learning process.
- Keep the learning time short and fun you will get better results.
- Review the cards with your child.
- Read the front of the card.
- Check your answer on the reverse side.
- Separate those he/she does not know.
- Review those he/she does know.
- Gradually work through the other cards.

These steps will help build your child's confidence with multiplication and division. Enjoy the rewards!

"Teacher, Teacher"

Three or more players.
Each player takes a turn as "Teacher."
The Teacher mixes up the flashcards and holds one card up at a time.
First player to yell out "Teacher, Teacher,"
will have the first chance to give the answer.
If his/her answer is right he/she receives 5 points.
If his/her answer is wrong, he/she will not receive any points.
Move on to the next person until someone answers correctly.
The next round someone else is teacher.
Repeat each round.
Reward the different levels, everyone wins!

Time Challenge

Follow the directions for "Teacher, Teacher" and add a time to it.
Increase the point system to meet the Time Challenge.
Reward the different levels, everyone wins!

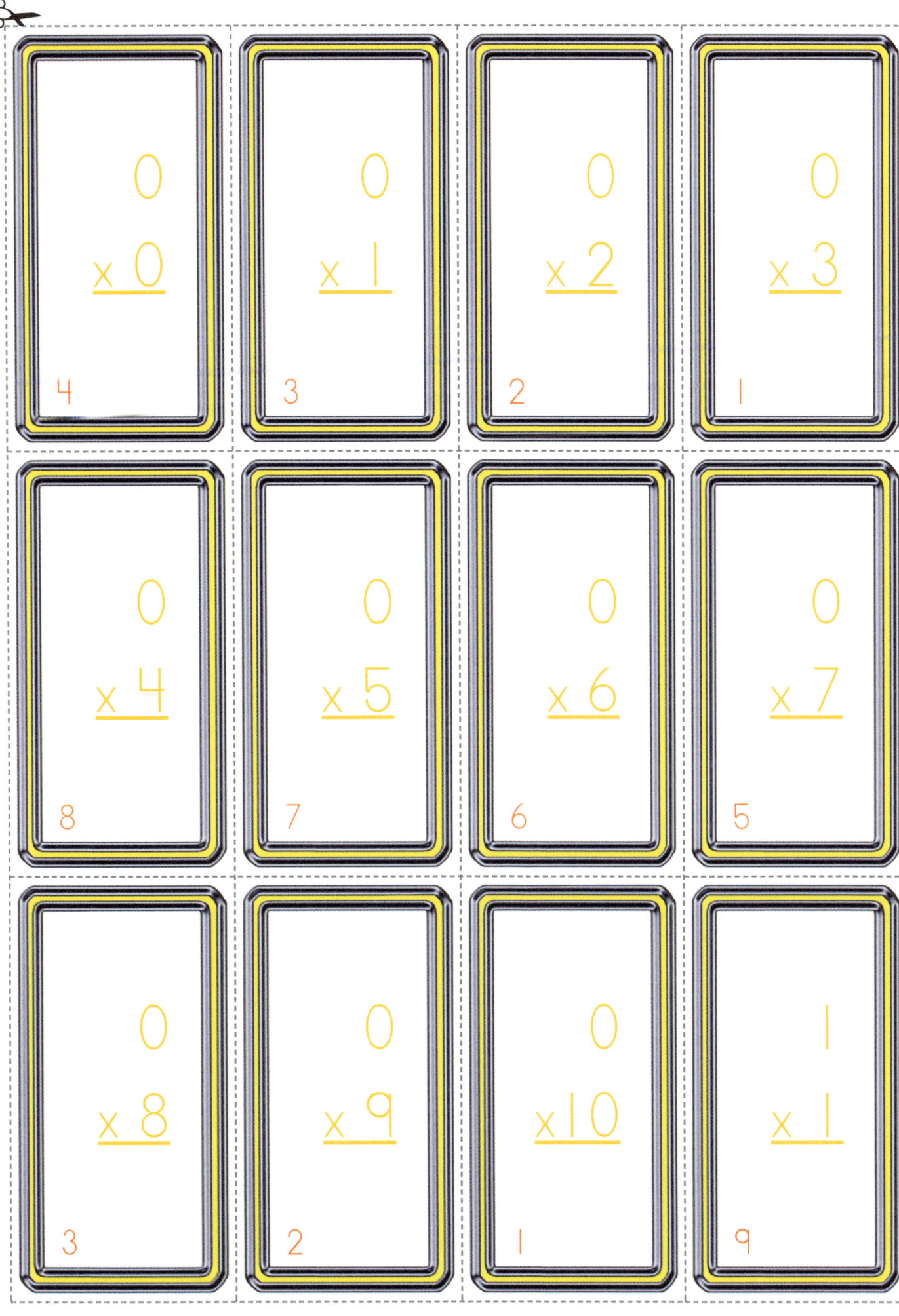

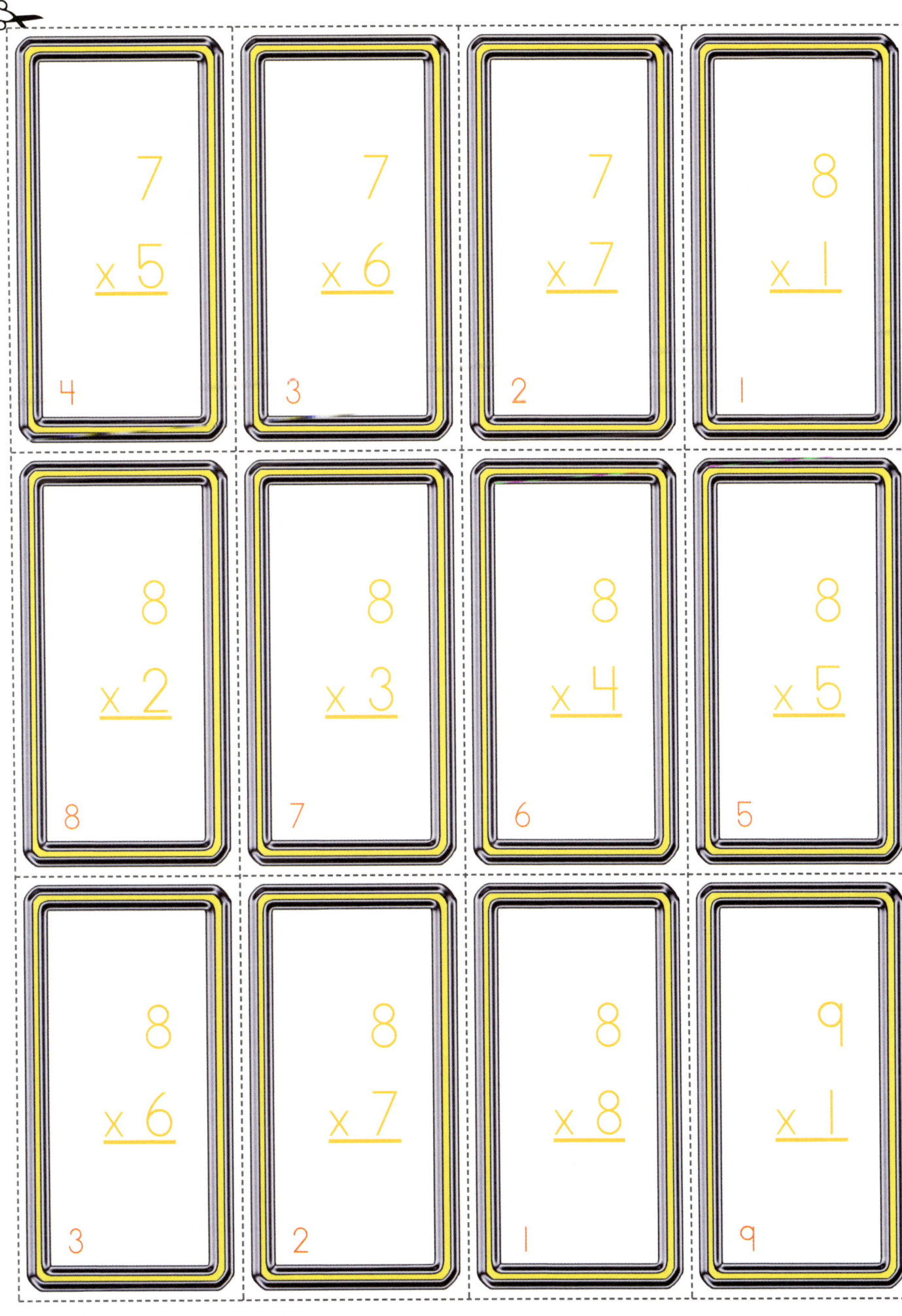

Certificate of Completion
(Certificado de Cumplimiento)

Awarded to
(Otorgado a)

_____

for the completion of *Bridges*
(por completar *Bridges*)

_____ _____
Parent's Signature   Teacher's Signature
(Firma del Padre)   (Firma del Maestro)

bridges